Great Couples
of the Bible

ENCOUNTER.
This splendid scene in the sixteenth-century Farnese Book of Hours, painted by Giulio Clović in the Renaissance style, employs an exuberant repertoire of decorations to frame an intimate scene: a man and a woman meet one another and each reaches out impulsively to the other. Here, the two are King Solomon and the Queen of Sheba, who has traveled to Jerusalem.

EYES MEET.
Detail from a woodcut by Albrecht Dürer, cf. p. 34.

DOMINE·AD·AD
IVVANDVM·ME·FE
STI   NA

Great Couples of the Bible

HERBERT HAAG

DOROTHEE SOELLE

KATHARINA ELLIGER

MARIANNE GROHMANN

HELEN SCHÜNGEL-STRAUMANN

CHRISTOPH WETZEL

Translated by Brian McNeil

NOVALIS

"Then the Lord God said: 'It is not good that the man should be alone; I will make him a helper as his partner.'"

GENESIS 2:18

GREAT COUPLES OF THE BIBLE
Published in Canada by Novalis
10 Lower Spadina Avenue, Suite 400
Toronto, ON M5V 2Z2
Canada

Phone: 1-800-387-7164
Fax: 1-800-204-4140
E-mail: books@novalis.ca
Website: www.novalis.ca
<http://www.novalis.ca>

English translation © Augsburg Fortress
2006. Translated by Brian McNeil from the
German, *Schön bist du und verlockend.*
Große Paare der Bibel, published by Herder
Verlag, Freiburg/Basel/Vienna, 2001/2003.
All rights reserved. Except for brief
quotations in critical articles or reviews, no
part of this book may be reproduced in any
manner without prior written permission
from the publisher.

A production of EMB-Service for
Publishers, Adligenswil.
© 2004 EMB-Service for
Publishers/Motovun Book GmbH,
Lucerne.

ISBN 2-89507-559-X

Canadian cataloguing data for this book is
available from Library and Archives
Canada.

Printed in Italy.
09 08 07 06 1 2 3 4 5 6 6 8 9 10

THE FIRST COUPLE.
A circle, symbolizing perfection and eternity, surrounds the Garden of Eden. The fountain of life with its gothic decoration is in the center. The pictures in the garden tell the story of the fall, *God's sentence, and the expulsion of the first human couple, Adam and Eve, who now begin their life together on earth. Miniature in the fifteenth-century "Very Rich Book of Hours of the Duke of Berry."*

CONTENTS

PROLOGUE

"Paradise is love. Every lover was in paradise for fleeting moments. But whoever lives in God's love lives there for good." Ernesto Cardenal

In the biblical stories that are the substance of this book, we celebrate the struggles of women and men to love, and we find time and again the intimate connection between erotic and divine love.

What eros is to sexuality, mysticism is to religion. In fact, the preferred place of mystical experience is eroticism. As the Talmud says, "Behold, the mutual love between you and God is like the love of man and woman." And that is how we should understand being human; it is being in love. Martin Buber summed up this understanding in a simple sentence, "In the beginning was relationship."

Yet classic Christianity has not always affirmed this biblical ideal. In many discussions, eros and more particularly sex have nothing to do whatsoever with holiness and God's love. But if it is true that mystic-erotic energy has often subverted and transcended the patterns of patriarchy within the old monotheistically formed cultures, we may ask whether this same sacred power within us does not also know how to transcend today's arrangements of sexual consumerism and of the little private paradise within the world of consumer goods. Religion is therefore indispensable particularly for people who love. For religion still names our poverty and reminds us still of the power in us that holds together and heals. Religon still speaks of the sacredness of life for all that we can locate in love.

To embrace God means to embrace a process—a process of love, a process of going forward, a process of infusing everything. Only with our partnership can that love become incarnate in our world every day. This book aims to bring divine and human love closer together again and to say, with St. Teresa of Avila, "There is only one love."

BRIDE AND BRIDEGROOM. *One of the favorite biblical themes of Marc Chagall was the poems celebrating love in the Song of Songs. This painting, from 1956, is entitled* Song of Songs I.

LOVE, EROS,
AND SEXUALITY

This book is about the people we meet in the Bible – about the way they relate to one another, and above all about love, eros, and sexuality. We have perhaps become accustomed to the idea that love and eros are not particularly important in the Bible, but this view owes its origin primarily to the church's sexual morality and to a dualistic anthropology or idea of persons which makes a fundamental distinction between spirit and matter, soul and body. If we actually take a look at the history of Israel, we find a completely different situation. Love and passion bring human joy – as well as intrigue and suffering – to people in the Bible too, and leave their marks on their relationships. We today are only gradually and with difficulty rediscovering the insight that the human person is a unity: but the people of the Bible took this as a matter of course. This means that one can conceive of the entire intellectual realm, as well as all the feelings and ethical evaluations, *only* within the structure of the human body. We cannot continue to understand the human person who lives today as a composite of body and soul (or spirit) within which the body with its needs is the inferior part; similarly, it is inconceivable that the human person should dissolve into his or her component parts at death. He or she dies as a complete person.

THE HUMAN PERSON IN THE BIBLE'S PERSPECTIVE

This means that it ought not to be difficult for us to approach the Bible's anthropology. Our modern understanding of the human person corresponds in an astonishing way to the thinking of the Old Testament. This anthropology is already anchored in the story of human origins. In the more recent creation narrative (Gen 1:1-2:4a), which is the fruit of theological reflection and belongs to the source P (that is, the Priestly document), written in the mid-sixth century before Christ, we are told: "So God created *adam* in his image, in the image of God he created him; male and female he created them" (Gen 1:27). Accordingly, God created the human person in one single act in a twofold form, man and woman, created at the same time and equal in value. The human person is understood from a higher perspective (so to speak) as a unity. This, however, is not an initial monad that – as in many myths – is subsequently shattered by the separation of the genders. On the contrary, *this* initial unity retains at the same time an initial distinction. The two genders are bound together by a profound inherent relatedness, because both man and woman are human persons. The specific gender is not the totality of a person, but is *one* distinguishing mark of a person – and *all* the distinguishing marks

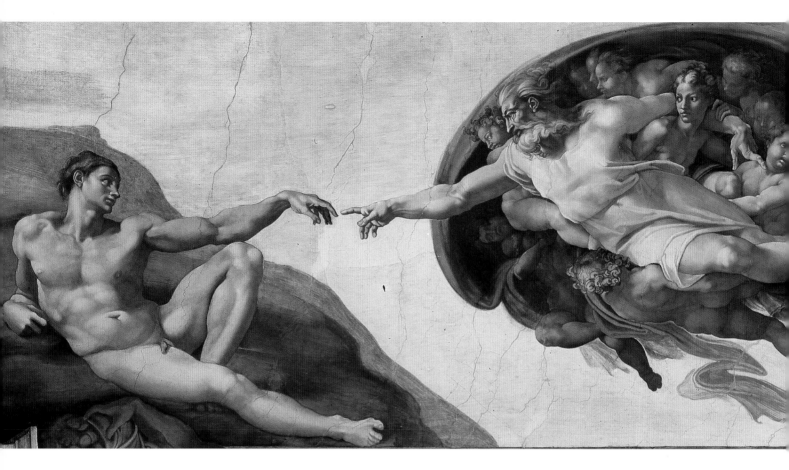

THE HUMAN PERSON
RECEIVE A SOUL.
*The traditional title of this scene in
Michelangelo's cycle of pictures on the ceiling
of the Sistine Chapel (1508-1512) is* The
Creation of Adam, *but it would be more
appropriate to speak of Adam as receiving
life, or a soul. A spark leaps across from the
Creator's finger to the finger of the first
human being and "vitalizes" his beautiful
body: Adam "awakens" in body and mind.
One bold element in this depiction of the
creation story is the figure of Eve, who is
embraced by God's left arm.*

belong to the structure of the person.

This is what the first creation narrative means when it first employs the Hebrew *adam* (a singular collective concept, comparable to the English noun *people*) and then differentiates the substance of this concept by means of the plural: "male and female he created them." But both genders are meant in the first and the second parts of verse 27. If one gender alone rules, or one gender rules over the other, this does not carry out the creator's will.

The use of language here emphasizes the unity in duality: they are two genders, yet one human person. This is raised to a higher level by the fact that man and woman together are the image of God – of a God who is not defined in terms of gender, but displays both masculine and feminine traits. The repetition of the phrase "image of God" shows how important this affirmation is. Here, contrary to what some Christian interpreters hold, scripture is surely not thinking of the physical form of the human person – e.g., the fact that we walk upright – and still less of the intellect (or spirit) which the human person might have in common with God. Rather, the human person is charged here to continue the creation: "God blessed them, and God said to them, 'Be fruitful and multiply'" (Gen 1:28). This means something tremendously significant: the human person is to take the position of God and continue the creator's work. This is why the Jews considered the commandment to procreate as the first and most important precept which God gave human beings as soon as he had created them; this is the position taken in the *Shulchan Aruch*, the authoritative code of legislation in Judaism. Accordingly, love and sexuality are not excluded from this anthropology: they form part of the vital functions which are essential to the human person, and reflection on them prescinds (at least initially) from any moral evaluation. The fundamental rejection of sexuality which we find in the Qumran sect and in the early and mediaeval Christian monastic foundations did not exist in Israel. Israel would have found absurd the notion that sexuality could prevent or disturb one's relationship to God.

THE UNITY OF BODY AND SOUL

We find another approach to the understanding of the human person in the older creation narrative, which follows the more recent narrative at the beginning of the Book of Genesis (2:4b-25). It is attributed to the Yahwist author, and was written in the tenth century before Christ. Here, there is a different accent: "Then the Lord God formed *adam* from the dust of the ground [*adamah*], and breathed into his nostrils the breath of life; and *adam* became a living soul" (2:7). This is a literal translation of the well-known verse which introduces us to the human person on earth: *adam* formed of *adamah*. What surprises us here is not the image of God as a sculptor forming the human person from clay and then giving him life with his own breath, for the Bible shows us on every page a God who behaves like a human being, and the creation of the human person from the earth was a widespread motif in the Near East. Rather, it is surprising that the breath of Yahweh makes the clay figure a "living soul." This seems paradoxical: the bestowal of life makes the body, not a living body, but a living soul. (The New Revised Standard Bible translates: "the man became a living being.")

The author's words make it clear that "body" and "soul" did not mean quite the same to the Hebrews as to us; indeed, he does not have any word for "body" or "soul" taken on its own. When he distinguishes the two, this is not in the sense of a division of the human person into two separate components, but in the sense of an articulated unity. Here, body and soul are different aspects of one totality. Just as the whole human person is "soul" (i.e., a living being), so too the whole human person is "flesh" (i.e., a frail being). This is why the whole human person can be called either soul or body (Ps 44:26; Song 3:1ff.; Mt 6:22f.), and this is why the Hebrews can say that the human person – the soul, the flesh – thinks, hopes, wishes, loves, lives, and dies. And this gives a new dimension to the words: "and they become one flesh" (Gen 2:24) which explain why man and woman belong together. Desire and yearning for one's partner are there from the beginning of creation. The internal organs of the body are the bearers of the feelings of the psyche and of our ethical deci-

THE COMPANION.
This detail from Michelangelo's ceiling fresco The Creation of Adam *shows Eve. The Creator, surrounded by angels, stretches out his right arm with his finger pointing to Adam. Meanwhile, he shelters Eve with his left arm as she looks at the man who is awakening to life. The message of this unusual depiction is a new kind of interpretation of the biblical description of the woman (who has in fact not yet been created!) as "a helper as partner" of the human being. Michelangelo's depiction is revolutionary, since the woman appears here as a pre-existent being. Despite this, in another scene Michelangelo takes up the traditional motif of the creation of Eve.*

sions – think of the many contexts in which we speak of the "heart." The Bible can even attribute feelings to our limbs: Ps 51:10 says that the "bones you have crushed" will "rejoice" when Yahweh forgives sin.

This makes the body indispensable in everything that the human person does. We need the body in order to praise God. The entire body participates in prayer; even today, Jews rock back and forth when they pray. In his anxiety that he might utter something untruthful, the human person prays: "Set a guard over my mouth, O Lord; keep watch over the door of my lips" (Ps 141:3). Whatever the human person does, thinks, or feels, he or she experiences himself or herself holistically. The biblical account of the earliest story of our race relates that Adam and Eve experienced sexual union for the first time immediately after being thrown out of paradise (Gen 4:1). This is surely meant to indicate that, in the rough reality of this life, sexuality and love provide consolation and a sense of being at home. While they were in the bliss of paradise, it seems not to have occurred to the two human beings that they might have intercourse; now, when things are going badly, they discover each other in this way. Sexuality is the expression of a warm human relationship (cf. Prov 5:15-19; the Song of Songs), and therefore promises enjoyment and joy.

SENSUALITY.
Some have held that the Garden of Delights *which Hieronymus Bosch depicted on the central panel of an altarpiece is meant as a warning against sinful excesses, but scholars today take a more nuanced view. The* Garden of Delights *(ca. 1480/1490) is understood as an interpretation of the world in which natural sensuality, which originally belonged to paradise, is manifested in innumerable forms. This means that the alleged "dreamer" Hieronymus Bosch turns out to be a "realist" with acute psychological insights.*

LOVE PLAY.
Scenes of tender charm, portraying sensual pleasure, underscore the title: Garden of Delights.

LIGHT AND DARK.
In the Song of Songs, the desirable bride praises herself: "I am black but beautiful" (1:5).

HERMETIC.
This detail in the so-called Garden of Delights depicts the hermetic togetherness which is brought about by sensual love (above).

BEAUTIFUL MEN, BEAUTIFUL WOMEN

Accordingly, it would have been unthinkable to the people of the Old Testament that they should neglect their bodies. Personal hygiene and attention to the way one looked were taken for granted. They bathed in a river

"Naomi her mother-in-law said to her, 'My daughter, I need to seek some security for you, so that it may be well with you. Now here is our kinsman Boaz, with whose young women you have been working. See, he is winnowing barley tonight at the threshing floor. Now wash and anoint yourself, and put on your best clothes and go down to the threshing floor.'"

RUTH 3:1-3

CARE OF THE BODY.
The painting of the nude Bathsheba by Heinrich F. Füger (ca. 1700) emphasizes the care of her body. A bath in water is followed by sunbathing, with a sheet held up to ward off curious glances.

where possible, or else in their gardens or on the roofs of their houses, and without any prudishness – for otherwise, David would not have been able to observe Bathsheba, as she bathed without any attempt at concealing herself. The extravagant use of ointments, perfumes, and fragrant herbs shows how much importance was attached to care of the body. These give a positive feeling and express both prosperity and satisfaction. A moving example of loving extravagance is found in the New Testament, in various versions (Jn 12:3ff.; Mt 26:6-13; Mk 14:3-9) which relate how a woman comes up to Jesus and anoints his feet with genuine nard, or else stands behind him, breaks open the bottle, and lets the precious nard oil, estimated to be worth the yearly wages of a laborer (Jn 12:5), flow down over Jesus' head. The whole house is filled with this fragrance. And Jesus defends the woman against the reproaches of his disciples.

Personal hygiene was essential before an intimate sexual encounter, as we see in many verses of the Song of Songs, as well as in the story of Queen Esther, who prepared herself for a whole year with oil of myrrh, balsam, and fragrant herbs for her encounter with the king (Est 2:12).

Naturally, the use of cosmetics makes people beautiful – and for the people of the Bible, it is beauty, more than anything else, that triggers love. The New Testament shows only a pale interest in women, and never says of any woman (not even of the mother of Jesus) that she was beautiful; but the Old Testament speaks again and again of the beauty and charm of Israelite women such as Sarah, Rebekah, Rachel, Judith, and Esther. Bathsheba attracts the notice of David because "she was very beautiful": he had her fetched, and slept with her (2 Sam 11:2ff.). We are also told explicitly that men such as Joseph, David, and Absalom were beautiful. The most vivid portrait of male beauty is the praises of the beloved in the Song of Songs. These people are aware of their physical attractiveness, and the women seek passionately to win the favor of the men.

EROTICISM AND PHYSICAL TENDERNESS

If sexuality is to become a cultured bodily language, a number of requirements must be fulfilled. As a young person, one must learn to experience joy in one's own body; one must sense that one can be attracted or rejected by others; one must experience one's own impetuous vitality; there must be a growing need to assume responsibility for one other person; indeed, one must accept the reality of jealousy and of an instinctive desire to possess the other person. In order to cope with all this, one must be able to tackle conflicts, to show consideration for the other, and to live in fidelity – qualities essential to a good relationship.

It is only in very recent times that the important role of tenderness for the human person has been rediscovered – not only in the sphere of sexuality, but for life in common as a whole. The loss of tenderness was due to traditional sexual morality, which was afraid to touch. A prudishness hostile to the human body had cast suspicion on physical tenderness, which was thought to be connected to sensuality or to domination by one's bodily urges. But physical tenderness allows one to show affection to another person without coming excessively close, since it does not seek to take possession of the other; it expresses empathy and respect. Tenderness accepts the other person, taking him or her seriously. This is why it bestows a sense of belong-

TENDERNESS.
This detail from Giotto's fresco The Meeting at the Golden Gate *in the Arena Chapel in Padua (1405/1306) shows the tenderness with which Joachim and Anne embrace.*

TOGETHERNESS.
If we examine this mediaeval book illumination, we see that it depicts themes which are not centrally important in the biblical manuscripts, but nevertheless deserve to be portrayed. One example is the couple in the tendrils of a border of the fifteenth-century Ottheinrich Bible *(above).*

ing, warmth, and harmony. And this is why it must go hand in hand with sexuality. For without physical tenderness, sexuality becomes inhuman.

"Eroticism" tends to be understood as a non-sexual love, but it is found only in persons with the gift of sexuality. Sigmund Freud repeatedly warned against separating eroticism from sexuality: to speak of the one is to speak of the other. They belong together, even if eroticism operates on a different level. Just as it is impossible for a cultured manner of eating to emerge where people's lives are dominated by famine, so it is impossible for eroticism to emerge where sexual needs enslave people. Accordingly, eroticism presupposes the experience of a culture of sexuality.

"Hesiod says that these two – the earth and Eros – first came into being after chaos. But Parmenides writes of the primal generative force: 'The first of all the gods whom it created was Eros.' There is a general agreement that Eros is one of the oldest gods. As one of the oldest gods, he is at the same time the creator of the highest good things. If one wishes to lead a beautiful and worthy life, neither relatives nor positions of honor can compare with love in supplying what is necessary for one who wishes to lead his whole life in a fine and worthy manner."

PLATO, *SYMPOSIUM*

A DUBIOUS TRIUMPH.
The title of this painting by Giovanni Baglione (ca. 1602) corresponds to the ecclesiastical demonization of sensuality (the motif of the child indicates that sensuality is something congenital to the human person): the victory of the heavenly love over the world, the flesh, and the devil.

The best way to understand the many levels and forms of eroticism is to consider the origin of this word. In Greek mythology, Eros, the god of love, is the primal god at the beginning of the world. His is the power that brings the world into existence. He helps it come into being, since his orientation is towards life. He overcomes all that is dead, and reconciles opposites. According to Plato, he is rooted in yearning and longing, and strives toward that which is new. He is never content with what he has already attained but is ablaze with enthusiasm for something higher. Hence, eros is the tension between reality and the object of one's dreams. Our creativity stems from the possibility for which we yearn, the possibility we envisage. What Freud calls "sublimation" is based on eros: in other words, intellectual and artistic achievements which are apparently unrelated to sexuality are in reality the product of the sexual urge. Eroticism is cultivated and sublimated sexuality. Seen in this light, eroticism is a humane introduction to sexuality. From the reverse perspective, we can say that one who sees (for whatever reason) that his life will be celibate can become the author of great cultural achievements in the religious, artistic, and intellectual spheres. Freud goes so far as to maintain that without sublimation, there would indeed be no culture at all.

THE EXPERIENCE OF LOVE

It follows that no love, no committed relationship, no act of creativity is possible without eros or eroticism. But how did people concretely experience love? We have different notions of "love" today. The breaking open of the gender pattern has brought about a tremendous plurality of behavior on all societal

and personal levels, and love is a matter for the absolute freedom and intimacy of each individual. Nevertheless, people in all ages are attracted by a partner who is different from their own selves, because he or she incorporates a part of ourselves for which we long. And we need this partner, if we are to reach those regions of living and of experience which we cannot reach on our own. Sexuality and love are the bodily expression of our yearning for this "other."

The intimate encounter of Ruth and Boaz on the threshing floor ends in marriage. And it is certainly true that marriage provided the model for relationships in ancient Israel. The laws governing sexuality were conditioned by

TWO KINDS OF LOVE?
This painting by Titian is known by the title Heavenly and Earthly Love *(1515/1516). This probably refers to the view in classical antiquity that love was both "heavenly" and "earthly."*

tradition and culture, and women were societally dependent on men. The real goal was the continued existence of one's family and clan, since child mortality was high and life expectancy low. It is only these facts that allow us to understand polygamous marriage. In principle, weddings were a private matter, not subject to religious institutionalization. The fathers agreed on a dowry and married off their children, in the conviction that love would surely appear later on; and this is how marriages are still arranged in the Orient today.

The example of the clash between Sarah and her servant Hagar, which led to the expulsion of the maid (Gen 16:4ff.), is an example of the tensions that could easily arise when a man had more than one wife; another example is the jealousy which the childless Rachel felt for Leah, who had borne several children (Gen 30:8) – Rachel pleads desperately with her husband, "Give me children, or I shall die!" (30:1). In the same way, the childless Hannah sees herself humiliated by her "rival" Peninnah, who "had children" (1 Sam 1:2-6). At the same time, the story of the two wives of Elkanah shows that a husband's love was not necessarily dependent on this factor: he does not reject Hannah because of her childlessness, but comforts her: "Am I not more to you than ten sons?" (1:8). And he gives her a double portion of food.

The marriage laws reflect a patriarchal society, but we also find much evidence of love and tenderness in the relations between men and women. It is probably this experience that underlies the expression "to know," which the Old Testament employs for sexual intercourse. This verb encompasses more than sexuality and love (two concepts which we separate from each other today), and it does not refer primarily to an intellectual knowledge or insight:

"Then the Lord God said, 'It is not good that the man should be alone; I will make him a helper as his partner.'"
GENESIS 2:18

WEDDING.
This diptych in a Hebrew manuscript written in Italy in 1435 is found in a chapter dealing with laws about marriage and divorce. In the right half, the bridal couple makes their entry; on the left, the bridegroom puts a ring on the outstretched finger of the bride's right hand, probably with the words: "See now, you have been consecrated to me through this ring according to the law of Moses and of Israel."

it designates a comprehensive act of understanding, involving the entire human person, heart, spirit, and senses. It means that each experiences and becomes familiar with the other, thanks to a wholly personal relationship in which the partners are discovered as man and as woman.

THE LAWS ARE SILENT ABOUT LOVE

The marriage laws were strict, and the threshold for a husband to divorce his wife was low – trifling grounds sufficed. At the same time, however, there are no restrictions in the Old Testament on the free intercourse of a married or single man with an unmarried woman; the ethical law appears to take no notice of this question, with the one exception of the rape of a girl. The legislation, however, understands this as a crime against property: a father would not be able to get so high a dowry for a daughter who had been raped. Both the Song of Songs and the narratives confirm that the official morality of Israel did not restrict sexuality to marriage. The entire sphere of love, eroticism, and sexuality was so immensely valuable that it was counted among the incomprehensible things of this creation (Prov 30:18f.):

> Three things are too wonderful for me;
> four I do not understand:
> the way of an eagle in the sky,
> the way of a snake on a rock,
> the way of a ship on the high seas,
> and the way of a man with a girl.

Here, the ethical ideas of the Old Testament agree with those elsewhere in the ancient Orient, for example, in Babylon and Egypt. And there is no evidence to indicate that Jesus took any other position than this.

JESUS AND THE ADULTERESS

It is at any rate striking that sexuality clearly was not a theme that interested Jesus at all. He says nothing in the Gospels about prostitution, fornication, or the prescriptions about ritual purity in connection with sexuality. Nor are we told that he condemns homosexuality, masturbation, or premarital or extramarital intercourse – although the Christian church appeals to the Bible when it prohibits all these forms of behavior. Jesus mentions only adultery and divorce, and each time he speaks in favor of the woman involved. The ten commandments forbid adultery, and the frequent quotations in the New Testament show that there was a general awareness of this point. Jesus' own attitude is made explicit only in the scene when a woman caught in adultery is brought to Jesus (Jn 8:2-11), with the demand that he decide whether the

FORGIVENESS.
This panel from Michael Pacher's Altar of St. Wolfgang *(ca. 1480) is an impressive illustration of the narrative in John 8. We should note the upright stance of the woman who has been accused of adultery, when she appears before Jesus. Those who are really accused are the men who accuse her, especially because their hidden intention is to set a trap for Jesus.*

penalty of stoning, as laid down in the law, should now be carried out. Jesus' lenience towards sinners was well known, and the "scribes and Pharisees" intend to challenge him to see whether he will infringe the law of Moses. But he refuses to play the judge, and the trial ends with an acquittal: "Neither do I condemn you." He does of course add: "From now on do not sin again," thus defining the woman's action as sin. But at the same time, he holds a protecting hand over her.

MARY AND JOSEPH

There were certainly a number of reasons for Jesus' tolerant behavior vis-à-vis the adulteress, and probably the most important lay in his own biography. Matthew's infancy narrative relates that Joseph wished to dismiss Mary, his betrothed, without making any public fuss, when he noticed that she was pregnant (1:18). Since a fiancée was legally in the same situation as a wife, this would have been perfectly possible, and a divorce could be justified on much more trivial grounds than the fact that the woman was expecting the child of another man. It was enough for the man to find something objectionable in his fiancée: this might be a moral defect, but it might simply be that he found another woman more beautiful than his own, or even (on a rather lax view) that she had put too much salt in the soup. In the case of Mary, however, who was suspected of adultery, Joseph could have had her stoned, or at least put her to public shame by accusing her of adultery before a court. That would have closed all the doors to Mary in polite society: in villages, everyone knows everyone else.

Joseph did not do this, and this is why Matthew uses the biblical word "righteous" here. Joseph must have loved Mary very much. And she herself was a strong personality, who was deeply one with him. Luke presents her as an active woman of faith. The Magnificat (Lk 1:45-55) undoubtedly gives a truer picture of her than the subsequent theological over-paintings and the pious kitsch. After all, the couple had other children too. Mark's Gospel relates that his closest relatives – his four brothers and his sisters, and indeed even his mother – could not make any sense of Jesus. The whole family is presented in one single sentence (6:3), based on an old tradition which attests the historical knowledge that Mary was the biological mother of Jesus. Joseph is not mentioned in this context, and this may indicate that Mary was a widow; it may also hint at polemic related to Jesus' illegitimacy. Matthew and Luke have long infancy narratives in which angels appear, but it was in Nazareth that the family led its daily life, and questions such as: "Is not this the son of Mary and brother of James and Joses and Judas and Simon, and are not his sisters here with us?" (Mk 6:3) do not suggest that Joseph and Mary had become the object of any

THE PARENTS OF JESUS.
In the Urbino Bible *(1476-1478), the illuminations at the beginning of Matthew's Gospel depict both the wedding of Mary and Joseph and the birth of Jesus. These pictures illustrate the last entry in the genealogy of Jesus (Mt 1:1-17): "Jacob was the father of Joseph the husband of Mary, of whom Jesus was born, who is called the Messiah."*

ESPOUSALS.
*This title (*Sposalizio *in Italian) is given to depictions of the betrothal or marriage of Mary and Joseph. This painting, with the temple of Jerusalem in the background, is an early work (1504) of Raphael (above).*

Iesu christi filii dauid: filii abraham. Abraham au
tem genuit ysaac. Ysaac autem iacob genuit:
Iacob autem genuit iudam et fratres eius. Iudas
autem genuit phares et zaram de thamar. Pha
res autem genuit esrom. Esrom autem genuit
aram. Aram autem genuit aminadab. Ami
nadab autem genuit naason. Naason autem
genuit salmon. Salmon autem genuit booz
de raab. Booz autem genuit obeth et ruth.
Obeth autem genuit iesse. Iesse autem genu
it dauid regem. Dauid autem rex genuit sa
lomonem ex ea que fuit urie. Salomon aute
genuit roboam. Roboam autem genuit a
biam. Abias autem genuit asa. Asa autem
genuit iosaphat. Iosaphat autem genuit io
ram. Ioram autem genuit oziam. Ozias au
tem genuit ioatham. Ioatham autem genuit
acaz. Acaz autem genuit ezechiam. Eze
chias autem genuit manassem. Manasses au
tem autem genuit amon. Amon autem genu
it iosiam. Iosias autem genuit iechoniam et
fratres eius in transmigratione babilonis. Et
post transmigrationem babilonis: iechonias
genuit salathiel. Salathiel autem genuit zo
robabel. zorobabel autem genuit abiud.
Abiud autem genuit eliachim. Eliachim

autem genuit azor. Azor autem genuit sadoch
Sadoch autem genuit achim. Achim autem
genuit eliud. Eliud autem genuit eleazar.
Eleazar autem genuit mathan. Mathan
autem genuit iacob. Iacob autem genuit iu
rum marie: de qua natus est iesus qui uoca
tur christus. Omnes ergo generationes abra
ham usq, ad dauid generationes quattuorde
cim. Et a dauid usq, ad transmigrationem ba
bilonis generationes quattuordecim. Et a tris
migratione babilonis usq, ad xpm generati
ones quattuordecim. Xpi autem generati
o sic erat. Cum esset desponsata maria ma
ter iesu ioseph. antequam conuenirent in
uenta est in utero habens de spiritu sanc
to. Ioseph autem uir eius cum esset iustº
et nollet eam traducere: uoluit occulte di
mittere eam. hec autem eo cogitante ecce
angelus domini in somnis apparuit ei di
cens. Ioseph fili dauid noli timere accipere
mariam coniugem uxorem. Quod enim in e
a natum est de spiritu sancto est. Pariet au
tem filium. et uocabis nomen eius iesum. Ipse
enim saluum faciet populum suum a pecca
tis suis. Hoc autem totum factum est ut ad
impleretur quod dictum est a domino p

"Now as they went on their way, he entered a certain village,
where a woman named Martha welcomed him into her home.
She had a sister named Mary."

LUKE 10:38

MARY AND MARTHA.
*Mary and Martha, here depicted by
Tintoretto (ca. 1580), were two of the
female disciples of Jesus whose story is told
in the Gospels. According to John 11:1,
they were the sisters of Lazarus in the
village of Bethany.*

special esteem in their village. At any rate, the Joseph of iconography, an old man at the side of the picture who tends a fire or looks helplessly away while Mary gives birth, has nothing to do with the reality in Nazareth. Jesus came from a completely normal family.

JESUS AND WOMEN

Another reason why Jesus showed the adulteress so much understanding is his attitude to women in general. We know from the Gospels that he was accompanied not only by men disciples, but by women disciples too. Our sources indicate that his behavior towards women was natural, free, unaffected – in a word, normal. Just as he healed other sick persons, he healed women too. Women followed him, gave him financial support, and welcomed him into their homes. In Jewish society at that time, this offended against every rule of propriety: it was unheard of, indeed disgraceful, for women to leave their own families and to have the courage to share the itinerant life of another man. Jesus' unreserved acceptance of them and their service attests his own sovereign attitude vis-à-vis the customs of his age. The Gospels mention several of Jesus' women friends by name: Mary and Martha in Bethany, Mary of Magdala, Joanna, Susanna, and "many others" (Lk 8:1-3; 10:38-42). He did not reject the tax collectors and other sinners; nor did he reject the prostitutes. He laid his hands on women and let himself be touched by them – something that certainly gave offense to some. At any rate, the women were fascinated by him and loved him. Is there any reason not to call these relationships "erotic"?

What are we to make of the woman who comes up to Jesus from behind during a meal and anoints his feet with precious anointment, weeping, kissing his feet, and drying them with her hair (Lk 7:36-50)? All the city knows that she is a "sinner," and hence ritually impure. And yet, her love is greater than that of Jesus' host, Simon. Doubtless she recognized in Jesus a kind and understanding man who did not join in the universal condemnation. Before this, she was a despised outsider. After the encounter with Jesus, she realizes that she still has a future ahead of her.

Much has been written about the kind of "love" Jesus meant when he said: "Her sins, which were many, have been forgiven, for she has shown great love" (7:47). Is this the "love" for other men, which had driven her hitherto, or is it "love" for Jesus, since she knows that he understands her? Whatever the answer, Jesus encountered here love in a very concrete and realistic manner, without prudishness or inhibitions. In this exuberant scene, conventions are shattered.

MARY OF MAGDALA

One of the women who stayed close to Jesus was Mary of Magdala. She is the first to be named among the many women who accompanied him from Galilee to Jerusalem in order to serve him. She followed him to the extent of standing under his cross, and she witnessed his death and burial. According to all four Gospels, she went on the first day of the week to Jesus' grave (John says she went alone, the other evangelists mention one or two other women who accompanied her). She was taking a risk: it could be dangerous to be seen at the grave of an enemy of the state. Mary is described as a disciple who went with Jesus on his journeys. Jesus had driven seven demons out of her. People at that time thought that illnesses were caused by demons; in modern terms, Jesus had freed her from a severe psychological illness which must have torn apart and lacerated her personality. It is hard to overestimate what this healing meant for Mary of Magdala: she came back to herself. It was a turning point in her life, and it is scarcely surprising that she clung to Jesus in gratitude and love. He also provided an economic basis for her life. It was impossible in society at that time for an unmarried woman to have a livelihood. If she did not have a man to protect her, she was forced into prostitution.

Mary of Magdala weeps in the early morning when she finds the tomb of Jesus open and his body not there. She cannot live without him, so she wishes to be bound to him at least in her grief. Perhaps she begins to be afraid of a return of her old illness. When she turns around, Jesus stands before her and asks why she is weeping. But she thinks he is the gardener, and asks him to tell her what he has done with the body of Jesus, so that she can fetch it. Then Jesus addresses her: "Mary!" (Jn 20:16). The voice is familiar: this is the tone in which he always spoke her name, and so he penetrates her grief and reaches her. She replies with the Hebrew expression: "Rabbouni!" ("My master!"). One can hardly imagine a more intimate dialogue, a more loving and tender encounter, than these two words which reveal the love that unites these two persons and their lengthy common history. No one loved Jesus like Mary. His reaction – "Do not hold on to me!" – suggests that her spontaneous reaction is to embrace him. It is not by chance that this scene is set in a garden, for this recalls the Song of Songs and paradise, both of which symbolize love.

Mary is then charged by Jesus to proclaim his resurrection to the disciples. This is why Augustine calls her *apostola apostolorum*, "the female apostle of the male apostles." In the apocryphal gnostic literature, she is portrayed as an intimate friend of Jesus and as a rival to Peter. This situation generated a crisis of authority, or possibly a struggle for power, in the early church.

MARY OF MAGDALA.
Numerous legends grew up around this female disciple, honoring the "sinner" as a saint under the name "Mary Magdalene." This enchanting portrait is a detail from Raphael's altarpiece, with St. Cecilia as the main figure (1514).

TAKING THE WRONG PATH

The human affection and the positive attitude to eros which we see here are a part of the message of the New Testament, even if they are seldom put into

"Jesus said to her, 'Mary!'
She turned and said to him in
Hebrew, 'Rabbouni!'
(which means Teacher).
Jesus said to her, 'Do not hold
on to me, because I have not yet
ascended to the Father.'"
JOHN 20:16F.

NOLI ME TANGERE.
*This is the Latin translation of the words spoken
by the risen Jesus to Mary of Magdala, "Do not
touch me!" (Jn 20:17). This miniature dates
from ca. 1195 (above).*

A RELATIONSHIP OF LOVE?
*This painting by Peter Paul Rubens of
Jesus with the "sinner" Mary of
Magdala anticipates the modern view
that the woman disciple, who had been
healed and converted, and Jesus himself
were drawn to each other by a mutual
erotic attraction (right).*

words. However, this must not allow us to forget that an admonitory, rigid attitude to love, eros, and sexuality gradually gained the upper hand. Paul's convic-
tions on this subject were fundamentally hostile to eros – the relatively rare positive affirmations, as in 1 Cor 11:11f., do not really alter the picture – and they
laid down the guidelines for Christian moral theology. The so-called catalogues
of vices in the Pauline and Pastoral Letters repeatedly mention, often in a prominent position, two concepts, *porneia* and *akatharsia*, which are usually translated as "fornication" and "impurity." Nor does Paul have anything encouraging
to say about love and marriage. Sexual intercourse exists only in the ghetto of
matrimony, and even there is tolerated only out of necessity, in order to avoid

greater ills. Marriage seems to be merely a safety valve for exorbitant sexual urges, when we read: "If they are not capable of practicing self-control, they should marry. For it is better to marry than to be aflame with passion" (1 Cor 7:9). All other sexual relationships are condemned. All this sounds very hostile to eros, and critics from many different standpoints have accused the New Testament of hostility to the body and of sexual inhibition.

The reasons for this ascetic rigorism may lie in part in the biography of Paul himself, who did not succeed in finding a harmonious and affirmative attitude to his own body. In part, the imminent expectation of the return of Christ may have caused a lack of interest in having children and continuing the human race; and when he failed to return, this expectation may have given way to world-weariness. Other influences came from Greek and oriental philosophy. The Stoic ideal of *apatheia* (literally, "passionlessness") culminated in a refusal to pay any attention to the body; the ideal of a life devoid of all needs, preached and practiced by the Cynics, attached no value at all to the body or pleasure. In addition, eastern doctrines proclaimed a strict dualism between light and darkness, good and evil, spirit and matter, soul and body. The unity of body, soul, and spirit – which the Old Testament had taken for granted – was definitively abandoned and replaced by a division into two levels, which were assessed differently.

This provided the background for the ascetic life of the hermits, which was chosen by the adherents of apocalyptic, beginning with John the Baptist. Gnosis too, a movement composed of many various elements, tended to reject sexuality. The detachment of eros from religion left only a naked sexuality behind: the body became the gate through which evil entered, and this made it necessary to despise everything connected with sexuality. People seem not to have noticed the contradiction here of the positive attitude to human beings which Jesus proclaimed, nor the antithesis to the doctrine of the resurrection, which (appealing to Gen 2:7) included the body too: "It is sown a physical body, it is raised a spiritual body" (1 Cor 15:44 – here, Paul is in fact contradicting himself!). And the creed speaks literally of the "resurrection of the flesh." Hence, the bodily dimension is essential, and it must be so, for Christianity is a religion that understands the human being as a holistic person who is unthinkable without bodiliness.

There is no irreconcilable antithesis between love and sexuality in the Bible, or between eros and religion. Indeed, we must ask whether one in whose life eroticism has not fully developed can be religious at all; the simple fact that the language of those who pray recalls the language of those who love (e.g., Ps 63, or the writings of the mystics) suggests that our answer must be negative. Let us imagine what an erotic church might be. It would be much more interested in tenderness than in power. It would devote its energy to celebration, rather than to moral regulations. It would help people to emerge from isolation and to overcome their alienation from the very ground of their being.

JOHN AND JESUS.
This depiction of Jesus' baptism in the waters of the Jordan also symbolizes baptism in the Spirit, by means of the dove in which the Holy Spirit descends. In the Renaissance style, the bodies have a form reminiscent of those trained in the gymnasium of classical antiquity (from the sixteenth-century Farnese Book of Hours).

BIBLICAL COUPLES

A FAMILY.

The two parts of this picture depict how the family of the patriarch Jacob came into being: he meets Rachel at the well (Gen 29:9-12), is accepted by Laban as his son-in-law, and is reconciled with Laban (symbolized in the stone monument they set up) after he has fled in secret with his two wives, Leah and Rachel, the maids Bilhah and Zilpah, and all their children (Gen 31:45-53).

When we think of the great women and men of the Bible, especially of the Old Testament, we see a large number of completely individual persons. The church, art, and literature help us make a link between these figures and our own experiences of what it is to be human. And such common Christian names as Esther, Judith, Rebecca, Ruth, and Sarah, or David, Joseph, and Tobias suggest that we look at the stories originally linked to these names.

If we examine the Bible, we will discover that Esther, Rebekah, Ruth, and Sarah, and David, Joseph, and Tobias are each the half of a couple. It is only in their relationship to their partner that we can discern their humanity: "Male and female he created them," as we read in the first (and more recent) creation narrative at the beginning of the Book of Genesis. The reason for this is akin to the situation of the animals of earth, who were created on the same day: human beings are couples, so that they may "multiply." They are however distinguished from the animals by the fact that, as man and woman together, they are an "image" or "likeness" of God. The creator's will – "Let us make *adam* in our image, according to our likeness" (Gen 1:26) – is the basis for human fruitfulness and "multiplication," as well as for the human domination over animals, plants, and the whole earth.

As soon as we lose sight of the fact that man and woman together are made in God's image, this quality pales into something neutral, something that is applicable only to an abstract "human person," something bereft of all fruitfulness and of all resemblance to God. This means that the "human person" is excluded from a human existence that is "fruitful" in more than a merely biological sense.

Dorothee Soelle's meditation at the end of this book ("Where there is love, there is God") both sums up and further elaborates the meaning of such an existence.

From the biblical perspective, existence as a human person, as man and woman, as a couple has both an origin and a goal to which it is oriented. It is perhaps questionable whether we can truly speak of a "straightforward" union between man and woman, in the sense that a straight line is the shortest union of two individual points. At any rate, alongside such "straightforward" relationships we find many detours and false turnings in the relationships of the couples whose stories are presented in the following chapters. We should note that the concept of "couple" is not the same thing as a monogamous married couple. As king, David was entitled to have many wives. Three of these – Michal, Abigail, and Bathsheba – had very different relationships to their partner, David, and tradition sheds a very different light on each of them. These three stories are preceded by a look at the couples in the period of the patriarchs and matriarchs, and at Ruth and Boaz, to whom the Bible dedicates a book that is mirrored with great affection in the work of many artists. The centerpiece is the Song of Songs, a collection of love poems which has had a great impact on religious history. We also find, however, couples in whom lust and hatred dominate the relationship between men and women, culminating in treachery (Delilah and Samson) and murder (Judith and Holofernes). The "resemblance to God" gives way to a distance from God: a theme which finds expression in the figure of Job, who is despised by everyone, including his (unnamed) wife.

THE CHILDREN OF ISRAEL.
The second pair of pictures in the Crusader Bible *(ca. 1250) shows Jacob wrestling with the angel after he has crossed the ford of Jabbok with his two wives, the two maids, and his eleven sons. In this scene, Jacob is given the name Israel, which means: "he who contends with God" (Gen 32:23-33). The right half portrays the reconciliation between Jacob and his brother Esau. When the latter asks who all these people are who accompany Jacob, he receives the reply: "The children whom God has graciously given your servant" (Gen 33:5). These "children of Israel," borne by Leah, Rachel, Bilhah, and Zilpah, are the ancestors of the people of Israel.*

ADAM AND EVE

(Genesis 2 and 3)

BOOK OF GENESIS.
The sixteen pictures in the Hamilton Bible
*(ca. 1350) give an overview of the first book
of the Bible. The scenes begin with the
creation of the world and of human beings,
depict the beginning of human life on
earth, and go as far as Pharaoh's dream
in the story of Joseph (opposite page).*

THE FALL.
*The first human couple with the tree of the
knowledge of good and evil in the center of
the Garden of Eden: a miniature in a
Hebrew manuscript of the Bible from
northern France (ca. 1280/1290) (above).*

When we speak of the first human couple in the Bible, we usually call them "Adam and Eve," but these names are no older than the tradition of the last centuries before Christ. The older biblical text, in Gen 2 and 3, does not speak of an individual couple, but simply of the human person, whom we meet in the dual articulation of man and woman. The text intends to make fundamental affirmations about the relationship between the two genders, not to tell the story of what happened to two specific individuals. In these ancient narratives, the woman has a leading role; she takes the initiative and has a significant dialogue with the snake. The man is more passive. This means that – if we want to retain the traditional names – it would in fact be more appropriate to speak of the story of "Eve and Adam."

These two chapters are embedded in a larger narrative framework which, like all the ancient oriental creation myths, begins with the creation of the world and of the human person and culminates in a terrible destruction, the so-called flood. The biblical storytellers adopted this framework from creation to flood, and this is why we must not isolate the two chapters which speak of the relationship between man and woman, as Christian tradition has mostly done. Above all, however, they must not be read as historical accounts which follow a logical sequence in their narration of how things got the way they are, or how things came into existence originally. Scholars identified the genre of these narratives two hundred years ago, and we must cordon off the mythical narrative in Gen 1-11 from the subsequent historical narratives of the Bible. The primal history speaks of things that are universally valid, things that are human – indeed, often things that are all too human!

For this reason, these narratives do not supply us with an historical "before and after." All the older naïve or literal interpretations which held that Gen 2 was writing about a human being before sin and Gen 3 about human beings after the so-called fall are untenable. This historicizing perspective has long been left behind. Rather, chapters 2 and 3 must be read in parallel: Gen 2 relates how God created the human person (or humanity) and how the relationship between man and woman was intended to be, while Gen 3 tells us how this relationship actually functions. In Gen 3, the narrator tells how he experiences the people of his own age, who transgress the commandments, who have lost their mutual trust, who accuse one another; he tells us how the man rules over the woman. This is how the author, probably a theologian in the period of the kings of Israel (tenth to sixth centuries before Christ), sees reality. Gen 3 describes how the human being is – and always was.

IN principio creauit deus celu 7 tra.
Terra aut erat manis 7 uacua. et te
nebre erat sup facien abissi. 7 spus
dei ferebat sup aquas. Dixitq3 ds.
Fiat lux. 7 facta est lux. Et uidit de
us lucem q3 eet bona. 7 diuisit lu

cem a tenebris. appellauitq3 lucem diem 7
tenebras noctt. Factuq3 est uespe 7 mane.
dies unus. Dixit quoq3 ds. Fiat firmame
tu in medio aquar. 7 diuidat aquas ab
aquis. Et fecit deus firmamtu. 7 diuisitq3
aquas que erant sub firmanito. ab hijs

These two chapters in the Hebrew Bible describe the fundamental relationship between man and woman, that is, the relationship between the genders. Gen 4 then speaks of another relationship, that between brothers, and relates the first murder. The relationships between tillers of the soil and cattle breeders, and between dwellers in the countryside and in the city, also find expression in this narrative. Finally, Gen 6:1-4 speaks of the relationships between heavenly beings and earthly women. Again and again, the theme is the basic relationship between various persons or groups, and between the two genders. And this sequence begins with the relationship between woman and man.

We find the affirmations applicable to all human beings at the beginning of Gen 2. *Adam* – best translated "earthling," since his origin is *adamah*, the soil that is cultivated – is initially bound to this soil, on which "he" must work. The narrative expresses the link between the earthling and the earth by telling the earthling that "he" must return to the earth: in other words, "he" will die. This earth plays a central role in the continuation of the primal history. In Gen 4, Cain is driven from the cultivated soil after he murders Abel. God says to him: "Your brother's blood is crying out to me from the ground! And now you are cursed from the ground, which has opened its mouth to receive your brother's blood from your hand" (4:10f.). Finally, in the flood, all human beings apart from Noah and his family are "blotted out from the earth," because "the wickedness of humankind was great in the earth, and every inclination of the thoughts of their hearts was only evil continually" (Gen 6:5-7). Only the fish are exempt from this punishment; everything that has the breath of life and lives on the earth must drown. This is the first relationship indicated in Gen 2, that is, the relationship of the human person to the earth on which he lives and works.

It is only at the end of chapter 2 that God creates the woman, because God sees that the earthling is alone and that it is not good for him to be alone. Until that point, the gender of the human person is not yet determined; it is only after the creation of the woman that *adam* becomes a man. Hebrew has specific terms for "man" and "woman," and these are employed only after the creation of the woman; the term for "woman" is mentioned first. It is only thanks to the creation of the woman that the human being becomes a man.

The author uses great skill in his account of how the woman is created. First, God creates the animals, to see whether the human being will find anything suitable, a being that corresponds to his own self – for God had said, "I will make him a helper as his partner" (Gen 2:18). This concept of "help" was utilized by a long tradition, almost two thousand years old, as evidence of the inferiority of woman and of her subordination to man. A wife was understood as a kind of servant maid or housekeeper for her husband. Indeed, Augustine understood her exclusively as an aid in the procreation and education of children; this church father held that, for every other work, a man would be a better "help" for a man, and his exposition of Genesis had a lasting influence in

THE CREATION.
The dome in the vestibule of San Marco in Venice, decorated with mosaics (ca. 1220) (opposite page).

PARADISE.
The left wing of the Heuwagen Triptych *by Hieronymus Bosch (ca. 1490) (above).*

the Middle Ages. None of these interpretations actually does justice to the meaning of the biblical text itself. The term for "help" which is used here designates a specially qualified partner. It is applied above all to God, where a human being is in a hopeless situation and finds no help. Many of the Psalms employ this term when they appeal to God for aid. And this means that it cannot be used in Gen 2 to speak of a subordinate helper. The text refers in the first instance to a decisive help given to a person who is alone – and it refers to both man and woman, since it is not good for *adam* (that is, the human person in general) to be alone.

When he creates the woman, God does not simply fashion a new creature from the earth. Rather, he takes a rib from the human person and constructs a woman out of it, then he brings this woman to the human person. The man's exclamation (2:23) is the high point of this chapter. These are the only words in this narrative which take the form of poetry:

This at last is bone of my bones
and flesh of my flesh;
she shall be called Woman,
for out of Man this one was taken.

The word "this" is the first and the last word in the Hebrew text. It expresses the joy that the human person – now for the first time called "man" – has finally found the partner who is right for him. The formula about bone and flesh is used in other passages of the Book of Genesis too, affirming that another person belongs to the same tribe or clan, i.e., is equal in rank. It emphasizes the close link between the two sexes. Since they are of the same substance, they are continually attracted to each other – this is the meaning of the metaphorical story about the rib, which tradition has mostly expounded as the woman's disadvantage although in fact it affirms exactly the opposite. The skill God employs in

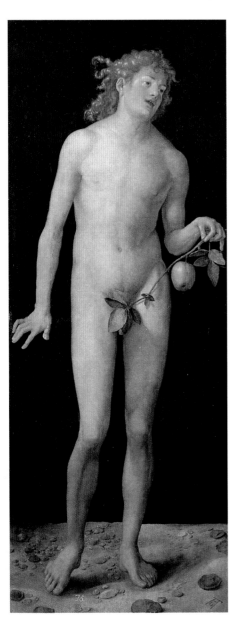

IDEAL IMAGE OF THE HUMAN BEING.
Albrecht Dürer's depiction of Adam and Eve (1507) does indeed include allusions to the "fall," but is devoted primarily to the ideal of male and female beauty in the Renaissance style.

creating the woman is meant to express the mutual relationship of the sexes, an original unity which seeks to become a unity in an endless series of new couples. This is how the biblical author envisages the ideal relationship between man and woman, as God intended it: a relationship of joy and confidence, and of complete equality. Their confidence is expressed above all in the last sentence in the chapter: "And the man and his wife were both naked, and were not ashamed." This lack of embarrassment, and the complementarity of man and woman which Gen 2 describes, are central elements in the model proposed by the theological author for the relationship between the sexes. A related text is the Song of Songs, which employs the language of poetry, drawing especially on metaphors associated with the garden and fruits, to describe the unembarrassed relations between man and woman.

THE GARDEN OF EDEN.
In their shared work Adam and Eve in Paradise/The Fall *(ca. 1620), the Baroque painters Peter Paul Rubens and Jan Brueghel the Elder suggest a comparison with the uninhibited eroticism of the Song of Songs.*

THE SEDUCER.
In his painting of the fall (ca. 1470/1475), Hugo van der Groes sticks to the biblical text: the temptation is the work of the serpent. The woman is the first to act, while the man merely takes part in what she does (right).

SEPARATION OF THE SEXES.
Albrecht Dürer's woodcut (ca. 1510) contains an interpretation of the "fall" as the beginning of an alienation between man and woman. Adam's face expresses the tragedy of this confrontation.

Gen 3 goes on to describe the reality of relationships between men and women. The author's experience shows him that things are not how they ought to be: the relationship between men and women is one of domination and subordination, and is marked by distrust, sin, and violence. Joy is absent.

In her dialogue with the snake at the beginning of this chapter, the woman comes to realize that it would be good to eat the fruit of the forbidden tree. She does indeed have a theological conversation with the snake, in which she defends God; but in the end, she takes some of the fruit. She herself eats, and so does the man who is her companion. He had been there all along, but he is completely silent throughout this scene: all he does is eat. Immediately, they lose their uninhibited naturalness and see that they are naked – and their nakedness is now a problem, so they cover themselves with fig leaves. When they hear God strolling in the garden, they hide like little children with bad consciences. The text vividly describes how trust is lost, first between the human beings and God, and then between the man and the woman, who begin to accuse each other, the man affirming that it was the woman who gave him the forbidden fruit. These recriminations shatter their original unity.

God then addresses the three characters – the snake, the woman, and the man – in poetic words which are not "judicial verdicts" (as some interpreters still hold) but rather descriptions of the state of affairs in their lives. The biblical author formulates in these texts the situation he knows from his own days. He begins with the snake, the only genuine seducer in the biblical text: it must crawl on its belly and eat dust.

God tells the woman about the tribulations of pregnancy and giving birth, and says that she will be oppressed by her husband: the author sees a situation in which men dominate women as contrary to God's will. He has already described (in Gen 2) how the relationship between men and women ought to be. The pains involved in becoming a mother, and the oppression by her husband, are a perversion of the original state of things, which was meant to bring joy. A woman who resists this perversion is acting correctly, in accordance with God's will, just as much as a man who employs tools that will reduce his "sweat" when he works in the fields. Both the wearisome toil of the man on the soil and the pains of the woman are signs that an original trust, a God-given naturalness, has been lost. Not only the relationship between the sexes has been disrupted: the relationship between human beings and the creation is likewise problematic.

It is only at the close of the narrative that the woman receives the name *Hawwah* ("life"); in later translations, this becomes "Eve." In the Hebrew Bible, this name is found only here and in the first verse of Gen 4:

> And the human being knew his wife Hawwah,
> and she conceived and bore Cain.

With this name, as we see in chapter 4, the woman becomes a mother. In Gen 2 and 3, her motherhood is not yet mentioned, because the author is concerned with the relationship between the sexes, whose dealings seem almost childlike, natural, naïve. The question of whether they already had sexual intercourse in the Garden of Eden has been much discussed, but if we follow the biblical text, it is likely that it is only outside the garden (i.e., in Gen 4) that intercourse and

EXPULSION FROM PARADISE.
An illustration to John Milton's epic Paradise Lost *(1667). In Milton's poem, Adam is the protagonist; in a vision, the archangel Michael reveals to him the path to redemption, which God has decreed in his salvific plan.*

procreation occur. The two chapters can also be read as a portrait of the stages by which human beings become adults: first they are like children, then they grow up, discover their sexuality, and lose their naturalness. Unfortunately, this narrative has often been interpreted as implying that there is something fundamentally negative about sexuality, so that it would be with the appearance of sexuality that sin, humankind's falling away from God, begins. Nothing in the narrative of Gen 2 and 3 supports such a reading. Although an explicit sexual encounter between the first human beings is not mentioned before 4:1, the reason why chapters 2 and 3 have nothing to say about this may be that the author took it as a matter of course.

This extreme narrowing-down in the understanding of the text was made possible in the Christian tradition by the identification of women with sexuality and bodiliness, so that the entire responsibility for the so-called "fall" was laid on Eve's shoulders. The fact that it is the woman who takes some of the fruits of the tree and gives them to her husband who stands beside her, was generally held to show that she bore the greater share of guilt (or indeed the totality of guilt) for human sin. On this view, the man took part in her transgression of God's prohibition only in a passive manner, as a "gentleman," so to speak. Augustine says that Adam did not want to leave Eve alone in her distress. But none of these excuses for the man is supported by the text itself. According to the entire tradition of ancient oriental images, it is always a woman who is linked with a tree (and a snake), for the simple reason that it is women who prepare and serve food. It would be unthinkable for this iconographic tradition to do what Michelangelo did at a much later date, namely to portray the man reaching out to the tree. Artists in older times were much more bound by the standard forms than in the modern period, where all the possibilities may be exploited. In the first millennium before Christ, the pictorial unit woman-tree-snake was so firmly established that an author could not arbitrarily depart from it. This means that all attributions of guilt to the woman are completely unjustified expositions of the text. The only reason that they were able to survive so long was that the exposition and translation of the Bible was exclusively reserved to men throughout the Christian tradition – and these men imported their own self-understanding, their societal role, and their interests into their interpretation of the text.

The biblical authors lived and wrote in a patriarchal society. This makes their egalitarian picture of the partnership between man and woman all the more astonishing. Clearly, they saw an equilibrium both in nature and in the relationship between the sexes; if this was disturbed, the result was disorder, destruction, and violence. Unlike the later Christian tradition, the biblical tradition is not hostile to women or to the body. This judgment is confirmed by the Song of Songs, which with great freedom of spirit contains songs about the erotic interplay between men and women.

"Then the Lord God said, 'See, the man has become like one of us, knowing good and evil; and now, he might reach out his hand and take also from the tree of life, and eat, and live forever.'"

GENESIS 3:22

CHANGE OF ROLES.
Michelangelo's "fall" on the ceiling of the Sistine Chapel activates Adam, who reaches out his hand greedily to take hold of the fruit, while Eve passively allows a fig to be handed to her (opposite page).

MORTALITY.
Michelangelo's fresco of the expulsion from the Garden of Eden (ceiling of the Sistine Chapel, 1508-1512) gives the human beings, who are now condemned to mortality, the form of Titans.

THE ANCESTORS

Chapters 12 to 26 of the Book of Genesis tell the stories of the ancestors. The composition of these passages began with ancient oral narratives and sagas. A second stage, with narrative cycles and collections of texts, culminated in the continuous presentation of the history as a whole. This process took a long time, from the tenth to the sixth century before Christ, and this explains why there are many discontinuities and contradictions; some narratives are handed on in various versions.

These Old Testament texts deal with the early period of Israel, 1200-1000 before Christ, in which it was organized as a tribal society. The ancestors are nomads who live in tents, breed cattle, and move continually from place to place. They come from Mesopotamia in the East and settle in the land of Canaan, which had been promised to them. Society is ordered along patriarchal lines, but the women in the ancestral period take many initiatives and are very active. There is no separation between men's and women's spheres of work; both are involved in working with the cattle, and both are involved in guaranteeing the continued existence of the family through their children. It is in the stories of the ancestors that the people of Israel come into being.

The three ancestral couples, the great models who initiate the history of Israel, are not presented as glorious heroines and heroes, nor as saints. We see them with all their human qualities, their strengths and weaknesses. Their relationship to God is reflected in their human relationships. All the ancestors have very long lives: for example, Abraham lives for 175 years, Sarah for 127. This extreme old age symbolizes a fulfilled, successful life. When such a long life is bestowed on someone, it is a sign of God's fidelity.

The narratives about the ancestors are not romantic love stories. The biblical vocabulary is often brief and businesslike; feelings are hardly ever described, and can only be glimpsed between the lines. Here, the primary importance of love and eros is in connection with fertility. The ancestral mothers are beautiful, but initially infertile. It is God who causes this infertility, and it is God who ends it. These women, initially childless, are thus a symbol of God's grace. It is they who continue the lineage of the promise. God and God's promises are the point of reference for their whole existence. Their stories are charged with a tremendous tension between childlessness and the promise of a numerous progeny. Their relationships display such typically human behaviors and problems as jealousy, sibling rivalry, cheating, or despair caused by childlessness. Even if the world has changed since then, these aspects have not lost their relevance to us.

THREE PATRIARCHS.
A Russian icon (ca. 1830/1840) depicting the patriarch Abraham in the center, with Isaac and Jacob, who protect the souls of the dead (like the soul of the poor Lazarus in the parable, who is "carried away by the angels to Abraham's bosom" (Lk 16:19-31) (opposite).

HOSPITALITY.
A fourteenth-century Russian icon depicting the "three men" (Gen 18:2) who visit Abraham and Sarah in the grove of Mamre (above).

ABRAHAM AND SARAH
(Genesis 11-23)

When we meet Abraham and Sarah, it is taken for granted that they are a married couple. We know nothing of their life before they married. To begin with, their names are Abram and Sarai; it is only when God makes a covenant with them that they are renamed Abraham ("father of many peoples") and Sarah ("princess"), because many peoples and kings are descended from them. Their home is Ur in Chaldea, in Mesopotamia.

Sarah is infertile. Nevertheless, Abraham receives God's promise: "I will make of you a great nation, and I will bless you, and make your name great, so that you will be a blessing" (Gen 12:2). His descendants are to be as many as the stars of heaven. The marriage of Abraham and Sarah is marked from the outset by this dissonance between the divine promise and a reality which contradicts it. In hope, they leave their country and their relatives and make their way to the promised land of Canaan, wandering through it from north to south.

A famine compels Abraham and Sarah to move on to Egypt, which is fertile thanks to the Nile. Since his wife is beautiful, Abraham fears for his own safety and presents her as his sister: "I know well that you are a woman beautiful in appearance; and when the Egyptians see you, they will say, 'This is his wife'; then they will kill me, but they will let you live. Say you are my sister, so that it may go well with me because of you, and that my life may be spared on your account" (12:11-13). Abraham wants to save his own neck at Sarah's expense. There is no discussion between them here: Sarah is a silent victim. In Egypt, Sarah is taken into Pharaoh's house, and Abraham receives gifts of cattle, men and women servants. His fear thus proves to have been completely unfounded. But God intervenes on behalf of the woman who has been abandoned to her fate: he inflicts plagues on Pharaoh, who then calls Abraham to account: "What is this you have done to me? Why did you not tell me that she was your wife? Why did you say, 'She is my sister,' so that I took her for my wife? Now then, here is your wife, take her, and be gone" (12:18f.). Early Jewish interpreters cover up Abraham's scandalous action in handing over his wife to adultery: an angel intervenes and strikes Pharaoh with a stick before he can approach Sarah.

After achieving prosperity in Egypt, Abraham returns with his family to the promised land. The marriage remains childless, and Sarah attempts to solve

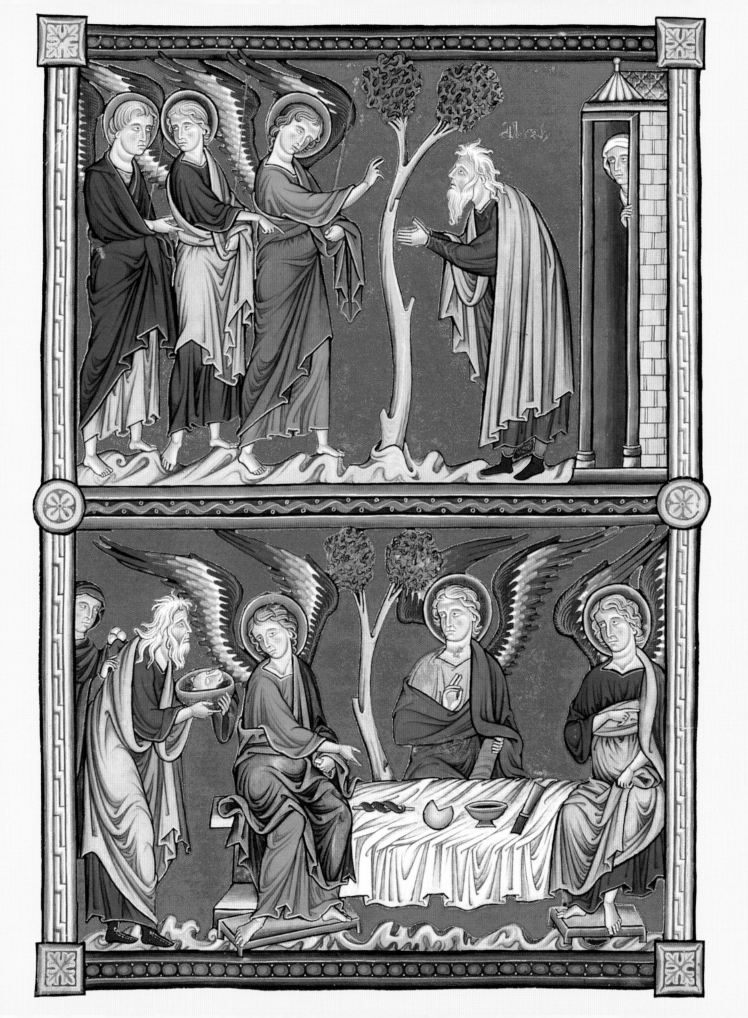

"If Abraham was justified by works, he has something to boast about, but not before God.
For what does the scripture say? 'Abraham believed God, and it
was reckoned to him as righteousness.'"

PAUL, LETTER TO THE ROMANS 4:2-3

FAITH AND OBEDIENCE.
*The mosaic in San Vitale in Ravenna
(ca. 550) links two scenes: at the
meal in the grove of Mamre, Abraham
believes the promise that Sarah will bear a
son (Gen 18:1-33); when God demands
that Abraham offer in sacrifice his
son, Isaac, who has been born in a
miraculous manner, he obeys
(Gen 22:1-19).*

the problem of childlessness by giving Abraham her own slave Hagar as a wife. But Abraham and Sarah cannot resolve the conflict which arises when Hagar becomes pregnant. Her vicarious act of giving birth "on behalf of" Sarah is a failure.

God makes a covenant with Abraham and seals it by means of circumcision. Sarah too is included in God's promise to Abraham. God blesses her and says that she will bear a son. His name is to be Isaac, and God will make a covenant with him and with his descendants.

The name of their longed-for son (meaning "he laughs") comes from the unbelieving laughter of the parents. When Abraham hears this promise, he falls on his face and laughs, and asks: "Can a child be born to a man who is a hundred years old? Can Sarah, who is ninety years old, bear a child?" (17:17). Sarah's laughter likewise gives her son his name. One day, three men – through whom God speaks – visit Abraham and Sarah at the oaks of Mamre. They find

Abraham sitting outside his tent at midday. He greets them and displays a lavish hospitality. The men ask about Sarah and tell Abraham that she will have a son in a year's time. Sarah is listening at the entrance to the tent. She and Abraham are old; their time of fertility is past, and she views the situation realistically. "So Sarah laughed to herself, saying, 'After I have grown old, and my husband is old, shall I have pleasure?'" (18:12). But nothing is impossible for God. When Sarah recognizes who it is that is speaking through the three men, she is terrified and denies that she has laughed. But God addresses her directly: "Oh yes, you did laugh" (18:15). This is the only passage in which God addresses her directly – and here, she is rebuked. Otherwise, it is always Abraham who receives promises from God and converses directly with him.

Now the birth has been predicted very concretely: Sarah is to give birth one year from now. But the fulfillment of this promise is postponed by the insertion of a second narrative in which Abraham abandons his wife. This time,

OBEDIENCE AND REWARD.
This seventeenth-century tapestry illustrates the happy ending of the story of "Abraham in Gerar" (Gen 20:1-18): Abimelech restores to Abraham his alleged "sister" Sarah, obeying the instruction God has given him in a dream. God rewards Abimelech by putting an end to the infertility in his family.

she is handed over to Abimelech in Gerar, a town in the land of the Philistines, between the Mediterranean and the Negev desert. In this version of the story, God warns Abimelech in a dream, thus preventing the scandal of adultery.

The miracle of God's promise is greater in Sarah than in the other ancestral mothers. She is ninety years old when her son Isaac is born, i.e., far beyond the age at which a woman can give birth; and Abraham is one hundred. But this longed-for event is described in brief sentences, with few words: "The Lord dealt with Sarah as he had said, and the Lord did for Sarah as he had promised. Sarah conceived and bore Abraham a son in his old age, at the time of which God had spoken to him. Abraham gave the name Isaac to his son" and circumcised him when he was eight days old. "Now Sarah said, 'God has brought laughter for me; everyone who hears will laugh with me.' And she said, 'Who would ever have said to Abraham that Sarah would nurse children? Yet I have borne him a son in his old age'" (21:1-7). God makes Abraham and Sarah laugh, and this joy at the birth of the child, so long awaited, is contagious.

But the parents' love for Isaac is put to a harsh test. God makes a terrible demand of Abraham: "Take your son, your only son Isaac, whom you love, and go to the land of Moriah, and offer him there as a burnt offering on one of the mountains that I shall show you" (22:2). All Abraham's hopes of numerous descendants repose in this son – and now he is to be sacrificed. Abraham obeys and sets out with Isaac, who notices that something is wrong and asks his father: "Where is the lamb for a burnt offering?" Abraham's reply is brief: "God himself will provide the lamb for a burnt offering, my son" (22:7f.). The tension increases: Abraham makes the wood ready, binds Isaac, and lays him on top of the wood on the altar. He is already stretching out his hand to take the knife and slaughter his son, when an angel of God intervenes from heaven at the last minute and calls out to Abraham: "Do not lay your hand on the boy or do anything to him; for now I know that you fear God, since you have not withheld your son, your only son, from me" (22:12). Instead of Isaac, a ram is offered as a burnt sacrifice.

"He did not weaken in faith when he considered his own body, which was already as good as dead (for he was about a hundred years old), or when he considered the barrenness of Sarah's womb. No distrust made him waver concerning the promise of God, but he grew strong in his faith as he gave glory to God, being fully convinced that God was able to do what he had promised."

PAUL, LETTER TO THE ROMANS 4:19-21

THE PROMISE.
This miniature in the Octateuch *(a manuscript of the first eight books of the Bible, written in Smyrna in the eighth century) concentrates on the core of the scene at the oaks of Mamre: a son is promised to Abraham and Sarah. Their gestures express the faith with which they accept the promise.*

This story confronts our faith even today with a question: What kind of God is this, who requires a father to slaughter his son? The fact that this cruel deed is not carried out is no consolation. The story remains terrible, and theologians have discussed it for centuries. In Christianity, Abraham is interpreted as the model of one who seeks God, of one who believes unconditionally. The Jewish tradition employs the Hebrew term *aqedah*, the "binding" of Isaac, because he is only bound by Abraham, not actually killed in sacrifice. The "binding" of Isaac suggests how one might make some sense of inexplicable suffering, martyrdom, and persecution.

The biblical narrative does not mention Sarah here. Although the mother is just as much affected as the father, the only actors here are Abraham and God. In Jewish interpretations, Sarah is an important figure and is considered a prophetess. One mediaeval midrash asks: Where was Sarah when Abraham led Isaac off to sacrifice? It replies that Abraham managed to separate Isaac from Sarah only on the pretext that he was taking their son to a house where he would receive an exceptionally good education. They take a tearful leave of one another; then Satan visits Sarah and tells her that Isaac has been offered in sacrifice. Sarah dies of grief.

In Genesis, Sarah's death is in fact related after the "binding" of Isaac. She dies at the age of 127 in Kiriath-arba-Hebron. After lamenting Sarah's death and weeping over her, Abraham purchases from a Hittite the cave of Machpelah in the grove of Mamre and buries her there. This fulfills the promise that Abraham would possess the land: the first piece of territory that belongs to his clan is Sarah's burial place.

After her death, Abraham married another wife, Keturah. He bequeathed everything to his favorite son Isaac. He gave presents to the sons of his concubines and sent them away eastward, as far as possible from Isaac. He then died at the age of 175, "an old man and full of years" (25:8). Isaac and Ishmael buried him too in the cave of Machpelah. The tomb of the ancestors is venerated in Hebron to this day.

Abraham and Sarah had a very eventful marriage, with the distress of their childlessness, the promise by God, the birth of their son, and then the new danger to which he was exposed. The principal elements structuring their relationship were their wanderings, their childlessness, and their parenthood. Artists tend to portray them as elderly people. They stay together through the ups and downs of life together. They do not live in an unbroken symbiosis; there are times when Abraham takes an initiative on his own, and hands Sarah over to foreign rulers because he fears for his life, and it is he alone who bears responsibility for the sacrifice of Isaac. Sarah's initiative, when she tries to obtain a child using her maid Hagar as a proxy, leads to a marital crisis. Abraham is in a continuous dialogue with God, and Sarah is involved only indirectly in this relationship. The love of the oldest of the ancestral couples is expressed in the fact that, despite all the difficulties, they are unconditionally loyal to each other.

"Isaac said to his father Abraham, 'The fire and the wood are here, but where is the lamb for a burnt offering?' Abraham said, 'God himself will provide the lamb for a burnt offering, my son.'"
GENESIS 22:7-8

FATHER AND SON.
Rembrandt's etching (1645) is a detail from the story of the sacrifice of Isaac: we see Abraham giving an evasive answer to his son's question about the sacrificial lamb. Is he secretly hoping that he will not need to sacrifice his own son?

ISAAC AND REBEKAH

(Genesis 24-28)

The marriage between Isaac and Rebekah is an arranged marriage. Abraham sends his oldest servant to seek a wife for Isaac in his homeland, Mesopotamia; and Rebekah is the woman he finds. The woman whom Abraham seeks for his son Isaac must be willing – like Abraham himself – to leave her country and her family and go to the promised land.

The servant, furnished with gifts and a great caravan of camels, sets out and stops at the well outside a city, where the women come out to draw water. He prays to God for success in his undertaking: the right woman is to be the one who answers his request and gives water, not only to the servant, but also to his camels. Before he has finished speaking, Rebekah comes to the well. She is the daughter of Bethuel and the granddaughter of Abraham's brother Nahor and his wife Milcah. In other words, she is a descendant of the relatives whom Abraham had left behind in the east, in Mesopotamia. She is very beautiful, and is a virgin. Rebekah gives water to the servant, then to the camels, thus showing that she is the right woman. The servant gives her jewelry of gold and asks that he may spend the night in the house of her family. While Rebekah runs ahead to the house of her mother, the servant thanks God for this happy outcome.

The servant is received with lavish hospitality in the house of Laban, Rebekah's brother, and he asks for her hand in marriage for his master's son. The family consents, in obedience to the will of God, but they ask Rebekah whether she is willing to depart with Abraham's servant. When she says, "I will," they send her on her way with a blessing: "May you, our sister, become thousands of myriads; may your offspring gain possession of the gates of their foes" (24:58-60). Rebekah and her maids set off on camels, accompanying Abraham's servant.

Rebekah and Isaac meet for the first time near the well of Lahai-roi in the Negev, the southern region of the land. After she was thrown out by Abraham and Sarah, Hagar experienced deliverance there by a messenger from God and gave the well this name: "well of the Living One who sees me" (16:14). At evening, Isaac is walking in the fields when he lifts his eyes and sees camels approaching. When Rebekah lifts her eyes, she sees Isaac and descends – indeed, falls – from her camel. She asks the servant: "Who is the man over there, walking in the field to meet us?" When she hears that he is Isaac, she takes a veil and covers herself. Isaac brings Rebekah into the tent of his mother Sarah. She becomes his wife, and he loves her: "So Isaac was comforted after his mother's death" (24:65-67). In comparison with the detailed account of the wooing of Rebekah, the account of her first meeting with Isaac is concise and matter-of-fact. In this arranged marriage, love grows only after the wedding. It is not some-

BRIDE AND BRIDEGROOM.
After Eliezer has successfully asked for her hand in marriage, Rebekah meets her bridegroom, Isaac. In the biblical text, she veils herself, but here – in a detail from a painting by the Neapolitan Baroque artist Andrea Vaccaro (ca. 1650) – she goes to meet her future husband in full awareness of her beauty, with an openness that is almost provocative (opposite page).

ASKING FOR A BRIDE.
This miniature in the Wenceslaus Bible *(ca. 1400) shows how Rebekah gives water to the camels of Abraham's servant, Eliezer. It is here, at the well outside the town, that he paves the way for Isaac's marriage to Rebekah.*

SECRECY.
Rembrandt's painting The Jewish Bride *(ca. 1665) probably takes as its subject the alleged "siblings" Isaac and Rebekah, who are observed by Abimelech (opposite page).*

AN EXCEPTIONAL WOMAN.
Rebekah quenches Eliezer's thirst (Gen 24:18). As the painting of the Spanish Baroque artist Bartolomé Estéban Murillo emphasizes, she does something that no other girl at the well would do.

thing to be taken for granted, as we see from the emphatic way in which the author mentions it.

Like all the ancestral mothers, Rebekah is initially unfruitful. After Isaac prays to God, she becomes pregnant with twins. When the unborn children struggle together in her womb, she asks God what this means, and receives an oracle concerning their birth: "Two nations are in your womb, and two peoples born of you shall be divided; the one shall be stronger than the other, the elder shall serve the younger" (25:23). The firstborn has red hair all over his body, like an animal's skin. He is given the name Esau ("red"); the second twin is called Jacob, a name which contains two meanings – first, "heel," since he is holding his brother's heel when he emerges from the womb; but also "cheating." Esau, the firstborn, becomes a hunter, and Isaac prefers him, because he loves eating game. Jacob is a more domestic man, and stays close to the tents; he is Rebekah's favorite son. The brothers are rivals from the very beginning. As the firstborn, Esau has legal advantages, but he treats his rights lightly. One day, when he

comes home hungry from the field, he sells his rights to his brother for a plate of lentil stew.

A third parallel narrative telling how the ancestral mothers were handed over to a foreign ruler involves Isaac and Rebekah. Like Abraham and Sarah, they leave their land because of a famine and come to Abimelech, the king of the Philistines, in Gerar. God confirms to Isaac the promises of territory and of numerous descendants which he had earlier made to Abraham. Like Abraham, Isaac too disowns his wife. He fears that the men of Gerar might kill him because of her beauty, so he pretends that she is his sister. One day, Abimelech looks out of a window and sees Isaac fondling Rebekah. He is furious, and demands that Isaac explain why he has concealed the fact that she is his wife. Isaac admits that he acted, not out of concern for Rebekah, but prompted by his own (unfounded) fears. The story has a happy ending, and Abimelech gives his protection to Isaac and Rebekah. God's blessing accompanies Isaac here and gives him a rich harvest.

"When Isaac had been there a long time, King Abimelech of the Philistines looked out of a window and saw him fondling his wife Rebekah."

GENESIS 26:8

TWINS.
The miniatures in the Wenceslaus Bible *(Ca. 1400) depict Rebekah in childbed with Esau and Jacob, then the parents with their growing twins. In both pictures, Rebekah holds Jacob in*

her arms. Finally, with the help of his mother, Jacob cunningly obtains Isaac's blessing for himself (below).

"And the Lord said to Rebekah, 'Two nations are in your womb, and two peoples born of you shall be divided; the one shall be stronger than the other, the elder shall serve the younger.'"

GENESIS 25:23

The rivalry between Esau and Jacob casts a shadow over the relationship between Isaac and Rebekah. After getting hold of Esau's right of primogeniture by a trick, Jacob also contrives to obtain his father's blessing. Isaac, by now old and blind, calls his firstborn son Esau and asks him to hunt game and prepare a delicious meal, so that he may bless him before he dies. Rebekah overhears these words and sends her favorite son Jacob to fetch two young goats for Isaac. She prepares the food her husband loves. She accepts the responsibility for what Jacob does, because the oracle about the birth of her children had told her that Jacob was the one who would inherit the promise of God. Rebekah's plan succeeds, although the blind Isaac becomes suspicious and tries with his remaining senses to find out whether the man standing before him is truly Esau. He is convinced when he smells Esau's clothes (which Jacob is wearing) and the skins of the kids, which his son has tied to his hands and throat, and he blesses Jacob, the second-born son on whom the divine promise reposes.

When Esau comes to his father with the game he has caught, Isaac and his firstborn son recognize the trick, and their shock and bitterness is great. The blessing of the firstborn has already been pronounced, and all that Esau receives is a minor blessing. Now he waits only for his father to die, so that he may take his revenge on Jacob. Accordingly, Rebekah advises her favorite son to leave the country and flee to her brother Laban. Jacob departs after his parents have asked him to seek a wife among their own relatives. The blessing with which his father sends him on his way is a comprehensive confirmation of God's blessing of Abraham.

The Book of Genesis shows us Isaac and Rebekah in various phases of their marriage. At the beginning, there is the vivid story of her wooing, in which God reveals that Rebekah is the right wife for Isaac. At the beginning of their day-to-day married life, Isaac loves Rebekah, and they wait together for a long time before children are born. In their midlife years, we see Isaac disowning Rebekah; but we also see him fondling her, and this indicates that they had a tender physical relationship. The birth of their sons brings a distance between them, and in their old age, the central element is their antithetical relationship to their sons. Their relationship is dominated by Isaac's love for Esau and Rebekah's love for Jacob. This marriage is no idyll. On the contrary, deceit stands in the background – both in Gerar, when Isaac disowns Rebekah and presents her as his sister; and later on, when Rebekah orchestrates the deceit her favorite son Jacob practices on Isaac, presenting him as Esau. This relationship, which develops from initial love to subsequent mutual deceit, shows that the ancestors are not perfect. They too have their weaknesses.

JACOB AND LEAH AND RACHEL

(Genesis 29-53)

The relationship between Jacob and the two sisters Leah and Rachel is an unhappy eternal triangle which shows us the ups and downs of daily life in a polygynous marriage.

The love story between Jacob and Rachel begins idyllically. Fleeing from his brother Esau, Jacob travels eastward and sees a well in a field, surrounded by flocks of sheep. When he talks to the shepherds, he learns that he is close to his goal, Haran, and his uncle Laban, his mother's brother. During this conversation, Laban's daughter Rachel, a shepherdess, comes to the well with her father's sheep. When Jacob sees her, he rolls the stone from the mouth of the well and waters the sheep. Then he kisses Rachel and weeps loudly. Such a kiss in public is an unusual action. It is a joyful kiss between relatives; but it is also the beginning of Jacob's great and tragic love for Rachel.

Jacob informs Rachel that he is Rebekah's son and thus her relative, and she hurries off to tell her father. Laban arrives, greets Jacob warmly as his sister's son, and invites him into his house. He has two daughters. The older, Leah, has weak eyes; the younger, Rachel, is very beautiful, and Jacob falls in love with her. The two men work out a deal. Jacob is a refugee looking for a safe place to live, and has no means of paying for a bride. Accordingly, "Jacob served seven years for Rachel, and they seemed to him but a few days because of the love he had for her" (29:20).

After the seven years, he asks Laban to give him his wife: his time is up, and he wants to marry her. Laban does not reply, but acts. He holds a great feast for the whole neighborhood, but in the evening it is not Rachel, but his older daughter Leah whom he brings to Jacob, and he sleeps with her. When he realizes in the morning that he has slept with Leah, he upbraids Laban angrily and demands an explanation. Laban replies calmly: "This is not done in our country – giving the younger before the firstborn" (29:26). But if Jacob serves another seven years, Rachel too can become his wife. Jacob accepts the deal. He sleeps with Rachel too, and loves her more than Leah. On their marriage, Leah is given Zilpah as maid, and Rachel is given Bilhah.

The text does not explain why Jacob, who is completely in love with Rachel, does not at once realize that he is sleeping with the wrong woman. In the Talmud, the deceit is explained by stating that Rachel had told Leah about the signs she and Jacob had agreed upon for their wedding night. This means that Rachel herself helps her sister not to be recognized as Leah: Rachel wants to avoid bringing shame upon her sister, who has certain privileges because she is older.

"Leah said to Rachel, 'Is it a small matter that you have taken away my husband? Would you take away my son's mandrakes also?'"
GENESIS 30:15

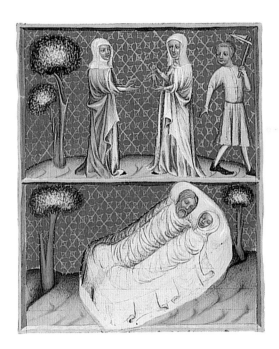

LOVE POTION.
This miniature in two parts from the Wenceslaus Bible *(ca. 1400) shows (above) the quarrel between Leah and Rachel about the mandrakes which Reuben had brought to his mother Leah, whom Jacob now despised; these were regarded as an aphrodisiac. Below, we see Jacob sleeping with Leah once again.*

GREETINGS.
The detail reproduced below from a drawing (ca. 1460) by the Dutchman Hugo van der Goes shows the first meeting between Jacob and his cousin Rachel.

This drawing may have provided the model for the depiction of the ensuing meeting between Jacob and his uncle Laban on a sixteenth-century Brussels tapestry (opposite page).

After "completing the week" with Leah, Jacob is finally wedded to Rachel, for whom he has longed. He pays the agreed price for Rachel, seven further years of service, only after he has married her. The story shows that this polygynous marriage with the two sisters does not function smoothly. They compete with one another to get what they do not have: Leah for Jacob's love, and Rachel for children. With their maids, Rachel and Leah build up the house of Israel. Their experience is reflected in the names they give to their children, to whom the twelve tribes of Israel trace their origin. In this phase, Jacob's feelings are not mentioned. His love for Rachel and his angry disappointment were described at the time of his marriage, but now we are told the story from the perspective of his two wives.

God is on the side of those who are at a disadvantage. He sees that Leah is unloved, neglected, indeed hated. And that is why he makes her fertile, while Rachel initially remains childless. Leah conceives and bears four sons, one after the other: Reuben ("See, a son!"), Simeon (God "hears"), Levi ("companion"), and Judah ("praise"). In the names she gives her sons, Leah expresses both her gratitude to God and her abiding hope – which remains unfulfilled – that her husband will love her.

When Rachel realizes that she is not becoming pregnant by Jacob, she reacts with envy of her sister, who is blessed with children. Rachel's great yearning is not for Jacob's love, but for children. In her despair, she appeals to Jacob to give her children. She would rather die than remain childless. Jacob responds to her desperate plea with anger: "Am I in the place of God, who has withheld from you the fruit of the womb?" (30:2). It is not Jacob, but God who is responsible for fertility or infertility. In her despair, Rachel herself (like Sarah) now takes the initiative to solve the problem, and gives Jacob her maid Bilhah as wife, "so that she may bear upon my knees and that I too may have children through her" (30:3). The vicarious child-bearing of a slave woman for her mistress, an ancient Israelite form of surrogate motherhood, was a legitimate institution in the Old Testament: the child born to a husband and to the slave woman of his wife was adopted by the act of bestowing a name, and was then considered the legitimate offspring of the wife and her husband. This had unfortunate results in the case of Sarah, but now the vicarious birth works well for Rachel. Bilhah becomes pregnant and bears two sons, and Rachel gives them the names Dan ("judge," because God has given her what she considers her rights) and Naphtali ("wrestler," because "With mighty wrestlings I have wrestled with my sister, and have prevailed," 30:8). Leah follows Rachel's example and gives Jacob her maid Zilpah as wife. She bears two sons, and Leah gives them names signifying joy: Gad ("good fortune") and Asher ("child of happiness").

The first conversation between Rachel and Leah involves bartering love for fertility. Leah's firstborn son Reuben finds mandrakes in the field, and brings them to his mother. The roots of these plants have a human-like form, and they

"Then Rachel and
Leah answered Jacob,
'Is there any portion or
inheritance left to us
in our father's house?
Are we not regarded
by him as foreigners?'"
GENESIS 31:14-15

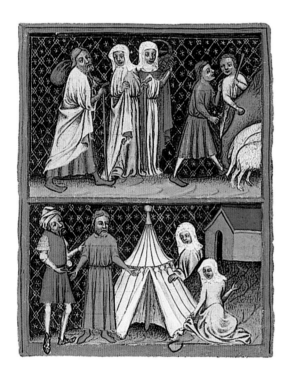

SEPARATION.
This miniature in two parts from the
Wenceslaus Bible *(ca. 1400) shows
Jacob with Leah and Rachel leaving the
women's home, and Laban who
catches up with them and accuses
them of theft. Jacob's wide open hands
are a gesture which pleads his innocence.*

were considered an aphrodisiac in the ancient east. Rachel hopes that they will make her fruitful, and she barters with Leah, offering her one night with Jacob in exchange for the mandrakes. Jacob is the plaything of his two wives here. When he comes home from the field in the evening, Leah comes to meet him and informs him: "You must come in to me; for I have hired you with my son's mandrakes" (30:16). So he spends one night with her. The barter brings Leah more success than Rachel: Jacob sleeps with her once more, God hears her, and Leah bears two more sons and a daughter: Issachar ("hire"), Zebulun ("honor"), and Dinah ("judge").

It is only now that God "remembers" Rachel and makes her fertile. She becomes pregnant and gives birth to a son. "She said, 'God has taken away my reproach'; and she named him Joseph ['he adds'], saying, 'May the Lord add to me another son!'" (30:23f.). At last, Rachel has her son – but one son is not enough for her.

After Rachel has given birth, Jacob goes to Laban and says that after serving him for fourteen years, he now wishes to return to his own land with his wives and children. But Laban does not want to let him go, since he has become rich thanks to Jacob's work, which is blessed by God. Laban and Jacob make a new agreement, which gives Jacob a share in Laban's herd and allows him to breed his own animals. Jacob remains with Laban for another six years, together with his family. He is so skillful and successful in breeding the animals that his own herd grows, while Laban and his sons become jealous.

Now God intervenes, charging Jacob to return home and promising his aid. Jacob calls his wives to him out in the field and discusses the situation with them. The two sisters had hitherto been rivals, but now they both agree that their father has cheated not only Jacob, but also themselves, by selling them but taking no money for them on their marriage. They argue that the wealth that Jacob has acquired out of Laban's property belongs to them too, and to their children. Without hesitation, they resolve to go with Jacob wherever his God will lead them.

Jacob, with his family and his numerous flocks, sets out to go to Isaac in the land of Canaan. They leave in secret, without taking their leave of Laban, and Rachel takes revenge on her father by stealing his teraphim (figures of the gods for domestic worship) while he is away shearing the sheep. Three days after their flight, Laban finds out what has happened, gives chase, and catches up with them seven days later in the mountains of Gilead. He demands an explanation of the sudden departure and of the theft of his domestic gods, but assures him that he will not do him any harm, since Jacob is protected by God. Jacob, who knows nothing of the theft of the teraphim, tells Laban: "I was afraid, for I thought that you would take your daughters from me by force. In the presence of our kinsfolk, point out what I have that is yours, and take it" (31:31f.). Laban searches the tents of Jacob, Leah, and two maids, but finds nothing. Rachel has put the teraphim in the camel's saddle in her tent, and is sitting upon it. She excuses herself to her father for not standing up, since she is having her monthly period – so Laban finds nothing. After a vehement argument, Laban admits that God is on Jacob's side, and makes a covenant with him, which contains a clause guaranteeing the safety

JUSTIFICATION.
The scene depicted in the late Gothic miniature of the Wenceslaus Bible *(opposite page) is the subject of this Baroque painting (ca. 1650) by Bartolomé Estéban*

of Rachel and Leah: Jacob must not ill-treat them, nor may he take any additional wives. It seems cynical of the despotic Laban, who initiated the unhappy eternal triangle, that he should formulate this clause protecting his daughters. Jacob and Laban part company at the border of the promised land. On the following morning, Laban kisses his children farewell and blesses them, returning to his own land of Haran.

Jacob does not know what awaits him in the promised land, in the region of Edom: is Esau still angry with him? Accordingly, he sends ahead servants bearing gifts to appease his brother. Before he meets Esau, he lines up his wives and their respective children in keeping with his own esteem for them: first the maids

Murillo. In both cases, Rachel prevents Laban from discovering the household gods which she has stolen: "Let not my lord be angry that I cannot rise before you, for the way of women is upon me" (Gen 31:35).

HAEC SVNT NOMINA

filioz isrl qui ingressi sunt in egyptu cum Iacob
singuli cu domib; suis introierunt Ruben: Syme
on: Leui: Iudas: ysachar: zabulon et Beniamin
Dan: et Neptalim: Gad: et Aser: Erant igitur
omes anime eoz q egressi sut de femore Iacob
septuagita. Ioseph aute in egypto erat. Quo
mortuo et universis frib; eius omni q, cognatio
ne sua: filii isrl creuerut et quasi germinantes
multiplicati st. ac roborati nimis impleuerut
terra. Surrexit interea rex nouus super egyptu
qui ignorabat Ioseph. Et ait ad pplm suum. Ecce
ce populus filioz israel multus et fortior nobis e
Venite sapienter opprimamus eu: ne forte mul
tiplicetur: et si ingruerit contra nos bellu: ad
datur nris inimicis: expugnatisq, nobis egredi
atur de terra. Prepofuit itaq, magistros operu:
ut affligeret eos oneribz: edificaueruntq, urbes
tabernaculoz Pharaom Phiton: et Ramesses
quatoq, opprimebant eos: tanto magis multi
plicabantur: et crescebat. Oderantq, filios isrl
egypti: et affligebat illudentes eis: atq, ad a
maritudine perducebant uita eoz operibus
duris luti et lateris: omni q, famulatu quo in
terre opibus premebantur. Dixit aute rex e
gypti obstetricibus hebreoz: quaz una uoca
batur Sephora: altera Phua: precipies eis. Qn

obstetricabitis hebreas: et partus tepus aduene
rit: si masculus fuerit interficite eu: si femina
reseruate. Timuerunt obstetrices deum: et nõ
fecerunt iuxta preceptu regis egypti: sed con
seruabat mares. Quibz ad se accersitis rex ait
Quid nã est hoc quod facere uoluistis ut pueõs
seruaretis: Que rnderut. Non sut hebree si
cut egyptie mulieres. Ipe enim obstetricãdi
hent scientia: et priusq ueniamus ad eas pa
rut. Bene ergo fecit deus obstetricibz. Et cre
uit pplus cofortatus q, est nimis. Et qa timue
rut obstetrices deu: edificauit illis domos. Pre
cepit aute Pharao omni pplo suo dicens. Quicqd
masculini sexus natu fuerit: in flume proicite:
quicqd femini reseruate. · C II ·
Gressus est post haec uir de domo leui accepta
uxore stirpis sue: q cocepit et peperit filium.
Et uidens eum elegante: abscodit mensibz tribz.
Cuq iam celare non posset: sumpsit fiscelam
scirpea: et liniuit ea bitumie ac pice: posu
it q, intus infantulu: et exposuit eu in carep
to fluminis state procul sorore eius: et con
derate euentu rei: Ecce aute descedebat fi
lia Pharaonis ut lauaretur in flumine: et pu
elle eius gradiebatur p crepidine aluei. Que
cu uidisset fiscella in papirione misit una de

with their children, then Leah with her children, and finally Rachel with Joseph. Jacob's fears prove unfounded: Esau runs up to him, embraces him and kisses him in friendship. The brothers are reconciled, and Jacob goes with his family and his flocks to Sichem in Canaan, where he settles.

God charges them to go to Bethel, where Jacob builds an altar. On the road from Bethel to Ephrath (Bethlehem), Rachel dies giving birth to her longed-for second son. She gives him the name Ben-oni (which can be translated, in view of her impending death, as "son of my doom," but also as "son of my vigor," since this is the son to whom Rachel has given all her vital force); but even before she dies, Jacob gives his son another name which sounds very like the first, Benjamin ("son of the right hand" or "son of joy"). Rachel is buried where she dies, and her tomb is a place of pilgrimage even today, above all for childless women who pray that they may conceive and for pregnant women praying for an easy delivery. Jacob moves on to Hebron, where he meets his father Isaac. When Isaac dies at the age of 180 years, old and full of years, he is buried by his two sons, Esau and Jacob.

The relationship between Jacob, Rachel, and Leah is an unhappy eternal triangle, with unfulfilled wishes, where each of them has something another wants. Jacob loves Rachel, and this love is the most important thing of all to him; but it is not really clear whether she loves him. Rachel can indeed be sure that Jacob loves her, but that is not as important to her as the motherhood for which she must wait so long. Leah is not loved by Jacob, but she bears him one child after another. This polygynous marriage is kept together, not so much by love, but by a kind of family solidarity. They stick together against Laban, the father of Rachel and Leah, and against Esau, the brother of Jacob; they stick together in flight and struggle.

The spheres in which Jacob and his two wives live are cattle-breeding and the family. At the beginning, Rachel is presented as a shepherdess, but Jacob takes over this task from her. Both Jacob and his two wives attach great importance to having children, since this entails the growth of the people of Israel: the story of the people is narrated as the story of a family.

"These are the names of the sons of Israel who came to Egypt with Jacob, each with his household: Reuben, Simeon, Levi, and Judah, Issachar, Zebulun, and Benjamin, Dan and Naphtali, Gad and Asher."
EXODUS 1:1-4

A LARGE FAMILY.
The illumination at the beginning of the Book of Exodus in the Urbino Bible, *which illustrates the first verses, recalls how Jacob (Israel) and the "sons of Israel" moved from Canaan to Egypt (opposite page).*

FLIGHT TO CANAAN.
The painting Jacob's Journey *(ca. 1650) by the Italian Baroque artist Giovanni Benedetto Castiglione depicts Jacob's flight with Leah, Rachel, their children, and all his possessions from Mesopotamia to Canaan.*

JUDAH AND TAMAR

(Genesis 38)

"He went over to her at
the road side, and said,
'Come, let me come in to you,'
for he did not know
that she was his
daughter-in-law."

GENESIS 38:16

A PROSTITUTE'S WAGES.
*For the service which Judah expects from
Tamar, as depicted in the* Vienna Codex
2554 *(ca. 1210), the alleged prostitute is to
receive a goat kid. The miniature depicts
Judah and the unveiled Tamar.
Judah, who is on his way to the sheep
shearing, gives her his staff and his signet
ring as pledges (miniature from the*
Wenceslaus Bible, *ca. 1400) (opposite page).*

The name of Tamar occurs with that of three other women from the
Hebrew Bible in the genealogy of Jesus. In genealogical tables of this kind, a
patriarchal society was usually interested only in men, who are listed as follows:
"X begot Y." In Matt 1, however, we find Tamar, Rahab, Ruth, and Bathsheba.
Why are these women mentioned among the ancestors of Jesus, and what do they
have in common?

Tamar is the first of the four women in this list. She was a Canaanite, i.e.
a foreigner. Her name means "date-palm," a biblical symbol of fertility – but it
seems that she cannot become a mother. But Tamar is a woman who knows what
she wants and who acts resolutely in order to get it. It is obvious that the story of
Judah and Tamar in Gen 38 has its origin in groups of women. It must be older
than the Book of Ruth, since 4:12 of that book refers to Tamar when a blessing
is pronounced on Ruth. We can easily imagine both these stories being handed
down in groups where women told one another about their successes, and about
the tricks they sometimes played on men.

Judah, one of the sons of Jacob, is the main character. On him rests the
blessing of God's promise, and it is his descendants who will be centrally important for the people of Israel. Accordingly, it is Judah and his wife Shua who are
blessed with three sons, and who dominate the story at the beginning. The future
of the clan seems assured. When Judah seeks a wife for his firstborn son Er, he
finds Tamar and the two are married. Nothing is said about any consent on
Tamar's part. Nor is Er consulted about his wishes. Here, the father of the clan
follows the customs of that time when he looks for a wife for his son.

However, the hopes set on this marriage remain unfulfilled, since Judah's
oldest son dies without begetting a son. The Levirate law required the brother-in-
law of the widow, i.e., Er's next oldest brother, to take the place of the dead man.
He is obliged to beget a son on behalf of Er, so that his brother's name may not
die out. Hence, Tamar is given to Onan as his wife. But Onan is aware that any
child whom he will beget will be counted as Er's, and Gen 38:9 tells us: "He
spilled his semen on the ground whenever he went in to his brother's wife, so that
he would not give offspring to his brother." (In the Christian era, this led to the
coinage of the word "onanism" for masturbation.) Onan displays a lack of solidarity with his brother, and Yahweh puts him to death: the biblical text unam-
biguously interprets his sudden death as a punishment.

Judah has still one son, the youngest, but he does not want to give him
to Tamar, since he is afraid that he too might die. So he sends Tamar back to her

dinck sprach iudas zu thamar
seiner snur · Bis ein wittwe in
deines vaters hous / vntz bis
mein sun sela ge wechset wenne
er vorchte das er ouch icht wür
de sterben · als seine bruder · Sie
gienk hin / vnd wonte in ires
vaters hous · Vnd do nu vol
gangen waren vil tage · do
starp die tochter sue · iudas
housvrowe · Vnd her noch der
clage nam her trost vnd gink
ouf zu den scherern seiner schaf
her vnd hyras der wolla mite
der schafmeister seiner hert · ge
gen tamna · Vnd das wart ge
saget thamarn seiner snur so
das ir sweher ouf gienge · ge
gen thamna die schaf zu sche
ren · Vnd sie legte von ir wg

want des witwetums · vnd
nam einen svmer mantil vnd

wandilte ir geperde vnd ire
wat · vnd satzte sich an des stei
ges wegscheide do man treit
het gegen thamna / do von
das gewachsen was sela vn
si nicht genomen hette tzu
einem manne · Do die ersach
iudas / do vorwente her sich
es were ein hure / wenne sie
hete trongen vochittert das
man sie nicht erkente · Nu
gienk er tzu ir ein vnd sprach
Las mich das ich bei dir lige
wenne her woste nicht das
sie were sein snur · Vnd si ant
worte · was wiltu mir geben
das du gebrouchest meines
beislafens · her sprach · Ich
wil dir senden einen bok ous
der hert · Vnd aber so sprach
sie · Ich leide was du wilt ist
das du mir empfant gibst
vntz bis du mir das gesen
dest das du mir gelobist · Do
sprach iudas · was wiltu
das ich dir gebe zu pfande
Vnd sie antworte · dein vigi
lein vnd dein achsil gespan
vnd den stab den du hast in
deiner hant · Dorumbe mit
einem beislafen empfienk
das weip / vnd stund ouff
vnd gienk von danne · vnd
legte abe die wat / die sie hatt
an sich genomen / vnd tat
an ir witwetum gewant

In Thomas Mann's four-volume novel *Joseph and His Brothers* (1933-1943), it is Tamar who asks to marry her brother-in-law (Judah's third son) after Onan dies. Judah is enraged: "What presumption on the part of this woman! Does she think I should give her the little sheep too, so that she can slaughter it? She is an Ishtar, who kills her bridegroom. She is filled with insatiable lust, she devours young men."

THOMAS MANN,

"JOSEPH UND SEINE BRÜDER"

father's house. Judah's fear that women may mean death to men is found in many fairy tales and myths, and also in the story of Lilith; this is why special protective measures were necessary on one's wedding night. We see this in the story of Tobias and Sarah, a woman whose seven earlier husbands had all died on their wedding nights: Tobias wards off the danger by prudent action and by prayer before the consummation of the marriage. In all these stories, there is something dangerous about the woman. They evoke a primal male fear that the woman may take the lead in love and sexuality. It is this fear that makes Judah blame Tamar for the death of his two sons, as verse 11 makes clear: "he feared that Shelah too would die, like his brothers." The biblical text, however, explicitly rejects this anxiety on Judah's part. In the case of Er, we are told that he displeased Yahweh, who therefore slew him; likewise in the case of Onan, the author underlines that he did something that displeased Yahweh, who therefore slew him too. Thus, it is God alone who is responsible for the deaths of the two older sons of Judah; or to put it more precisely, it is they themselves who cause their own early deaths by their deeds. Their death is God's punishment. Tamar is completely blameless, as the unfolding of the story shows.

Many years pass, Shelah has grown up, and Judah's own wife has died. As a widower, Judah still will not permit the marriage between his youngest son and Tamar, and now she takes matters into her own hands. She acts with determination and goes directly to the patriarch Judah himself, passing over his third and final son. After much reflection, she employs cunning to achieve her goal, i.e., to take her place in the line of those who pass on the promise of God to new generations.

From verse 14, where the main part of the narrative begins, it is Tamar alone who takes the initiative. She is not content to play the role of a victim, but puts off her widow's garments, conceals herself with a veil, and sits down at the entrance to the town. She knows that Judah will pass this place at the annual sheep shearing, which was the occasion for a great feast where alcohol flowed freely. He will assume that Tamar is a prostitute. She wears a veil because her plan can succeed only if Judah does not recognize her. They reach an agreement about her sexual services: he promises the unknown woman a kid from the flock (the going price for intercourse). Since he does not have the kid with him, he gives her three objects as a pledge, the insignia of a free man: his signet ring, his cord, and his staff. It is possible that a child will be conceived, and these pledges will permit Tamar at any time to prove the identity of its father. And this is the only important point for the narrator.

Once again, some time passes, until Tamar's pregnancy becomes public knowledge. In the meantime, Judah has attempted in vain to find the "prostitute" and to give her the kid he had promised. When he is told that Tamar has committed fornication, he pronounces the verdict: "Let her be burned!" (38:24). This makes it clear that she is still considered a member of his family; the link still exists. A simple act of fornication did not entail the death sentence – in the Old Testament, this penalty (usually by stoning) attaches only to adultery.

Now, however, Tamar's plan comes to fruition. She displays the pledges, thereby identifying Judah as the father of her child, and he is forced to revoke his verdict. Indeed, he is compelled, not only to acknowledge his paternity in public, but also to admit that he has acted unjustly: "She is more in the right than I, since I did not give her to my son Shelah" (38:26). The concept of justice which we find here, one of the fundamental concepts in the Hebrew Bible, goes far beyond the sphere of what is merely juridically correct. Tamar has acted in faithfulness to the norms of society because she wanted to gain what was hers by right, something that would benefit the entire clan of Judah. Her cunning and her reflection serve the implementation of a higher justice.

The last part of the narrative announces the outcome. Tamar gives birth to the twins Perez and Zerah. The motif of the birth of twins is probably modeled on the story of Esau and Jacob (Gen 25); the only one who is important for the sequence of generations is Perez, who is also mentioned in the story of Ruth, because he is one of the ancestors of David.

As a couple, Judah and Tamar come together somewhat "accidentally." Neither had the intention of initiating a lasting relationship; still less can we speak of "love" here. Rather, there is one clear aim, namely the continuation of the lineage of promise, which lies with Judah. The theologically interesting aspect of the story is the way in which it is told. As with David and Goliath, it is the small, defenseless partner, the weaker person, who outsmarts the stronger one despite all his weapons. And ultimately, it is God who is on the side of the weak and defenseless and helps them, though not in the sense that one who waits and is patient can automatically reckon on divine aid. Rather, the protagonist – here, Tamar – must take things into his or her own hands. Tamar does not let herself be marginalized and as it were ejected from the story. She is concerned about the future, and therefore she risks everything, even her own life, for if her plans do not succeed, she will be a meaningless person without any future. Tamar is a woman who enforces her own rights in a situation where she has been let down by the men who ought to have helped her. She risks her own life, and is therefore affirmed by God. In this story, Judah plays a somewhat passive, timid role. He is fearful and irresolute, but at the close he displays a sympathetic trait when he publicly admits his guilt. This couple, who have their place in the genealogy of David and of Jesus, have thus an unusual relationship, and this shows how various the relationships, marriages, and couples in the Bible are. They are not subject to any great moral judgment or condemnation. Tamar's conduct was often considered objectionable by subsequent Christian moral theology, but it is praised in the Bible itself: "She is more in the right than I," says Judah.

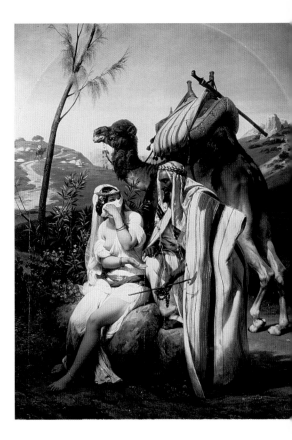

TAKING THE WRONG PATH.
In the realistic style of Orientalism, Horace Vernet (ca. 1840) shows Judah interrupting his journey to the sheep shearing in order to agree on a price with the supposed prostitute by the wayside.

RUTH AND BOAZ

(Ruth 1-4)

IN THE FIELD.
*The initial "I" is decorated with the
figure of Ruth, elevated from a
woman gleaning ears of corn to a reaper:*
Bible of the Duc de Berry
(ca. 1390) (above).

ON THE THRESHING FLOOR.
This miniature from the Wenceslaus Bible
*(ca. 1400) keeps close to the biblical verse:
"At midnight the man was startled, and
turned over, and there, lying at his feet,
was a woman!" (Ruth 3:8) (opposite page).*

Scholars disagree about when the short story we know as the Book of Ruth was written. Formerly, it tended to be dated to the seventh century B.C.E., in the middle period of the kings before the exile, and it was interpreted as a legitimation of David's Moabite ancestry. Today, the link to David is considered secondary, and Ruth is mostly regarded as a post-exilic text from the fifth century B.C.E. This book is primarily concerned with women and the stories of their lives and is consistently narrated from the women's perspective.

The Book of Ruth occupies a different place in the Hebrew and in the Greek canons. In the Hebrew Bible, it belongs to the *ketubim*, the "writings," between the Book of Proverbs and the Song of Songs. In Judaism, Ruth, the Song of Songs, Qoheleth, Lamentations, and the Book of Esther are the five *megilloth*, the "festal rolls" read at the Feast of Weeks, a harvest festival which celebrates the gift of Torah at Mount Sinai. In the structure of the Greek Bible (the Septuagint, which was adopted by the church), Ruth is one of the historical books. As David's prehistory, it stands between the Book of Judges and 1 Samuel. Since Ruth 1:1 dates the events to "the days when the judges ruled" and 1 Samuel tells the story of King David, Ruth's great-grandson, this book functions as a transition between the period of the judges and that of the kings.

There is a clear structure in the narrative. A famine forces the Israelite Naomi to leave Bethlehem with her husband Elimelech and settle in the neighboring country of Moab, where her two sons marry Moabite wives, Orpah and Ruth. After her husband and her sons die, and she hears that God has once again given bread to his people in Bethlehem (the name means "house of bread"), Naomi prepares to return. She charges her widowed daughters-in-law to return to the house of their mothers, so that they may find new husbands among their relatives. She does not want them to live with her as childless widows in a foreign land. Ultimately, Orpah is persuaded and parts company with her mother-in-law, weeping and kissing her. She returns to Moab, her native land, but Ruth remains with Naomi, assuring her of her fidelity and affection in these words: "Where you go, I will go; where you lodge, I will lodge; your people shall be my people, and your God my God. Where you die, I will die – there will I be buried. May the Lord do thus and so to me, and more as well, if even death parts me from you!" (1:16f.). Like Rebekah, she leaves her people and her country and cleaves to the God of Israel.

When Naomi arrives in Bethlehem with the Moabitess Ruth at the beginning of the barley harvest, people are astounded. Naomi still has some

relatives of her deceased husband in the town; these include Boaz, a respected landowner.

Ruth takes the initiative and decides to glean ears of corn in the fields for herself and Naomi. According to the Book of Deuteronomy (24:19), foreigners, orphans, and widows are entitled to gather sheaves that have been overlooked and lie on the ground. From Ruth's perspective, it is purely by chance that she gleans on the field of Boaz. The first encounter between the two takes place on his field when he comes from Bethlehem. He notices her and asks his reapers where she comes from, and why she is working so hard. He addresses her kindly as "my daughter" and invites her to remain in his field, advising her to join his maidservants. He forbids the male servants to molest her and says that she should drink with the others when she is thirsty. Ruth prostrates herself with her face to the earth and asks Boaz: "Why have I found favor in your sight, that you should take notice of me, when I am a foreigner?" Boaz's reply expresses respect for Ruth's behavior in abandoning everything in order to assist her mother-in-law, and he blesses her: "May you have a full reward from the Lord, the God of Israel, under whose wings you have come for refuge!" Ruth's reply displays both gratitude and affection: "You have comforted me and spoken kindly to me, my lord, even though I am not one of your maidservants" (2:10-13). Boaz invites her to eat, and she is "satisfied." The first encounter between the two is marked by Boaz's respect and generosity and by Ruth's gratitude.

She returns to Naomi with a plentiful harvest and with the leftovers from her meal. Naomi blesses Boaz: "Blessed be the man who took notice of you. ... Blessed be he by the Lord, whose kindness has not forsaken the living or the dead! ... The man is a relative of ours, one with the right to redeem (*goel*)" (2:19f.). The *goel* in ancient Israel was a relative who was obliged to offer assistance when the clan got into difficulties. If penury has compelled them to sell land which belongs to the family, he must buy it back, so that property can remain in the possession of his relatives even when they fall on hard times (Lev 25:23-25, 47ff.).

Ruth remains with her mother-in-law and accompanies Boaz's servant women until the end of the barley and wheat harvests. Now Naomi takes the initiative: she intends to bring about a marriage between Boaz and Ruth, not with the primary aim of securing descendants, but so that Ruth can find a place where she is safe and happy. Her plan is daring: Ruth is to wash and anoint herself and to go in festal garments to Boaz while he sleeps at the threshing floor. She is then to uncover his legs and lie down beside him. He will know what is to be done. Ruth agrees to this plan and goes to Boaz at the threshing floor. She waits until he has eaten and drunk and his heart is merry, and he lies down beside a heap of grain. She comes softly, uncovers his legs, and lies down beside him. This formulation is ambiguous and does not tell us precisely what happens between Boaz

"Salmon was the father of Boaz by Rahab, and Boaz the father of Obed by Ruth, and Obed the father of Jesse, and Jesse the father of King David. And David was the father of Solomon by the wife of Uriah."
MATTHEW 1:5-6

ADVICE.
This illustrated page of the Crusader Bible *(ca. 1250) emphasizes Naomi's role in giving good advice to Ruth (opposite page).*

AN ACT OF KINDNESS.
This miniature in the Octateuch *of Vatopédi Monastery on Mount Athos shows Boaz advising the unknown woman to glean ears of wheat only in his field. This is the beginning of their relationship.*

and Ruth; the "feet" or "legs" can also be a euphemism for the genital organs (cf. Ex 4:25; Deut 28:57). At midnight, Boaz wakes up and is startled to see a woman lying between his legs. He asks who she is, and she replies: "I am Ruth, your servant; spread the hem of your cloak over your servant, for you are the one with the right to redeem" (3:9). The Hebrew word for "hem" literally means "wing": Boaz is to take Ruth under his wings, just as the God of Israel takes human beings under his protection. God's action is manifested in the human action.

Ruth links the obligation of the *goel* to show solidarity to relatives in distress with the institution of Levirate marriage: if a man dies without children, his brother is obliged to marry the widow, and the first son born to this marriage is reckoned as the son of the deceased brother. If a man refuses to enter a Levirate marriage, the widow of his brother has the right to accuse him before the elders at the city gate. If he maintains his refusal, he is put to shame: the widow takes his shoe from his foot and berates him publicly (Deut 25:5-10). The legal institution of Levirate marriage aimed both at ensuring descendants for the deceased man and at giving protection to his widow.

BETHLEHEM.
The Urbino Bible *(1476-1478) opens the Book of Ruth with a landscape which shows Bethlehem and the "green land of Moab," where the action of the story is set. Elimelech and Naomi leave Bethlehem with their sons Mahlon and Chilion; and Naomi with her widowed Moabite daughter-in-law Ruth returns to Bethlehem.*

Boaz replies to Ruth's proposal with a blessing: "May you be blessed by the Lord, my daughter; this last instance of your loyalty is better than the first; you have not gone after young men, whether poor or rich. And now, my daughter, do not be afraid, I will do for you all that you ask, for all the assembly of my people know that you are a worthy woman" (3:10f.). Before he acts on her proposal, however, one obstacle must be overcome. There is another *goel*, who is in fact a closer relative. If this man is unwilling to marry Ruth, Boaz will do so. He sends Ruth home before daybreak, so that no one may see her – for that would ruin her good name – and gives her a present of barley. The second meeting between the two is marked by Ruth's unusual initiative, Boaz's kindness, and an erotically charged atmosphere.

While Ruth is on her way back to Naomi to tell her everything, Boaz goes to the city gate, the place where legal business is settled, and meets the other *goel* there. This man remains anonymous, in sharp contrast to the eloquent names of the other characters in the story – Naomi, the "pleasant" one, who on her return to Bethlehem would rather be called Mara, the "bitter" one; Ruth, whose name echoes both "friend" and "filled to the full"; and Boaz, whose name means "in him is strength." The nameless *goel* is willing to buy the field from Naomi, but not to enter a Levirate marriage with Ruth. Accordingly, the only potential *goel* is Boaz, since he wishes to do both these things. He calls the elders and the people to witness that he is acquiring Naomi's family possessions and taking Ruth as his wife, and this matter is confirmed when the anonymous *goel* takes off his shoe.

After this detailed narrative, the wedding and the birth of a son are noted only briefly: Boaz takes Ruth, she becomes his wife, he comes to her, and God grants that she become pregnant and bear a son. The women of Bethlehem rejoice with Naomi; Ruth, who loves her, is worth more than seven sons. The child whom she has borne gives joy to Naomi's heart and brings her life back. The women call the boy Obed ("servant"), and he will be the grandfather of David. The link to David (4:18-22) was added at a subsequent stage of composition, making Ruth the great-grandmother of David and the messianic female *goel* who prepares the way for the coming of the Messiah. The messianic hope of a *goel* (or "redeemer") looked to David, who came from Bethlehem; this hope continues in the New Testament, where Ruth is mentioned in the genealogy of Jesus (Matt 1:5; the parallel at Lk 3:32 follows the male line and mentions Boaz).

The blessing pronounced at her wedding incorporates Ruth in the ranks of the ancestral mothers of Israel. In the Book of Ruth, a Moabitess freely joins the people of Israel and marries an Israelite, in contrast to Deut 23:4-6, which forbids Moabites from becoming members of the community of Israel, and to the polemic of Ezra and Nehemiah against mixed marriages (Ezra 9-10; Neh 13:23ff.).

In terms of their background and social status, Boaz and Ruth are a very mixed couple: the socially prominent, rich landowner Boaz and the penniless refugee widow from Moab. But in their behavior and their character, they stand on the same level. The same Hebrew word, meaning "strong, able, worthy, courageous," is used of Boaz in the narration at 2:1 and of Ruth by Boaz himself at 3:11. In relation to Boaz, Ruth is the one who acts: he reacts to her initiatives.

The meetings between Boaz and Ruth in the field and the threshing floor are the center of the Book of Ruth. They take place in an atmosphere of acknowledgment, mutual respect, and kindness. The word for "favor, grace, goodness, loyalty, solidarity" is a leitmotiv in the book, both for God's action and for the relationships between Ruth and Naomi, and Ruth and Boaz. The word for "love" occurs only once, at 4:15, where it refers, not to the relationship between the husband and wife, but to Ruth's relationship to Naomi. Although the relationship between Boaz and Ruth contains very pragmatic elements – they wish to ensure the continued existence of the family – we sense again and again that it also contains an erotic charge.

INVITATION.
This miniature in two parts from the Wenceslaus Bible (ca. 1400) moves the meal to which Boaz invites Ruth from the field to a room with a table and benches.

"At mealtime Boaz said to her, 'Come here, and eat some of this bread, and dip your morsel in the sour wine.' So she sat beside the reapers, and he heaped up for her some parched grain. She ate until she was satisfied, and she had some left over."
RUTH 2:14

THE WOMEN IN DAVID'S STORY

Ideas associated with the figure of David, the shepherd boy who founded a kingdom, have been very influential throughout three thousand years of Jewish history and two thousand years of Christian history. Two "cities of David" symbolize the breadth of ideas involved here: Jerusalem – once the residence of Melchisedek, the Canaanite city-king and "priest of the Most High God" (Gen 14:18), which David made the political, cultic, and cultural center of his kingdom of Israel – and Bethlehem, the city where he had been born and where, according to prophecy, the Messiah would one day be born. The genealogical link between David and the Messiah Jesus Christ, which is made in the very first verses of the New Testament in the "genealogy of Jesus," is based both on the dynastic promise made to David about his descendants and on the messianic prophecy of Isaiah, who employs the image of the "root of Jesse" (cf. Is 11:1).

King David lives on in the widest sense in his dynasty, as ancestor both of the divinely authenticated kingship in Israel and of the messianic hope which was linked to this kingship; the fulfillment of this hope in Jesus Christ is the foundation of Christianity. Besides this, he more than any other figure in the biblical tradition personifies the basic situations and the whole spectrum of human existence. We can indeed see the ups and downs in David's life as related to the specific historical circumstances in which he established his kingship; but this biography has taken on a universal validity to which the Psalms bear a particularly eloquent testimony. The attribution of most of these poems to the psalmist David places his person in the context of a lyrical existentialism. And the epic and historiographical treatments of his life by the various Old Testament authors also display a wealth of forms which contribute to the vivid portrait of David, long before artists began to depict him in their own varied ways.

As the central character in the two Books of Samuel, David is involved in a network of relationships which possess an exemplary character, such as the encounter between the innocent, weak boy and the terrifying might of the proverbial Goliath, whom David kills with one single stone from his sling. The relationships between David and three women are also exemplary. Their impact is enhanced by dramatic scenes in which various kinds of behavior, on the part of men and women, are called into question. These three are Michal, David's first wife, who saves him in his hour of need and ends up a scoffer who is herself mocked, a woman who remains tied to her violent father Saul in a love-hate relationship; Abigail, who prepares David for his future office as king of Judah when he is persecuted by Saul, and then disappears from sight as the third wife in the king's harem; and Bathsheba, with whom David experiences the heights and the depths of human existence, the pleasure of sensual delight, blood-guilt and punishment, expiation and divine mercy, the fidelity of the woman he loves and her final elevation as queen.

"His firstborn was Amnon, of Ahinoam of Jezreel; his second, Chileab, of Abigail the widow of Nabal of Carmel; the third, Absalom son of Maacah, daughter of King Talmai of Geshur; the fourth, Adonijah son of Haggith; the fifth, Shephatiah son of Abital; and the sixth, Ithream, of David's wife Eglah."

2 SAMUEL 3:2-5

VICTORY.
Nicolas Poussin's allegorical painting The Triumph of David *(ca. 1630) follows classical models in giving the youthful David the goddess of Victory as his partner (opposite page).*

BODILY WARMTH.
This miniature from a Bible moralisée *(ca. 1410) shows Abishag, who is brought to the bed of David (now an old man) and takes her rest there. David's servants said: "Let a young virgin be sought for my lord the king, and let her wait on the king, and be his attendant; let her lie in your bosom, so that my lord the king may be warm" (1 Kg 1:2).*

"Rabbi Phinehas was wont to praise
music and song in high terms.
Once he said:
'Lord of the world,
if I could sing,
I would not allow
to you to remain in the
heights. I would badger
you with my
song until you made your
dwelling here
among us.'"
MARTIN BUBER,
STORIES OF THE HASIDIM

זהדוד המטן בנבל"

DAVID AND MICHAL

(1 Samuel 18 and 19; 2 Samuel 3 and 6)

avid's first marriage gets off to a bad start. Both the husband and the
father-in-law, each for his own reasons, see it as a means to an end. The
shepherd boy David is called to the court of King Saul in order to play the harp
and soothe the king whenever an evil spirit takes hold of him. The gratitude
and the trust that Saul feels towards his youthful benefactor are expressed in his
appointment of David as his armor-bearer. Indeed, "Saul loved him greatly" (1
Sam 16:21).

In the next chapter, another narrator takes up the tale. Here, we read
that David and Saul meet in the military camp in the Valley of Terebinths,
where the Israelites are drawn up in readiness to fight the Philistines. Three of
David's brothers are in the camp, and his father Jesse sends him with food and
with instructions to find out how his brothers are getting on. David sees how
the giant champion of the Philistines, Goliath, terrifies the Israelites, and is
impertinent enough to ask what reward the king has promised to the man who
is able to defeat this foreign boaster. His brother Eliab overhears this and puts
him in his place with the condescending sarcasm of an older sibling: "I know
your presumption and the evil of your heart; for you have come down just to
see the battle" (17:28). Others, however, inform the courtiers, and finally King
Saul himself, about the boy, and the outcome is a contest which flies in the face
of all human reason. God helps the weaker man to victory. It is only now that
David reveals to the king that he is the son of Jesse from Bethlehem, and it is
only now that he is entrusted with military tasks. His successes make him popular both with the people and with Saul's servants, but the king becomes angry:
"'What more can he have than the kingdom?' So Saul eyed David from that day
on" (18:8f.).

When he asked about the reward promised to the one who defeated
Goliath, David was told that the king would give his daughter in marriage to
the man who freed the Israelites from this scourge in human form. We are not
told whether such ideas were merely popular fancies – it sounds a little like a
fairytale – but at any rate, Saul himself offers David the hand of his daughter
in marriage, but first David must win praise on all sides as a military leader. To
outward appearances, this marriage will reward David by making him a member of the royal family; but in reality, the hope of marrying Saul's daughter is
meant to lead David to his death, for he is required now to be even more active
in the fight against the Philistines: "For Saul thought, 'I will not raise a hand
against him; let the Philistines deal with him'" (18:17). Fully expecting that his

THE PSALMIST.
*David plays the harp (from a manuscript
Miscellany, containing various texts
including Psalms, written in northern France
ca. 1380/1390) (opposite page far left).*

PSALM OF LOVE.
*Marc Chagall gives the songs of David an
interpretation which is rooted in the
mysticism of Hassidism with its openness to
the world: the praise of God finds one of its
many expressions in the union of bride and
bridegroom.*

THE FIRST MARRIAGE.
*This relief on a Byzantine silver vessel
(ca. 610/620) depicts the wedding of
David, who has won victories in the
struggle against the Philistines, with Michal,
daughter of King Saul (above).*

plot against David will succeed, Saul marries his eldest daughter Merab off to another man.

David is so much attracted by the prospect of becoming the son-in-law of the king, despite his lowly background, that he does not grasp the true intentions of his pretended benefactor. Not even Saul's failure to keep his promise, when he gives Merab in marriage to Adriel of Meholah (18:19), makes him suspicious, for the main point is not that he should marry one particular princess, but that he should marry a daughter of the king as his next step on the upward ladder.

THE BRIDAL PRICE.
David, as military leader, displays his trophies of victory and is rewarded with Michal, the king's daughter, as his wife. The illustration to 1 Sam 18:24 in the Crusader Bible *shows Saul himself presiding over the wedding.*

Now the perspective changes: "Saul's daughter Michal loved David" (18:20), a simple statement that is so significant precisely because it is quite separate from all the intentional deceits, actions, promises, and plottings at the court where Michal lives. And yet, her love too is turned into an instrument to gain the king's ends: "the thing pleased him," we are told in the same verse. His spies have informed him that David fears that he, as the son of a poor man, may not be able to afford the price one must pay to marry a king's daughter, so Saul makes him an attractive offer: it is enough that David bring him the foreskins of a hundred Philistines (as proof that he has killed them) before the year is out.

David kills twice that number before the time is up. The narrator does not tell us whether his zeal is prompted by his love for Michal, or whether he simply wants to give the king no occasion to break his promise a second time. Does he in fact know Michal? Has she urged him to act quickly? At any rate, the king has no longer any pretext for refusing to accept David as his son-in-law. The king sees the world in black-and-white terms: on the one side are his friends, on the other side his foes, and he is now filled with fear. The foes – whom he must fear even more than Philistines – are God (who has taken David's side) and his own daughter Michal, who loves her husband and thus cannot be used by her father to bring harm on David. "So Saul was David's enemy from that time forward" (18:29).

Michal acts resolutely to defend David. Above all, her courageous action saves him from mortal danger when she helps him escape from the murderers whom Saul has sent. This scene shows us for the first time Michal as a woman who reflects on a situation and acts with resolve. First, she ensures that David can leave his house through a window, climbing down on a rope or a ladder, without being noticed by Saul's henchmen. Her next goal is to give him a headstart before they start to pursue him: when those who have been sent to murder David force their way into the house, they accept her story that her husband is sick. Saul, however, cannot see why this should be a reason not to kill David, and sends them back. They demand proof that their intended victim is sick, and they are ready if need be to transport David in his bed to the king's palace and kill him there. Once again, time elapses in David's favor, for all they find in the supposed sick-bed is a domestic idol, presumably carved in wood. Michal has made it more realistic with a wig of goats' hair.

We can easily imagine how surprised the king's henchmen are when they uncover the trick that Michal has planned with such care and attention to detail in order to give David the chance to escape. Instead of the "enemy of the state," they drag the "traitor" into the palace – for that is how Saul sees his daughter, although he has surely sensed even before now that her love for David would bind her to him, and that her father would lose his power over her. "Why have you deceived me like this," he cries, "and let my enemy go, so that he has escaped?" The narrator reports Michal's reply without any commentary of his own: it is up to us whether we see this as a lie that Michal tells to protect herself in a desperate situation, or as an indication that she has deserted David in her heart and submitted anew to her father's will. She accuses David: "He said to me, 'Let me go; why should I kill you?'" (19:17).

At this point in the story, Michal is reduced to a woman with no will of her own, and Saul uses her as an instrument to further his own plans. We are told that he humiliates David by giving her in marriage to a man named Palti or Paltiel. After Saul's death, David becomes king in Judah and negotiates with

"Michal let David down through the window; he fled away, and escaped."

1 SAMUEL 19:12

THE FLIGHT.
Detail from a group of typological images on the theme of escape in a Biblia pauperum *(ca. 1430/1440). The Old Testament "types" are the flight of David from Saul and the flight of Jacob from Esau; the New Testament "antitype" is the flight of the Holy Family from Herod into Egypt.*

Abner, who had formerly served Saul, but now wishes to go over to David's side. David seizes this opportunity to enforce his own rights of possession – it is a matter of principle for him! He tells Abner, "Good; I will make a covenant with you. But one thing I require of you: you shall never appear in my presence

THE DANCING KING.
This picture (from a biblical history in German, ca. 1450) shows David entering Jerusalem with the ark of the covenant: "David danced before the Lord with all his might; David was girded with a linen ephod." According to Ex 39:2f., the ephod was one of the eight vestments of the high priest.

unless you bring Saul's daughter Michal when you come to see me" (2 Sam 3:13). Michal is "Saul's daughter," for whom David had paid the bridal price (3:14); he says nothing about having loved her in the past, nor about gratitude or compassion. And so the author simply passes over the first meeting of David and Michal after their long separation – we only hear about her second husband. When Michal is fetched, like a piece of merchandise, Paltiel "went with her, weeping as he walked behind her all the way to Bahurim. Then Abner said to him, 'Go back home!' So he went back" (3:16). We do not know whether he weeps because of what is happening to Michal, or because he had loved her, or even just because he was losing his property; but one brief order, and Paltiel no longer has any role to play in this transaction, which is governed by political interests.

We meet Michal one last time on the day of one of David's greatest triumphs, when he brings the ark of the covenant into Jerusalem, his capital. The terrible words with which she judges the king's dance before the ark bear eloquent witness to her deep sorrow and bitterness. It is as if the fate she has suffered for years, passively and in silence, compels her now to speak and free herself, but her outcry takes the form of a compulsive delight in mockery: "How the king of Israel honored himself today, uncovering himself today before the eyes of his servants' maids, as any vulgar fellow might shamelessly uncover himself!" (6:22). Michal sees him fallen from a tremendous height, from a king – and the memory of her once all-powerful father makes Saul the ideal representative of what a king should be – to a "vulgar fellow" who dances and exposes himself to the raucous laughter of the crowd. The narrator hints that Michal's loneliness may have been the reason why she measures her husband against her idea of what a king (or father) should be: she is not in fact a member of David's family, which consists of his wives Ahinoam and Abigail, Maacah, Abital, and Eglah, and his sons Amnon, Chileab, Absalom, Adonijah, Shephatiah, and Ithream (2 Sam 3:2-5), as well as various concubines. Polygamy, as a means of ensuring the birth of heirs who would continue the dynasty, was one of the privileges of a king, who had the resources to maintain such a household – and a harem, too. Despite being married to David, and despite living once again in the palace, Michal still remains the daughter of her father: "David returned to bless his household. But Michal the daughter of Saul came out to meet David …" (6:20). This sentence tells us: a stranger came out to meet the king. And this chapter, in which she makes her last appearance, ends with the annihilating words: "And Michal the daughter of Saul had no child to the day of her death" (6:23).

Christian art follows the Books of Samuel in portraying the contrast between Michal's help, which enables David to stay alive, and her mockery, which denies the new king of Judah any legitimation. Typologically speaking, the first scene sees Michal as a parallel to Rebekah, who helped Jacob flee from Esau, and both these scenes of escape prefigure the flight of the Holy Family to Egypt. As a mocker, in classical Christian depiction Michal embodies the synagogue, which has been struck with blindness and is unable to perceive the messianic work of redemption which is adumbrated in David and comes to fulfillment in Jesus Christ.

CONTEMPT.
The medallion on an illustrated page in the Romanesque Gumbertus Bible *(ca. 1200) depicts the verse: "As the ark of the Lord came into the city of David,*

Michal daughter of Saul looked out of the window, and saw King David leaping and dancing before the Lord; and she despised him in her heart" (2 Sam 6:16).

THE CITY OF DAVID.
This relief of the star of David, the symbol of his lordship, has been placed since ancient times on the city wall of the city of David, Jerusalem. In terms of the symbolism of numbers, the six points are derived from the six days of creation.

DAVID AND ABIGAIL

(1 Samuel 25)

The story of David and Abigail has been handed down to us in the form of a short novel (a word which literally means a "new event"). The external ring of the concentric narrative framework is formed by the situation of David in his political and military struggle against King Saul, who is pursuing him as his deadly rival: David is in the wilderness of Paran, in the northern region of the Sinai peninsula, with six hundred men. The second ring is formed by the regional lordship which David claims by virtue of his protection of the farmers who raise their cattle and sheep in this region: he considers the rich Nabal as his subject. The third ring is formed by the short space of time involved: one specific situation in the annual work of the farmers, viz., the period of sheep shearing, which ends in a lavish feast. These are the external conditions, the scenario; in the center, we see how the characters in the story interact.

David, the military leader pursued by Saul and dependent on material help, expects that the prosperous Nabal will pay the voluntary tribute for the protection that he has provided during the sheep shearing. To put it more precisely, David lays claim to a share in Nabal's prosperity in return for the fact that the farmer and his servants have been able to do their work undisturbed – something that could not at all be taken for granted. Nabal, however, whose name means "fool," belongs to the tribe of the Calebites, whose members have a reputation for exceptional rudeness and crudeness. He does justice to this reputation when he dismisses with a few words the ten messengers whom David sends to him with the polite request that they be allowed to take part in the feast. They wish him peace and remind him that his property (against all expectations?) has remained intact up to now, but Nabal closes his ears: "Who is David? Who is the son of Jesse?" (1 Sam 25:10). Is Nabal really unaware of events in the wider world? Or is he simply pretending to be ignorant? At any rate, this supplies him with what he himself sees as good reasons to get rid of the unwanted guests, although the "law of the wilderness" entitles them to receive hospitality: "Shall I take my bread and my water and the meat that I have butchered for my shearers, and give it to men who come from I do not know where?" (25:11).

Nabal reveals himself as an ill-mannered eccentric, a short-sighted man devoid of prudence. His behavior justifies David in laying aside his peacefulness and employing violence to seize what has been withheld from him, despite all his polite requests and exhortations. Nabal's servants are clearly better acquainted with the "law of the wilderness" and guess that this is how David will react.

OCCVRRIT
ABIGAIL, CVM
MVNERIBVSD̄
VIDI COMOTO

PRECIBVS ABIGAIL
PEPERCIT DAVID
DOMVI NABAL

TWO ENCOUNTERS.
The painting The Story of David and
Abigail *(1617, a copy of a lost work
by Hugo van der Goes) offers a synchronous
presentation of events. The individual
stages of the narrative take place
simultaneously in a wide landscape.
To the right – against the background of
Nabal's feast – we see the first*

One of them goes to their mistress and tells her about the danger that Nabal
has incurred through his stubbornness. Abigail, the mistress of the house,
immediately grasps what is at stake. She is very well informed about David and
praises him as a military leader who does not wish to seize booty for his own
personal gain but is "fighting the battles of the Lord" (25:28).

Abigail's acknowledgment of the religious legitimation of David as military
leader, and her acceptance of his demand for material support, are
expressed in the elaborate address she delivers when she goes to meet him. This
is the midpoint of the narrative, the intersection of two movements: David and
his armed men are marching towards the place where Nabal is enjoying the feast
at the end of the sheep shearing, but Abigail leaves this place in order to pro-

vide David with food which she has hastily packed: bread, wine in skins, slaughtered sheep, roasted corn, and cakes of raisins and figs. This portion of Nabal's feast is the material basis of the strategy which Abigail employs in order to ward off the impending disaster.

The narrator does not pronounce any judgment on Abigail, but leaves it to the readers to form their own opinion on the basis of the speech which he reports. Abigail begins with a *captatio benevolentiae*, i.e., words which ensure a benevolent hearing on the part of the one whom she addresses. She humbles herself and takes all the blame upon herself, excusing her husband by speaking of his stupidity – he is to some extent incapable of incurring guilt. Step by step, Abigail moves up from the mention of her reparation in the form of the pack-

encounter between Abigail and David, who rides high on his horse as he goes to fight against Nabal. To the left, we see the king bowing down to Abigail. He has repented and attained inner insight, and he raises her in gratitude and love to the status of queen.

ages she has loaded onto her donkeys, via the acknowledgment of David's legitimation, until she pronounces a prophecy: the Lord will appoint David "prince over Israel" (25:30). And then she moves one step further, by appealing to the human character of this man whom God has blessed; as the recipient of so many blessings, David is obliged to maintain a good conscience. After God has made him prince over Israel, his good conscience will be a source of security for him, since "my lord shall have no cause of grief, or pangs of conscience, for having shed blood without cause" (25:31).

This is the high point of Abigail's religious and moral exhortation, which implicitly declares that David has no reason to take vengeance. She then abruptly takes on a new role: the prophetess who speaks with religious and moral authority suddenly becomes the maid who brings a petition. At the same time, she bids him bear in mind her own share in David's salutary change of attitude, which is pleasing to God: "And when the Lord has dealt well with my lord, then remember your servant" (25:31).

David replies with praise of Abigail's prudence. This word sums up all the qualities that she displays in a situation of extreme peril: decisiveness, resolute action, judiciousness, and far-sightedness. He also expresses his admiration of her. Ensuing events justify Abigail's warning against incautious revenge on David's part. After Nabal awakens from his drunken stupor and Abigail tells him how she has saved his life and that of his servants, he suffers a stroke and dies soon after. David sees this as the act of God "who has judged the case of Nabal's insult to me, and has kept back his servant from evil; the Lord has returned the evil-doing of Nabal upon his own head" (25:39). He then sends messengers to tell Abigail that he wishes to marry her: his admiration of her prudence leads him to wish to have such a prudent woman in his household. The narrator, however, says nothing about David's motives. He moves back to the concentric framework around the story he has told, and presents the marriage with Abigail as part of dynastic politics: David first marries Ahinoam of Jezreel, a town in the tribal territory of Judah, and then the Calebite woman. At the same time, Saul dissolves David's link to the ruling royal house by giving his daughter Michal, who was married to David, in marriage to a man from Galilee named Palti or Paltiel. In this way, the narrative of David and Abigail leads back to the power struggle between Saul and David.

Abigail is mentioned only occasionally, and as it were glimpsed from a distance, in the further course of the First and Second Books of Samuel. Like Ahinoam, she too follows her husband David into exile among the Philistines (1 Sam 27:3). Both women are taken captive by the Amalekites, and rescued by David (1 Sam 30:5.18). When David is anointed king of Judah in Hebron after Saul's death, Abigail and Ahinoam are present. They bear two sons in Hebron: Ahinoam bears David's first-born, Amnon, and Abigail his second-born, Chileab. In the meantime, however, David has four other wives: Maacah, the daughter of

AN UNEQUAL COUPLE.
In his woodcut David and Abigail
(1509), Lucas Cranach the Elder exaggerates
the antithesis between the aggressive
man and the defenseless woman. We are
challenged to look beyond the outward
appearances and to grasp the "unheard-of
event" which this biblical story relates.

"Blessed be the Lord who has judged the case of Nabal's insult to me, and
has kept back his servant from evil."

1 SAMUEL 25:39

the king of Geshur, Haggith, Abital, and Eglah. Their children, born likewise in
Hebron, are Absalom, Adonijah, Shephatiah, and Ithream (2 Sam 3:2-5).

This makes the first encounter between David and Abigail all the more
precious, since it allows us to see this woman in her individuality. She is not
only equal in rank to the "hero" David; she moves him to repentance, to a literal change of direction. His wish to take her (or better: to have her) as his wife
probably means that something more is involved than her impressive prudence.
She has touched David's heart. It is surely not by chance that her speech in their
dramatic first encounter employs the vivid image of the "bag" in which all valu-
ables are kept, when she prays that the life of David – the life of the "beloved"
(which is the meaning of his name) – may be kept safe by God: "The life of my
lord shall be bound in the bundle of the living under the care of the Lord your
God" (1 Sam 25:29).

THE JUDGMENT OF GOD.
*An illustration of the story of Nabal's
death in the* Crusader Bible *(ca. 1250).
After he has slept off his drunkenness,
Abigail tells him what has happened.
Nabal suffers a stroke and dies a few
days later. Abigail wears the
headdress of a married woman;
after she is widowed, she marries David
as her second husband.*

"It happened, late one afternoon, when David rose from his couch and was walking about on the roof of the king's house, that he saw from the roof a woman bathing; the woman was very beautiful."

2 SAMUEL 11:2

LUST.
This section of the painting Bathsheba in the Bath *(ca. 1485/1490) by Hans Memling presupposes that Bathsheba has a maidservant who helps her put on her garment after her bath (opposite page). A detail shows David giving his servant a ring to bring to Bathsheba (above). Memling's painting depicted an example of unjust behavior and was probably one wing of a triptych of the type known as "image of justice" in the courtroom in a municipal building.*

DAVID AND BATHSHEBA
(2 Samuel 11-12)

Psalm 51, a request for forgiveness and a new creation, bears the title: "A Psalm of David, when the prophet Nathan came to him, after he had gone in to Bathsheba." After this biographical background, the Psalm itself – one of the seven penitential Psalms in the Christian liturgy – begins with a confession of sin:

"Have mercy on me, O God,
according to your steadfast love;
according to your abundant mercy
blot out my transgressions.
Wash me thoroughly from my iniquity,
and cleanse me from my sin.
For I know my transgressions,
and my sin is ever before me.
Against you, you alone, have I sinned,
and done what is evil in your sight."

These verses reflect the second part of a narrative which begins with events in the life of King David that appear to belong the category of "all too human" occurrences. The starting point, at least, might reckon with a benevolent nod on the part of the reader, but the very first sentence hints that the behavior of David deviates from what is expected of a king: at the time of year when kings usually go to war at the head of their armies, David sends his general Joab as his representative to fight against the Ammonites, and he himself remains in Jerusalem (2 Sam 11:1). The narrator seems less surprised by the fact that David feels erotic desire when he is walking on the flat roof of his house and sees a very beautiful woman bathing. Presumably, she was in the inner court-yard of a neighboring house, so that he could easily see her from his own roof. Ethnographically speaking, this reminds us of the bodily hygiene to which people in the Orient devoted particular care. A social historian will note that the king's actions display a reflex that is simply taken for granted: he inquires who the beautiful woman is, and invites her to his palace – or more precisely, he has her fetched. Clearly, this is done without any violence. And the fact that Bathsheba is married to a man named Uriah is no obstacle: David is putting into practice a "property right" which is more comprehensive than that of the restricted "bourgeois" situation of his subjects, and it appears to be no more

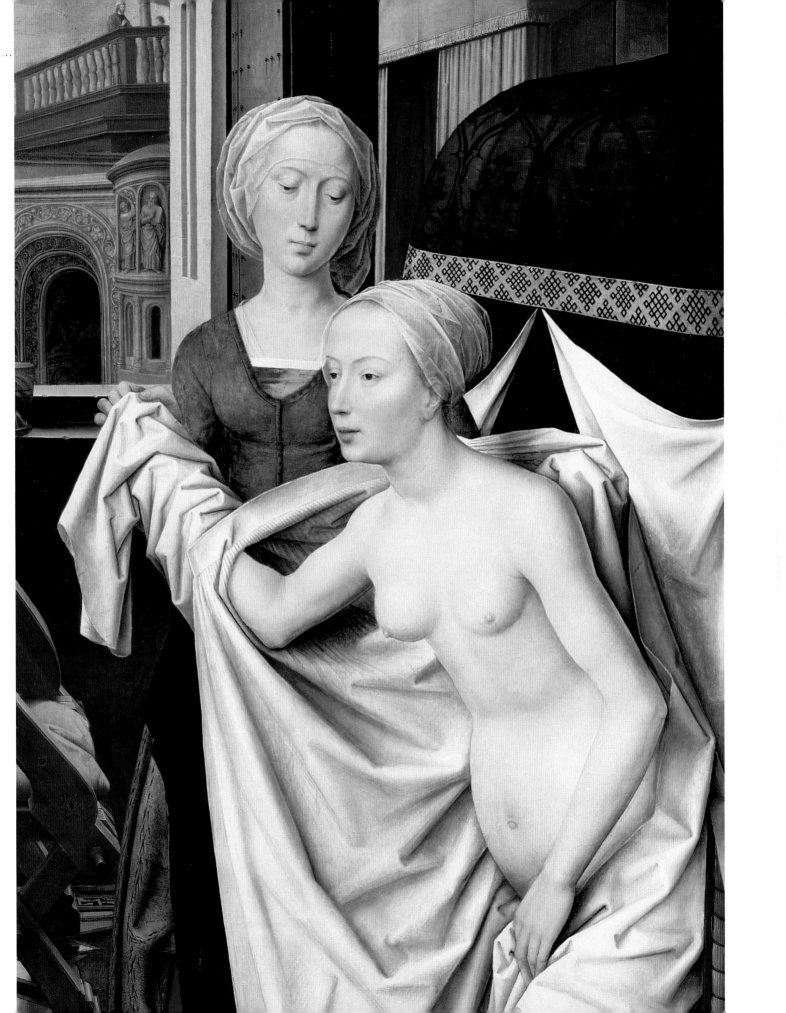

"In the letter David wrote, 'Set
Uriah in the forefront
of the hardest fighting,
and then draw back
from him, so that he may
be struck down and die.'"

2 SAMUEL 11:15

GUILT.
*This portrait of Bathsheba (ca. 1510)
is found at the beginning of
the penitential psalms in a* Book of Hours.
*It is accompanied by the scene in
which David gives Bathsheba's husband,
Uriah, the letter in which Joab is charged to
bring about Uriah's death.*

than one instance among many. David has intercourse with Bathsheba, who then "returns to her house" (11:4).

But appearances are deceptive: Bathsheba is pregnant, and David (for whatever reason) resolves to conceal his paternity by giving the impression that Bathsheba's husband Uriah is the father of the child. David has a sufficient number of legitimate children at his court; he does not desire an illegitimate child as well. Quickly, he organizes the planned deception. David easily finds a pretext for summoning Uriah, who is serving under Joab in the campaign against the Ammonites, to Jerusalem: he is to tell the king "how the war is going" and how Joab and the troops are faring (11:7). As a reward for his report, Uriah is to enjoy his house and his wife. Thereby, unknown to himself, he will have the impression that he is father of the child his wife is expecting.

Uriah, who has no idea of these plans, proves unexpectedly to be a subordinate who feels a particularly strong solidarity with his Israelite comrades who are fighting out in the open – perhaps because he is a Hittite, and hence a "foreigner." He refuses to receive a favor that would be his alone: instead of his own bed at home, he insists on sleeping in the uncomfortable military sleeping quarters of the palace guard. On the next day, when the king hears Uriah's argument – "The ark and Israel and Judah remain in booths" – this strikes him as far-fetched, even crazy. For what has the temporary housing of the ark of the covenant in a booth to do with Uriah's refusal to spend a comfortable night in his own home and to sleep with his wife? David decides to help this simple fellow on his way with a good meal and plenty of wine. But once again, Uriah remains true to his self-imposed asceticism.

As in a fairytale, the two first attempts to get Uriah to do what the king wants fail, because Uriah sees this behavior as wrong. They are followed by a third attempt, which does not belong to the world of fairytales with their happy endings: Uriah is murdered in cold blood, and the deed is covered up. The stubborn man is sent back to the battlefield, but the letter he bears contains his own death sentence. Joab, who is besieging the city of Rabbah, is to position Uriah at an especially dangerous place and abandon him there, once the enemy returns the attack. And this is what happens. Soon enough, Joab can inform the king that his commission has been carried out: the Hittite is dead. In order to forestall any idea of his own complicity in Uriah's death, Joab prepares his messenger for the meeting with the king, and cleverly covers up what has really taken place: if the king is furious and argues that the death could have been prevented, the messenger is to bring counter-arguments to convince him. But David receives the news of Uriah's death with complete calm, and dismisses the whole story with an unfeeling platitude: "The sword devours now one and now another" (11:25). Originally, Uriah was to have taken the role of the "father" of

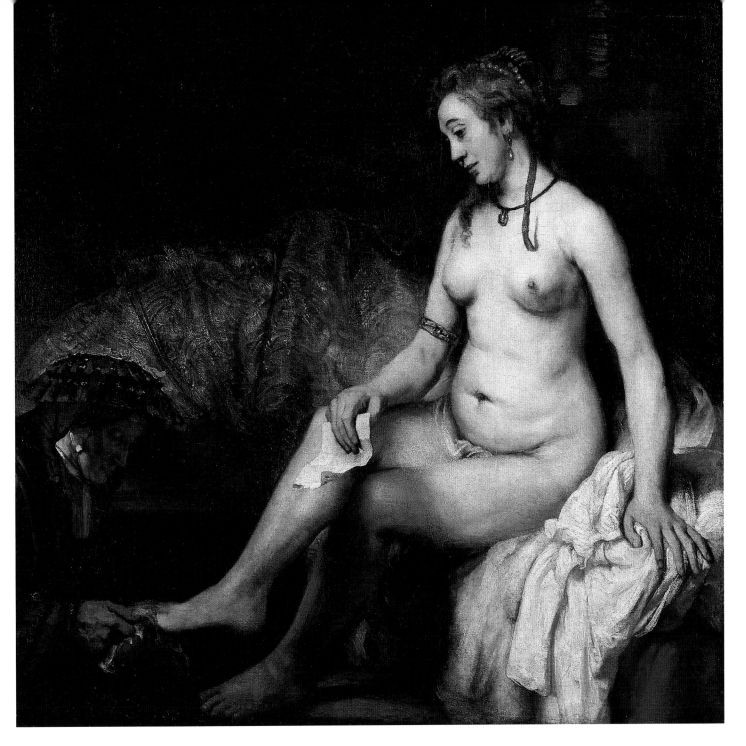

Bathsheba's child, but now the king has successfully eliminated him. Why is he so calm? An initial reflection may have been that he had got rid of the one man who could justifiably accuse him. But after the king's first plan fails, another solution presents itself: he will transform his illegitimate paternity into a legitimate fatherhood by marrying Bathsheba. But first, she must become a widow.

What of Bathsheba herself? The narrator goes to great pains to describe all the machinations of the king, but he has little to say about her. She is very beautiful; she accepts the wish of the king; after her husband's death, she performs the obligatory lamentation; after the period of mourning, she is brought

PREMONITION.
Rembrandt's painting Bathsheba with David's Letter *(1654) suggests that she has a premonition of the terrible consequences of her obedience vis-à-vis the king. Rembrandt's model was his mistress, Hendrickje Stoffels, who was accused of harlotry with the painter.*

INSTRUCTIONS.
The pictorial narrative of the Crusader Bible *(ca. 1250) makes appropriate use of body language to depict David as the dominant actor here. The messenger sent to Bathsheba must obey the instructions of the king, as must Uriah. Even when he makes love, the caressing hands of David take possession of Bathsheba.*

PRAYER FOR FORGIVENESS.
David at prayer: this miniature by Jean Bourdichon in a Book of Hours *from Tours (ca. 1480/1485) depicts King David as the author of the seven penitential psalms.*

to the palace, where she becomes David's wife and bears their son. She takes the initiative only once, when she sends word to the king: "I am pregnant" (11:5). Now she is queen (alongside others) and the mother of a legitimate son of the king. Is this then a happy outcome? No, for the chapter ends with these words: "But the thing that David had done displeased the Lord" (11:27).

It would be wrong to consider the outcome of the meeting and liaison between David and Bathsheba – the culmination of a love story which overcomes the barriers between high and low in society – as a happy ending. It is in fact exactly the opposite, and the prophet Nathan is charged to open the king's eyes to this reality. He employs the parable of the poor man whose single possession, a lamb that he has reared with love and care, is stolen and slaughtered by a greedy rich man who wants to keep his own herds intact (12:1-4). This parable, in which David recognizes that it is he himself who is the merciless rich man, has been included in the Koran (38:21-23) in the form of a concrete legal dispute which the king is asked to settle. "And David understood that We had exposed him to temptation. Then he asked his Lord for forgiveness and cast himself to the ground and turned to him in repentance. Then We forgave him this. He is allowed to draw close to Us and a beautiful dwelling is appointed for him" (38:24f.).

This is a short version of the Hebrew narrative of the punishment of David and of God's gracious mercy. The first child of David and Bathsheba dies, but she bears a second son: "The Lord loved Solomon and sent a message by the prophet Nathan; so he named him Jedidiah ['beloved of the Lord']" (12:24f.).

In this second part of the story, which is reflected in Ps 51, we hear little about Bathsheba. Is her role restricted to giving birth to a second son? We are challenged here to sense the deep bond forged between husband and wife by the pain at the death of their first child. This bond may be reflected in Bathsheba's role as royal counselor, when she secures the succession to the throne for her son Solomon and retains political influence even after David's death. Finally, Bathsheba takes on the identity of a woman who is aware of her rank and of the rights which this gives her, and who acts accordingly (1 Kg 1:19f.; 2:13ff.).

It is very important to note that the reserved perspective of the narrative gives no support at all to the depiction of Bathsheba – thanks to the "great beauty" of her body – as the embodiment of female seduction. This interpretation is found above all in art, where Bathsheba, along with Adam and Eve and Susanna (the victim of the two elders), was one of the few biblical motifs which permitted mediaeval artists to portray a naked body. In the Renaissance, when the noblest task was the depiction of the unclothed human body, the theme of "Bathsheba bathing" offered immense possibilities for artists to portray the sensuous relationship between the sexes. This tended to obscure another Christian tradition of interpreting the relationship between David and Bathsheba, which finds expression in the first chapter of Matthew's Gospel, where Solomon's mother Bathsheba, here called "the wife of Uriah," is one of only four women – the others are Tamar, Rahab, and Ruth – to feature in the genealogical tree of Jesus Christ, which begins with Abraham.

"Then David consoled his wife Bathsheba, and went to her, and lay with her, and she bore a son, and he named him Solomon."
2 SAMUEL 12:24

SUCCESSION TO THE THRONE. *Bernardo Strozzi's painting (ca. 1630) depicts David, Abishag, and Bathsheba pleading that her son Solomon should succeed (1 Kg 1:15-21).*

AHAB AND JEZEBEL

(1 Kings 21; 2 Kings 9)

Ahab and Jezebel are a couple who stick together, and make joint use of their power against other persons. They have different backgrounds: he is the king of Israel, she is a Phoenician princess, and their marriage serves the political and economic interests of Israel and Phoenicia. The Bible sees them as the embodiment of evil, both because they promote alien, non-Israelite cults and because they abuse their power to hurt innocent people. This has made them unpopular in subsequent history, and there are relatively few portrayals of Ahab and Jezebel in art and literature.

Ahab is a Hebrew name which means "brother of the father." The name Jezebel is connected to the Ugaritic word *zbl*, "prince," but it is interpreted in the Bible as "a pile of dung," in view of the dreadful fate that meets her: her body is to lie like dung on the field, so that she can no longer be identified.

The story of Ahab and Jezebel is related in the Books of Kings, which contain texts from the period of the kings of Israel (e.g., the cycle about Elijah from the ninth century before Christ) and reworkings of these texts in connection with the Deuteronomist historiography of the mid-sixth century before Christ. They are a good example of how history was written in ancient Israel. The basic data in the biographies of this royal couple are historical: Ahab, son of Omri, ruled the northern kingdom of Israel from 871 to 851 B.C.E., during the period when Israel and Judah were separate kingdoms. The stories of the conflict between Jezebel and Elijah and the expropriation of Naboth's vineyard have an historical background, but the details are later elaborations.

The Books of Kings relate the history of the kings as religious history, from the perspective of the prophets who attempt to keep monotheism free of all foreign cults and warn against apostasy from faith in Yahweh, the one God of Israel. The watering-down of monotheism is equated with harlotry. As in a monogamous marriage, Yahweh wants exclusive veneration. The royal house of Ahab and Jezebel does not meet this criterion, and this is why the religious verdict on Ahab is negative: he "did evil in the sight of the Lord more than all that were before him" (1 Kg 16:30).

We see an example of this conduct which displeases God in Ahab's marriage – as one element in the political alliances he sets up – with a non-Israelite woman, Jezebel, the daughter of Ethbaal, king of Phoenician Sidon. She is a worshiper of the Canaanite god Baal, and Ahab joins her in promoting the cult of Baal, a god whose special sphere was fertility and the weather; his female counterpart was Asherah. In Canaan, the cult of Baal and Asherah was practiced

alongside the worship of Yahweh. Ahab and Jezebel were proponents of a syncretism which embraced both cults.

Ahab builds a temple to Baal in his capital, Samaria, and Jezebel has one hundred prophets of Yahweh killed. This support of the cult of Baal brings them into conflict with the prophet Elijah, who upholds faith in the one God of Israel and opposes the fertility cults of Baal and Asherah. He assembles 450 prophets of Baal and 400 prophets of Asherah "who eat at Jezebel's table" (18:19), and the whole people of Israel on Mount Carmel. The divine verdict is displayed: Baal fails to appear, but Yahweh, the God of Abraham, Isaac, and Jacob appears in fire, thus demonstrating that he is the only true God. Elijah then has the prophets of Baal killed. When Ahab tells Jezebel about this, she threatens to kill Elijah, who flees south to Horeb, the mountain of God (1 Kg 19). Historically speaking, it is at least questionable whether the religious policy of the royal house was in fact so aggressive that prophets of other cults were slain; caution is suggested here by the fact that all the children of Ahab and Jezebel had names which included the divine name of Yahweh: Ahaziah, Jehoram, and Athaliah.

The only detailed narrative about Ahab and Jezebel is 1 Kg 21, the short story about Naboth's vineyard. The scene is Jezreel, the winter residence of the Omri dynasty on the eastern edge of the plain of Jezreel in northern Israel. Naboth, a Jezreelite – i.e., a "local" man – possesses a vineyard beside Ahab's palace, and the king wishes to use this as a vegetable garden. He does not actually need this piece of ground; he is taken by the fancy of extending the park around his palace. He negotiates with Naboth and proposes either a sale or an exchange for a better vineyard. But Naboth refuses to sell: he does not wish to part with the inheritance of his fathers.

At this, Ahab returns home despondently, lies down on his bed, turns his face to the wall, and refuses to eat. When his wife Jezebel asks him why he is so depressed, he tells her about his negotiations with Naboth, and she takes the matter in hand: "Do you now govern Israel? Get up, eat some food, and be cheerful; I will give you the vineyard of Naboth the Jezreelite" (21:7). This is how married life was for Ahab and Jezebel: the mighty king sulks like a little child because he cannot get something he wants, but his wife coaxes him to break his silence and tell her what is troubling him. She refuses to allow him to suffer defeat at the hands of his neighbor and takes the initiative.

She writes letters in Ahab's name to the elders and nobles in the city and seals them with his seal. She tells them to proclaim a fast and give Naboth the leading seat. The cultic community which assembles for the fast also has the function of a court of law. Naboth is given the leading seat in order that he may not become suspicious, but Jezebel has two "scoundrels" bear false witness that Naboth has blasphemed God and the king. He is then led out of the city and stoned. When Jezebel hears of his death, she says to Ahab: "Go, take possession

TWO KINGS.
Josaphat, the king of Judah, and Ahab, the king of Israel, in Ahab's capital, Samaria (1 Kg 22). The lower half of this miniature in the Wenceslaus Bible *(ca. 1400) depicts Zedekiah, who "made*

for himself horns of iron, and he said, 'Thus says the Lord: With these you shall gore the Arameans until they are destroyed'" (1 Kg 22:11). Instead of this, Ahab receives a mortal wound in battle (opposite page).

THE QUEEN.
The two sections of this miniature from the Wenceslaus Bible *illustrate the story of Naboth's vineyard (1 Kg 21). In order to get hold of this vineyard for her husband, King Ahab, Jezebel forges letters with his signature and seal, and a messenger brings these to the elders of the city. The lower half depicts the result of the false accusations: Naboth is stoned outside the city gates.*

of the vineyard of Naboth the Jezreelite, which he refused to give you for money; for Naboth is not alive, but dead" (21:15). And Ahab does as she says: he takes possession of Naboth's vineyard.

Jezebel shows here that she is an influential queen at her husband's side. Ahab had reluctantly respected Naboth's refusal to sell his family inheritance, but she takes a different view of the position of the king: she lays claim to an absolute royal authority with an arbitrary power over life and death. In order to achieve her purpose, she intrigues against an innocent man. It is she who takes the initiative, and this is why the Bible interprets her as a seducer; but her intention of expro-

"Concerning Jezebel the Lord said, 'The dogs shall eat Jezebel within the bounds of Jezreel.'"

1 KINGS 21:23

priating Naboth would not have succeeded without the complicity of Ahab and the elders. Ahab's seal is on the command to murder Naboth, and it is ultimately he who takes possession of the vineyard. The royal couple jointly disregard the ancient law of Israel which sees the will of a free citizen as setting a limitation on the will of the king, when it is a question of the citizen's own property. Ahab and Jezebel follow the Canaanite law, giving the king an absolute right to dispose of the property of his subjects. They treat an innocent man with wanton cruelty, consolidating their rule by enriching themselves at the expense of their subjects.

This legal murder of Naboth enkindles Elijah's wrath. He upholds the law of Israel, and proclaims God's sentence to Ahab: disaster will come upon him and his family. But when Ahab repents, fasts, and puts on sackcloth, Elijah postpones the realization of his threats: it is only in the days of Ahab's son that disaster will strike his house. The summary verdict on the activities of Ahab and Jezebel is negative: "Indeed, there was no one like Ahab, who sold himself to do what was evil in the sight of the Lord, urged on by his wife Jezebel. He acted most abominably in going after idols, as the Amorites had done, whom the Lord drove out before the Israelites" (21:25f.).

Ahab dies in battle against the Arameans, and Jezebel meets a terrible death: when she hears that Jehu is coming to Jezreel, she puts on her make-up and jewels and awaits him at the window of the palace where audiences were granted. Perhaps this signals her intention to take over the reins of power after the death of

the king. Jehu orders her to be thrown down from the palace window. His horses trample her, dogs eat her corpse, and all that remains is her head, feet, and hands.

The assessment of Ahab – and above all, of Jezebel – as archetypes of evil becomes increasingly negative, thanks to their mixture of arbitrariness, hunger for power, religious apostasy from faith in Yahweh, and erotic seduction. The Deuteronomist editors, well known for their tendency to demonize powerful women, draw a particularly negative picture of Jezebel, and the Revelation of John continues this Old Testament tradition. Here too, she is alleged to have sinned through a combination of religious and sexual seduction. Jezebel is the archetype of a sexually wicked woman, an adulterous harlot: she "calls herself a prophetess and is teaching and beguiling my servants to practice fornication and to eat food sacrificed to idols" (2:20).

A DISGRACEFUL DEATH.
This frieze in a Bible moralisée *(ca. 1410) tells the story of how the kings of Israel and Judah, Joram and Ahaziah, died (2 Kg 9:21-27), and how the widowed Jezebel was thrown down from the wall (2 Kg 9:30-37).*

ESTHER AND AHASUERUS

(Esther 1-10)

The relation between the Jewish woman Esther and the Persian king Ahasuerus involves power and the reversal of the balance of power: Esther, the Jewish woman who initially has no power, gains more and more influence until she achieves her goal of thwarting an imminent persecution of the Jews. The Persian king, initially powerful, proves more and more to be the powerless plaything of his subjects: he does everything that Esther asks him to do.

Her story is told in the Book of Esther, an exciting historical novel composed ca. 300 years before Christ. Legendary traits and fairytale details expand an historical core: King Ahasuerus – "Artaxerxes" in Greek – may be the historical Xerxes I (486-465 B.C.E.). The story is set in Susa (i.e., Babylon) among the descendants of the Jewish men and women who were exiled to Babylon.

The Book of Esther is transmitted in two strongly divergent versions, one in Hebrew and one in Greek. In the Hebrew version, it is the only book in the Bible in which God is not mentioned explicitly, although God works in the background to save the people and set them free. The Greek version contains numerous additions and expansions which speak explicitly of God and of his actions; these include prayers by Mordecai and Esther, and a dream of Mordecai's with its interpretation. The Book of Esther has a secular theology: God allows human beings to take their own initiatives. He is invisible, concealed in the vicissitudes of life.

Ahasuerus and Esther meet after the king has repudiated his first wife, Vashti, who had refused to show herself to the king's guests at one of his lavish banquets, where he desired to display the wealth and splendor of his kingly rule and the beauty of his wife to the princes and nobles of his domains. She was unwilling to be shown off as the king's most beautiful possession. He was enraged, and his counselors urged him to repudiate her, so that every man would be master in his own house.

Now the king looks for a new wife throughout the whole land. The most

beautiful virgins of the country are cared for and anointed with precious oils and perfumes for one year in his harem, then they are brought to the king and receive the rank of concubines. His changing moods decide when he wants to see them. One of these girls is the Jewish woman Esther, an orphan who grew up in the house of her cousin and adoptive father Mordecai. She has a lovely, charming appearance and pleases the king more than any other woman. She is chosen: Ahasuerus falls in love with her and crowns her queen. The name Esther echoes the word for "hidden"; her Hebrew name Hadassah means "myrtle." Esther conceals her Jewish origins from her husband, but she demonstrates her loyalty by telling him about a conspiracy that has been hatched against him: Mordecai has learned of the planned attack and saves the king's life. This is recorded in the royal chronicle.

Esther and Mordecai have an enemy at court, Haman, a high official who enjoys the king's favor. He hates Mordecai because he refuses to bow down before him. Haman persuades the king to issue a decree ordering the slaughter of the Jews; lots (*pur*) are cast to determine the date, and it is resolved that the decree will be put into action on the thirteenth day of the Jewish month of Adar (February/March). The situation of the Jews is hopeless, and Mordecai implores Esther to get the king to extend his protection to her people. She hesitates, for anyone who enters the king's presence without being summoned is sentenced to death; it is only when the king stretches out his golden scepter that one is allowed to draw near him. It is now some time since Esther herself was summoned to the king. But when Mordecai repeats his plea, she finally resolves to go to the king and plead on behalf of her people. First, she asks the Jews to fast for three days, hoping that this will give her solidarity and support in a grave situation. By taking this step, Esther puts her life at risk: she is completely at the mercy of the king's reaction.

On the third day, she puts on her royal robes and enters the inner courtyard before the palace where Ahasuerus sits on his throne. She employs the splendor of her robes of state in order to dazzle the king, and her plan works. The king reacts kindly and shows her his favor. He stretches out his golden scepter, which she touches, and then asks her: "What is it, Queen Esther? What is your request? It shall be given you, even to the half of my kingdom" (5:3). (The Greek version intensifies the drama at this point: after her

> "The king loved Esther more than all the other women; of all the virgins she won his favor and devotion."
>
> ESTHER 2:17

TERROR.
The verre églomisé *of Johann Creszenz Meyer (1778) attributes Esther's fainting to the terrifying character of the king, a man without self-control. We look at this picture and ask: What terrible deed will the king do now?*

prayer, Esther goes with two maids to the king and faints in his presence because he looks at her in furious anger, his face a fiery red. Then God softens the king's heart and he takes her kindly in his arms.) Esther's request is harmless enough: she invites the king and Haman to a banquet. "If it pleases the king, let the king and Haman come today to a banquet that I have prepared for the king" (5:4). When they are sitting with their wine, the king repeats his request, but now it is Esther who sets the tone. She keeps him waiting and invites him and Haman to yet another banquet on the following day.

Ahasuerus, who usually enjoys displaying his power, is completely subject to his wife here. Esther's character changed when she made up her mind to plead for her people: she is no longer the submissive girl but is now a courageous queen, conscious of her own dignity. She prudently employs her influence on the king in order to achieve her goal, the protection of her people from annihilation.

In the night between the two banquets, the king is unable to sleep, and he has extracts from the Book of Chronicles read to him. He notes that Mordecai has not yet been rewarded for making known the conspiracy against the king. Haman is standing in the outer courtyard: he has come to secure the execution of Mordecai. Ahasuerus calls him in, but instead of an execution, he charges Haman to honor Mordecai. At the king's command, Haman conducts his enemy,

THE AUDIENCE.
Hans Burgkmair's historical painting
The Story of Esther *(1528) draws our eye to the favor of the king, who touches his queen with his scepter, thereby bidding her present her request (Est 5:2). To the right of the king stands Haman, the mortal enemy of the Jews; as the painting tells us (to the right, in the background), he will end on the gallows.*

dressed in royal robes, on a horse through the city square, crying out before him: "Thus shall it be done for the man whom the king wishes to honor!" (6:9).

At the second banquet for Ahasuerus and Haman, Esther pleads to the king to spare her people, who are threatened by Haman – a request which reveals to her husband that she herself is Jewish. The king becomes very angry with Haman when he realizes that his own wife and her people are threatened with persecution. In fury, he rises from the banquet and goes into the garden. Haman, who is well aware that things have taken a very bad turn for him, kneels at Esther's couch and asks her to spare his life. When Ahasuerus returns from the garden, he interprets this as an attempt to rape his wife, and Haman is hanged on the gallows that he himself had erected for the planned execution of Mordecai.

Ahasuerus now rewards Esther and Mordecai by raising them to Haman's position and giving them the power that he had formerly enjoyed. Esther asks the king to tear up the decree of Haman that envisaged the slaughter of the Jews; instead, the king issues a new decree permitting the Jews to take revenge on their enemies in the Persian kingdom, and they do this on Adar 13 (in the capital, Susa, they kill their foes on Adar 14). On this day, which had been designated by lot (*pur*) for the annihilation of the Jews, they slaughter their foes. It is historically improbable that a blood-bath of this kind actually took place among the Persians. Rather, what we have here is a story written from the perspective of the oppressed. After this, Adar 14 (in the provinces) and Adar 15 (in the capital) are declared festal days, the feast of Purim. Mordecai and Esther send letters calling on the Jews to celebrate this feast, which is observed in Judaism up to the present day. Just as the Book of Esther has comic and ironic traits, so the feast of Purim is a joyful feast with boisterous banquets where so much wine is to be drunk that it is no longer possible to tell Haman and Mordecai apart. Presents and sweets are given to one's friends and to the needy, and children put on fancy dress.

Christians and Jews have interpreted the Book of Esther differently, and its influence has varied accordingly. Christian commentators even today often react with puzzlement to this text, taking their distance from it and calling it questionable from a religious and moral point of view. The church has never known quite what to make of the Book of Esther. It has been criticized for being too specifically Jewish, and the church has rejected the avenging murder of the Persians at the close of the book as morally unacceptable. In Judaism, however, this book is very well known and popular. It documents Esther's rescue of the Jewish people under threat, and it is read once a year in the synagogue at the feast of Purim. It is one of the five Megilloth, the "scrolls" for special feast days. Alongside Sarah, Miriam, Deborah, Hannah, Abigail, and Hulda, Esther is one of the seven prophetesses of Judaism.

Ahasuerus and Esther are an unequal couple – the mighty Persian king who demonstrates his splendor, and the beautiful Jewish virgin. It is a question of

A MISSION.
Superficially, we could say that the picture Esther on Her Way to Ahasuerus *by the Florentine Renaissance painter Filippino*

Lippo (ca. 1489) is depicting the verse: "Esther also was taken into the king's palace" (Est 2:8). But in this painting, she is not being "taken." Rather, she appears as a self-aware young woman who already senses that she has a mission to carry out.

power. The balance of power is not what it may seem: the king is the plaything of his princes and his counselors, of Haman – and ultimately of Esther herself, who embodies Jewish existence in the diaspora situation, in the tension between assimilation and resistance. To begin with, she adapts to the situation at the Persian court and conceals her Jewishness. But when she resolves to go to the king's presence although he has not summoned her, and to plead with him to avert the destruction of the Jews, she betrays her origins. Esther develops from a virgin chosen for her beauty to a self-aware queen who acts on behalf of her people and wards off the planned persecution of the Jews.

"Then King Ahasuerus said
to Queen Esther and
to the Jew Mordecai: 'See,
I have given Esther
the house of Haman, and
they have hanged him
on the gallows, because
he plotted to lay hands on the Jews.
You may write
as you please with
regard to the Jews, in the
name of the king.'"
ESTHER 8:7-8

THE KING LISTENS.
Esther's action to save her people begins when Ahasuerus prompts her: "What is it, Queen Esther? What is your request?" (Est 5:3). The painting of Esther's audience by Giulio Clovic in the sixteenth-century Farnese Book of Hours *concentrates on this moment.*

THE SONG OF SONGS

FULFILLMENT.
This second title of his painting The
Kiss *(1907/1908) is a homage by Gustav
Klimt to the sensual relationship of love
between man and woman (opposite page).*

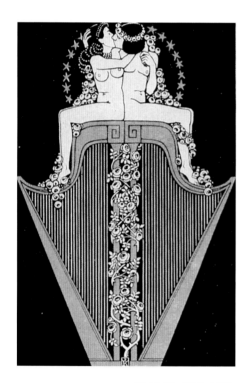

SONGS OF LOVE.
*Friedrich Wilhelm Kleukens
employed the motifs of two lovers and
a harp on the dust cover of a limited
edition of the* Song of Songs *(1909)
to emphasize that this biblical book has
its origin in erotic lyric poetry.*

Its status in the Bible. The Old Testament contains a short book, consisting of eight chapters and running to a few pages, which one could overlook – except for the fact that its contents are so explosive. It consists of love songs, full of eroticism and passion. Its title is a superlative; Goethe counted it among the most important books of world literature. What is the Song of Songs about? A young woman yearns passionately for her beloved. She must look after her brothers' vineyard, while he is taking sheep and goats to pasture. She seeks him in summer among the shepherds in the fields, she seeks him in winter on the streets of the city; she is fainting with longing for him. When he pictures her appearance, he describes her in images drawn from the exuberance of nature. He stands at her door, she lets him in, and they make love under the eyes of her mother. They make love in the vineyards, under apple trees, with flowers all around them. They are maddened by passion, which takes hold of them like a mighty fire, like a raging torrent.

These songs seem out of place in their venerable surroundings – for the Bible speaks of serious matters, like the history of Israel with Yahweh its God and the self-discovery of the people. Here no prophet is speaking because God has charged him to do so, nor is there any search for the meaning or the interpretation of life, such as we find in the Psalms. Indeed, the word "God" never occurs in the Song of Songs. Accordingly, both Jews and Christians have found it highly irritating that this love poetry should have been granted a place in the canon of the sacred writings. The synagogue began to understand the book in a metaphorical sense as speaking of the love between Yahweh and Israel, and the church followed this allegorical interpretation, reading the poems in terms of the relationship between Christ and the church, Christ and Mary, or Christ and the soul. But the more the text was praised, the less seriously was it taken, thanks both to a complicated attitude toward sexuality and to an increasing tendency to see women as less valuable than men – indeed, to see them as dangerous. This began in the third century before Christ (e.g., Qoh 7:27); Augustine handed it down to later Christian generations, and it continued into the modern period. Today, even the Catholic church has abandoned the allegorical interpretation.

The language of the poems. It must of course be admitted that the language of the text itself made its understanding more difficult. The Song of Songs employs a literary language with fixed rules: a poet could not simply write in any way he wanted. At most, he could introduce his individual note by the manner in which he took the various elements and produced a new composition. The principal styles used by ancient oriental lyric poetry were comparisons and metaphors, figures of speech

"Do not make jokes! There is no impoverishment here! Does not love make us rich?
When I hold you in my arms, my happiness equals every joy."

JOHANN WOLFGANG VON GOETHE, SULEIKA (1819)

that employ a word in something other than its original meaning. For example, when the young woman asks that the foxes be driven out of the vineyard, she is not talking about animals, but about other young men, and the "vineyard" is the field of love. This kind of language is seldom unambiguous; but it is precisely this mixture of precision and polyvalence that gives the Song of Songs its own special charm.

Comparisons are employed when something cannot appropriately be presented on its own terms alone; but since these poems come from another culture and a period far distant in time, we often do not understand the point of comparison, as we see in one classic example. When we read: "You are beautiful my love, ah, you are beautiful; your eyes are doves" (1:15), the statement is reduced to the two words "eyes" and "doves," which the text tells us are identical. The image and the comparison explain each other; they are in a sense interchangeable. Today, however, we know nothing about what the image "dove" expressed at that time; we must go back to literature, ancient art, or archeological discoveries. The similarities to the love poetry of ancient Egypt led to the erroneous idea that Solomon, famed for his cosmopolitan attitudes and tolerance, was the author of the Song of Songs, but in reality, this cycle was composed between the eighth and the sixth centuries B.C.E.

The language of the Song of Songs is permeated by erotic images and symbols, vividly depicting the fullness of life and vitality – the sweetness of honey, the intoxicating power of wine, apples and the apple tree under which the girl sits, the vineyard in which people work (symbolizing her body), grapes (symbolizing her breasts), a palm tree (evoking her alluring figure), and the widespread branches of the cedar (symbolizing the house of love). All kinds of fragrances remind her of the

SOLOMON.
The initial O of the first verse of the book in Latin: Osculetur me *("Let him kiss me!") in the* Winchester Bible *(ca. 1150) depicts King Solomon as the poet of the Song of Songs, with his beloved: "My dove, my perfect one, is only one, flawless" (below).*

HORTUS CONCLUSUS.
The painter known as the Master of the Upper Rhine employs the wall as a symbol in his painting The Little Garden of Paradise *(ca. 1400). This is drawn from the Song of Songs, where the bride is compared to "a garden locked"* (hortus conclusus *in Latin, 4:12). The identification of the bride with Mary led to the use of the metaphor of the "locked garden" as a symbol of Mary's virginity (right).*

seductive attractiveness of the man she loves: "nard and saffron, calamus and cinnamon, with all trees of frankincense" (4:14). Myrrh, the most expensive of all anointing oils, is mentioned frequently. Blossoms and fragrances evoke the love that reawakens after the lengthy winter rains.

Nature – mirroring love. Very many comparisons are drawn from nature: flowers, trees, blossoms, fruits, animals of all kinds, rocks. This is not surprising, since it is nature that determines the rhythm of life. After the rain, people long for the springtime (2:10-13). Their experience of the growth, the blossoming, and the wilting of nature is intense.

The beloved comes as a harbinger of spring at 2:8-14 (see the text in the margin), which recalls a serenade sung outside the loved one's door and is the most beautiful song about nature in the Old Testament. Nevertheless, the Song of Songs does not romanticize nature in the manner of much modern poetry. People in the ancient orient did not transpose their emotions onto nature; rather, nature awakened emotions in them. Every flower, every vineyard evokes the beloved, everything reminds the woman of the man she loves. These motifs do not require any explanation or justification, and they often take on a life of their own, as the poet is caught up in enthusiastic joy. Although many images are interchangeable, there is a nuance in the accents which the poets set: comparisons from nature tend to be used for the woman, comparisons from architecture tend more to be used for the man. It is he who woos; the expressions of yearning tend to be found on her lips.

Equality in love. If we now turn to the contents, we are immediately struck by the modernity of these poems: here we have two persons who enjoy a relationship of equality. They are equally important; they are sure of themselves when they speak, and have no hesitations. The actual words they employ may seem foreign to us, but the dialogue in the Song of Songs shows that they have equal roles. Indeed, the words sometimes seem like a duet, as at 1:15f.:

The man: "Ah, you are beautiful, my love, ah, you are beautiful;
        your eyes are like doves."
The woman: "Ah, you are beautiful, my beloved, truly lovely. Our couch is green."

They toss the ball one to another, until they utter a common wish or speak of a common experience. They express the same ideas, have the same feelings, and agree with each other. Often we have the impression that the woman is the more active partner, when she takes the initiative: "Come, my beloved, let us go forth into the fields … There I will give you my love" (7:11f.). She is the more courageous of the two. For the sake of her love, she risks her good reputation when she seeks her beloved at night in the city – and she is seized by the watchmen, who think she is a prostitute.

"The voice of my beloved!
Look, he comes,
leaping upon the mountains,
bounding over the hills.
My beloved is like a gazelle
or a young stag.
Look, there he stands behind
our wall, gazing in at the windows,
looking through the lattice.
My beloved speaks and says to me:
'Arise, my love, my fair one,
and come away;
for now the winter is past,
the rain is over and gone.
The flowers appear on the earth,
the time of singing has come,
and the voice of the turtledove
is heard in our land.
The fig tree puts forth its figs,
and the vines are in blossom;
they give forth fragrance.
Arise, my love, my fair one,
and come away.
O my dove,
in the clefts of the rock,
in the covert of the cliff,
let me see your face,
let me hear your voice;
for your voice is sweet,
and your face is lovely.'"
SONG OF SONGS 2:8-14

She speaks openly of her wishes and her needs: "Let him kiss me with the kisses of his mouth!" (1:2), "I am faint with love" (2:5). She throws her lover into confusion with the glances she throws him, then proclaims proudly: "His desire is for me" (7:11). When the first couple were expelled from paradise, a curse was pronounced: "Your desire shall be for your husband, but he shall rule over you" (Gen 3:16). But this has now been reversed: now, each partner is dependent on the other.

Is this love any different from the relationships between young people today? Like all who are in love, they want to be alone, and find a solitary place to be – for like all relationships of love, theirs is observed with inquisitiveness, suspicion, and disapproval. It is not only in the watchmen that the young woman encounters society (Song 3:3; 5:7); she must also appeal several times to the "daughters of Jerusalem" (who represent "high society" and uphold the rules of propriety in this world), "Do not disturb love until it is ready!" (2:7, etc.). In order not to be recognized and controlled by others, the lovers take on a variety of roles, imagining themselves as gardeners, shepherds, kings, or the owners of vineyards. Their relationship must at all costs remain hidden, and this is why they spend so much time out in the open, under trees, in the fields, and at night.

About beauty. Each longs continuously to see and admire the other – it is striking how prominent beauty is in the Song of Songs. It is beauty that impels their love and gives it urgency, and the couple repeatedly tell each other how beautiful they are: "Ah, you are beautiful, my love; ah, you are beautiful" (1:15, etc.); "How fair and pleasant you, O loved one, delectable maiden!" (7:6); "You are altogether beautiful, my love; there is no flaw in you" (4:7). The fascination each exercises on the other leads them naturally enough to exaggerate the difference to their surroundings, in order to emphasize the uniqueness of the one they love (2:2f.):

> "As a lily among brambles, so is my love among maidens."
> "As an apple tree among the trees of the wood,
> so is my beloved among young men."

Beauty generates erotic attraction, as we see above all in the descriptive songs which praise the partner in terms of the highest admiration. The picture that the woman paints of her beloved here recalls the Renaissance ideal of beauty which Botticelli realized with perfectly balanced harmony in his figures. Her friends ask: "What is your beloved more than another beloved?" (5:9), and her reply shows us her gaze descending from his head to his feet: "My beloved is all radiant and ruddy, distinguished among ten thousand ..." (see the full text in the margin of the opposite page).

This description of the beloved is one single sentence in the original Hebrew text – it is as if she cannot stop praising his beauty, while one impression follows swiftly on another, until at the end she cries out: "This is my beloved!" She does not describe him directly, and we are not informed about his height, the color of his eyes, or the expression on his face; but he stands vividly before us, a splendid harmony of formal perfection.

The garden of love. The peak experiences of love are not omitted. Some texts in the Song of Songs speak quite openly of intercourse, but usually this is clothed in metaphors. The image of the garden is particularly intense. When her friends ask her where her beloved has gone, and she replies, "My beloved has gone down to his garden, to the beds of spices, to pasture his flock in the gardens, and to gather lilies"

PASSION.
Love kindles "burning fires, a mighty flame": woodcut (1983) by Robert Wyss based on the Song of Songs (6:8).

"My beloved is all radiant and ruddy,
distinguished among ten thousand.
His head is the finest gold;
his locks are wavy,
black as a raven.
His eyes are like doves
beside springs of water,
bathed in milk, fitly set.
His cheeks are like beds of spices,
yielding fragrance.
His lips are lilies,
distilling liquid myrrh.
His arms are rounded gold,
set with jewels.
His body is ivory work,
encrusted with sapphires.
His legs are alabaster columns,
set upon bases of gold.
His appearance is like Lebanon,
choice as the cedars.
His speech is most sweet,
and he is altogether desirable.
This is my beloved and this is my friend,
O daughters of Jerusalem!"

Song of Songs 5:10-16

(6:2), we can be certain that he did not actually enter a real garden. Rather, this "garden" is not only the place of love, but the beloved herself. Even today, Arab men say that they "are going to paradise" when they visit their beloved at night.

And yet, this love is not without its problems and dangers. Many images hint at the dark aspects – though these only make the light shine more brightly. For example, the man stands early in the morning, trembling with cold and expectation, outside the door of his beloved, and he puts his hand through the latch – but when she opens the door in her excitement, he has departed (5:2-6). Why has he fled? Has his courage suddenly failed him? Was he afraid of getting too close to her? The love between these two is a continual searching and finding, but sometimes also a failure to find; they conceal themselves and present themselves, protect themselves behind a barrier and then pour themselves out in ecstasy.

Love and death – sacred or profane? At the close of the book, she asks her beloved to make her a seal and bind this on his heart. She looks for the greatest imaginable proximity to him; at the same time, she wants to be an amulet that will protect him from all that is negative – and from death itself. Love and death are envisaged as two mighty powers which keep each other in check. In order to resist death, love must have a powerful, indeed a violent dimension, namely the passion which is an elemental force, inexorable and not for sale (8:6f.):

> "Set me as a seal upon your heart, / as a seal upon your arm;
> for love is strong as death, / passion fierce as the grave.
> Its flashes are flashes of fire, / a raging flame.
> Many waters cannot quench love, / neither can floods drown it.
> If one offered for love / all the wealth of his house,
> it would be utterly scorned."

In this sense, the love of the two is a conspiracy against the darkness of the world. And clearly it is the woman, with her capacity for love, who can resist the forces hostile to life, whereas the man is at risk, emotionally speaking, and needs protection. This evaluation of love and sexuality shows that we cannot speak here of "profane" realities: this suffices to show why love and sexuality, central elements in human life, are given a place in the Bible. Yahweh (God) is not mentioned in the Song of Songs, but that does not mean that love is not holy.

The Song of Songs shows us an emancipated love between two young people who are not in the least thinking of marriage and family. Perhaps it was in fact possible in those days to avoid submitting to the strict marriage laws? At any rate, the biblical understanding of the human person takes a greater variety of forms than we sometimes think; it is no more subject to norms than are the ethical and dogmatic ideas of the Bible.

A BED OF FLOWERS.
The illustration by Åke Gustavsson in an edition of the Song of Songs (1971) takes up the motifs of the garden and flowers. The woman exults: "My beloved is mine and I am his; he pastures his flock among the lilies" (2:16).

SOLOMON AND THE QUEEN OF SHEBA

(1 Kings 10)

Those who paid a visit to Solomon entered a fairytale world. From far off, one could see the temple and the palace, radiant on their mountain. The king's house was surrounded by quarters for his mercenaries, with accommodation for horses and chariots, storehouses and administrative buildings. Jerusalem had taken on a completely new look. Work on the palace alone had taken thirteen years. It had columns and ceilings of cedar wood, and even its walls were paneled in wood and decorated with golden shields. On entering, the visitor came to a vestibule which opened out onto the most modern architecture: courtyards flooded with light, colonnades, rectangular windows and doors everywhere, and a throne room with the throne of gold and ivory, supported by lions, as its center. The only possible reaction was breathless amazement.

In those days, anyone as rich as that must also be very powerful, trading with many countries, controlling access roads, and exercising considerable influence; he must have good collaborators and highly qualified artisans. And Solomon ruled in great splendor. The goal of the buildings he erected was the integration of the heterogeneous population, and his politically motivated marriages created diplomatic contacts. During his reign, there was peace; culture blossomed, and a kind of "Enlightenment" occurred in intellectual life, marked by tolerance and a liberal spirit. For the first time, literature was produced in Israel. Solomon was a cosmopolitan who did not hesitate to accept influences from abroad, both in architecture and in the organization of the state. The twelve provinces were governed by a centralized bureaucracy. He went so far as to set up altars in honor of foreign gods, so that those of his workers who came from other countries could worship in Israel. In many ways, Solomon followed the model of Egypt; one of his foreign wives was in fact a daughter of Pharaoh. Egyptian love poetry had a considerable influence on the Song of Songs, the oldest parts of which may very possibly go back to the time of Solomon. It is no wonder that he became famous. All the world wanted to see Solomon's wealth and hear his wisdom. In order to win his favor, people came from afar and brought him presents worthy of a king.

The Queen of Sheba was one of those who could not stay at home. Was Solomon really so wise? Was he really so rich – even richer than she was? She had to find out. Sheba, in today's Yemen, was one of the richest cultures in ancient times. Together with several other small kingdoms in the southern Arabian peninsula, it had a monopoly on incense, myrrh, and other fragrances which at that time were indispensable for worship, and the taming of the camel led to a boom

AT JOURNEY'S END.
This miniature in the Wenceslaus Bible *(ca. 1400) depicts in a synchronous presentation the arrival of the Queen of Sheba before the walls of Jerusalem and her encounter with Solomon. One of the animals loaded down with presents is just disappearing through the city gate, and two busts in the city embody the king and the queen.*

in exports. Jerusalem must already have been importing large quantities of incense, spices, and cosmetics along the Incense Road. In his prophecy of future salvation, Isaiah makes Jerusalem the radiant center of the whole world, to which even foreigners will go on pilgrimage: "A multitude of camels shall cover you, the young camels of Midian and Ephah; all those from Sheba shall come. They shall

A LONG JOURNEY.
This fifteenth-century painting by Apollonio de Giovanni employs a varied landscape to underline the distance between the mythical Sheba and Jerusalem. Rich jewels display the wealth of the country from which the Queen of Sheba has set out with her caravan. Two gracious ladies-in-waiting in a sedan chair are likewise bedecked with jewels.

bring gold and frankincense, and shall proclaim the praise of the Lord" (60:6). In 1724, Johann Sebastian Bach took up this theme in his cantata "They shall all come from Sheba," in a majestic concert of music which sketches a brilliantly colorful picture of this solemn procession. Later, Jeremiah (6:20) and Ps 72 also mention Sheba.

The queen of this rich land has her camels saddled and loaded with all kinds of costly gifts; she herself mounts the dromedary on which artists have traditionally depicted her journey, and sets out with a great company through the desert towards Jerusalem, hundreds of kilometers away. She wants to put Solomon's knowledge to the test – this is the only reason that the Bible gives for her journey – and she is well prepared, having thought out difficult riddles to put to the king. If he answers correctly, she will acknowledge that he is a wise man. If he errs, however, he is no different from any other man.

Solomon successfully solves every riddle, for "Solomon's wisdom surpassed the wisdom of all the people of the east, and all the wisdom of Egypt" (1

"She came to Jerusalem with a very great retinue, with camels bearing spices,

Kg 4:30). This refers, not to his skill in government, nor to the sentence he pronounces when two mothers each claim that a child is theirs, nor to his encyclopedic knowledge, but to his experience of life and to his acuteness. We may find it strange that a queen should undertake such a long and wearisome journey in order to pose riddles to a king, but this was nothing unusual in olden times. The competition to solve riddles was an intellectual contest; like dreams, it belongs to religious psychology. A similar contest takes place between Samson and the Philistines (Judg 10:19).

Let us look at one example. According to Targum Sheni on Est 1:3, the first riddle of the Queen of Sheba was: "A wooden vessel for water, iron buckets,

and very much gold, and precious stones; and when she came to Solomon, she told him all that was on her mind."

1 KINGS 10:2

JERUSALEM.
A model of the temple built by King Solomon ca. 950 B.C.E. It was destroyed in 587 B.C.E. by the troops of King Nebuchadnezzar of Babylon (above).

STAGE-SETTING.
In his painting of the reception of the Queen of Sheba by Solomon (1890), Edward Poynter depicts a theatrical stage. Solomon's throne, the symbol of his wealth and wisdom, is equipped with sculptures of lions (1 Kg 10:19) (right).

they draw the stones up, they let the water flow." The answer is: a little tube containing kohl, a cosmetic which had been in use for a very long time. The intriguing point here is that the Israelites were forbidden to use such cosmetics.

After solving all her riddles, Solomon shows the queen all his wealth. He takes her through his palace, invites her to an opulent meal at which she is waited on by men in costly livery, and finally shows her the temple, where he offers his burnt sacrifices. The queen is so impressed that "there was no more spirit in her" (1 Kg 10:5). Solomon has demonstrated that he is not merely her equal in rank, but her superior. His fame is based on both wisdom and wealth, and her praise is unmeasured: "Your wisdom and prosperity far surpass the report that I had heard"

MARIB.
These steles are part of the remains of the palace near today's Marib in southern Yemen, which is linked to the mythical Queen of Sheba, who ruled in ancient Yemen and in Ethiopia.

(10:7). After they have exchanged precious gifts, the queen – who had been so sure of herself – travels back to Sheba.

This is the reason why this story is included in the Bible. It shows that Solomon is superior even to the rich, prudent, courageous, and charming Queen of Sheba, and this is narrated in the exaggerated style of propaganda. Soon after Solomon's death, the unity of the kingdom – which only a David could guarantee – collapsed. The northern tribes refused to acknowledge Solomon's heir, Rehoboam, and chose a king of their own, so that now there were two royal houses and two capital cities, Israel with Samaria and Judah with Jerusalem. Although the author of the Books of Kings, which were probably written in Jerusalem after

586 B.C.E., took the partition of the kingdom for granted, his sympathies lay with the southern kingdom, and he wanted to give his support to the Jerusalem dynasty. This little story served his purpose perfectly. It related the dream of ancient glories, in order to give hope when things had taken a turn for the worse.

The historical existence of the Queen of Sheba cannot be proven. However, at the end of the 1970s, German archaeologists using geomorphological methods demonstrated that a well-organized state existed in the territory of the legendary queen in the tenth century before Christ; and oral tradition preserved in the memory of the Arabian peoples a story of rich trading caravans of camels along the old Incense Road. It was from this happy Arabia that the legendary queen set out. In the East, the boundary between fairytales and historical traditions is fluid.

It is astonishing that the imagination of later times should have paid so much attention to this encounter. The story was elaborated in Jewish, Islamic, and Ethiopic, Coptic, and other Christian traditions. The allusions in the New Testament do not depart from the Old Testament context. When Jesus is asked for a sign, he replies that signs already exist, e.g., the people of Nineveh who experienced the greatness of Jonah, and the Queen of the South who bore witness to Solomon's wisdom. He himself, however, is greater than Jonah and Solomon (Mt 12:42). Another time, when he wishes to reveal God's care for humankind, he speaks in a parable about the lilies of the field and adds: "Even Solomon in all his glory was not clothed like one of these" (Mt 6:29).

The Jewish tradition (once again, according to Targum Sheni on Est 1:3) relates that Solomon understood the languages of the birds, the trees, and the winds. The evil spirits were servants at his court, and this made him lord not only over space and time but also over the material world. Once, when his court assembles, Solomon notes that the hoopoe is missing. It was believed that this migratory bird flew around in the world and discovered hidden treasures. When it at last arrives, it tells the king of the Queen of Sheba and her wealth: in her realm, the dust is more precious than silver, and the trees are as old as the world itself. Solomon then sends the hoopoe to invite her to visit him. The version related in the Koran (27:22-26) agrees with the Targum. In later Judaism and in Islam, it was believed that the queen had been possessed by an evil spirit and that Solomon fought against this spirit, in order to wrest her away from the worship of the sun and bring her to know the true God. It was said that when she entered the palace, she thought the glass floor was water – everyone saw her hairy legs and took her for a witch. The riddles she posed to the king doubtless also led to an association with the Sphinx. And so she became Lilith, the queen of the demons.

In the Christian tradition, the Queen of Sheba appears as a witness to the faith; she comes, a wise black woman, to pay homage to Jesus with the Wise Men from the East. She and Solomon are also identified with the lovers in the Song of

ROLE-PLAYING.
This Brussels tapestry (ca. 1550) depicts Charles V of France (king 1364-1380) and his sister Marie de Hongrie, who resided in Brussels, as Solomon and the Queen of Sheba. This role-playing is based in Charles V's nickname, "The Wise" (opposite page).

ANCESTOR.
This fifteenth-century Ethiopian miniature with its portrait of the Ethiopian-Yemenite "Queen of Sheba" and the king of Judah alludes to the tradition that Solomon was the ancestor of the emperors of Ethiopia. One of the titles of the last ruler of this dynasty, Emperor Haile Selassie I (deposed in 1974), was "Lion of Judah."

ox aduentt dominatoz dominus t regnū
in manu eius et potestas imperium. ps.
Deus iudicium tuum regi da et iustitiam
tuam filio regis. ORATIO.

Songs, who are seen as a typological representation of Christ and the church.

Nowhere, however, did the encounter between Solomon and the Queen of Sheba become more important than in Ethiopia, where it left very concrete traces: it is related that they had a son named Menelik, from whom all the Ethiopian emperors down to the twentieth century claimed descent. The motif of the seduction of the queen had a long prehistory, but it was only in the fourteenth century that it took a literary form, in the *Kebra nagast* of Jezhak of Axum. From that date, the Ethiopians were convinced that they were the chosen people of God, and that the Queen of Sheba surpassed Solomon in every way.

There are of course good reasons to see Solomon and the Queen of Sheba as a "great couple." The biblical account is so brief that it almost cries out for further details: "King Solomon gave to the Queen of Sheba every desire that she expressed" (1 Kg 10:13). These words may hint at intercourse; at any rate, they left the door open to a romantic interpretation, since the general reference to Solomon's granting her every wish may have suggested that it was not only on

ROYAL GIFTS.
This page from the fifteenth-century Turin-Milan Book of Hours *of the Duc de Berry draws a parallel between the adoration of the "kings" in Bethlehem (the main picture) and the visit of the Queen of Sheba in Jerusalem (at the bottom of the page). This can appeal to a biblical text, Ps 72, which is ascribed to Solomon (opposite page).*

"May the kings of Tarshish and of
the isles render him tribute,
may the kings of Sheba and
Seba bring gifts.
May all kings fall down before him,
all nations give him service."
PSALM 72:10-11

account of his wealth and his wisdom that she had set out on her journey to Jerusalem. Besides this, the Hebrew text at 1 Kg 10:2 ("when she came to Solomon …") employs a verb which is also a technical term for intercourse (e.g., Gen 19:34, where Lot "goes in" to his daughters). And it would surely be surprising if Solomon, to whom the Bible ascribes 700 wives and 300 concubines, had turned up his nose at his beautiful and exotic guest; he had indeed proved himself worthy of her love. The narrative has a third indication of a great love. The riddling contest is not only a power struggle; as the story of Samson's wooing of his bride reminds us (Judg 14:18), the suitor had to prove his worth by means of riddles. The Arabic tradition tells us that, after the riddles had been solved, Solomon and the Queen of Sheba married.

In the last analysis, then, the relationship between Solomon and the Queen of Sheba remains their secret. It can continue to fire our imaginations.

ETHIOPIAN LEGEND.
This pictorial narrative describes the journey of a messenger to Jerusalem; in the lower series of pictures, we see the journey of the queen herself. Solomon is the father of her son Menelik, the founder of the imperial dynasty of Ethiopia.

TOBIAS AND SARAH

(Tobit 7-8)

"Raphael was sent to heal
both of them: Tobit,
by removing the white films from
his eyes, so that he might see God's
light with his eyes; and Sarah,
daughter of Raguel, by
giving her in marriage to Tobias son
of Tobit, and by setting her free
from the wicked demon Asmodeus."
TOBIT 3:17

A PICTURE TELLS A STORY.
*At the beginning of the Book of Tobit
in the* Urbino Bible *(1476-1478), the
main picture describes the contents of the
story in three simultaneous scenes:
Tobias and his companion take leave
of Tobit and Anna; the two companions
proceed on their way; and they return
with Sarah. The medallions in the border
begin at the bottom left with the worship of
idols (Tob 1:5); above this, we can recognize
Tobias with his parents; at the top left,
Tobit receives prestigious commissions
from Shalmaneser (1:13). The central
medallion on the upper border shows
Tobit's care for prisoners – one of his
works of mercy (1:16) (opposite page).*

The Book of Tobit includes the story of Tobias and Sarah, a harmonious relationship which culminates in the marriage of the couple. Their narrative is embedded in a family history, and the wedding of Tobias and Sarah is the conclusion of some very dramatic events.

Each is an only child; they live far apart and know nothing of each other. The conclusion of the story shows how the geographical distance and other seemingly impossible difficulties are overcome. In fact, the story resembles a fairytale in many ways. It is not an historical account, but has "typical" characters. The Book of Tobit is set in the late period of the Old Testament in far-off lands, in the diaspora, and its events cover a wide area, as far as Persia.

Tobias's parents live in Nineveh and have fallen on hard times. Tobit, his father, has lost all his wealth. Then a good deed on behalf of his fellow Jews leads to the loss of his eyesight: he flaunts the prohibition by the king and buries a fellow believer, and then leans against the wall of his house, since contact with a dead body makes him ritually impure. The droppings of a bird fall into his eyes and blind him. This means that the only reason for Tobit's misfortune is his fidelity to the law of God (2:1-3:6). Tobias's mother Anna is a strong-willed woman who works to feed her family. She sometimes quarrels with her husband, when he treats her unjustly and harshly (2:11-14). This older couple is not portrayed so harmoniously as the young couple whom we meet later on in the story, but this is due to the intolerable situation in which they live. In order to relieve their distress, they send their only son Tobias to a foreign country to fetch the money that Tobit had left in trust with a relative, in the days when he was a wealthy man. His mother, with her many cares, would prefer to keep him at home, but his father insists on the journey, since this is his only hope of escaping from distress. Not only is Tobit poor; his blindness makes it impossible for him to support his family by working.

Tobias is the only son of his parents, and they live in a Gentile society. For Tobit, as a pious Jew, it is absolutely essential that Tobias find a wife from his own people, and even better, from among his own relatives. It is only in this way that the faith can be preserved and handed on. Tobit is a very pious Israelite, and before sending his son on his way, he repeatedly commands his son to marry only a wife from his own tribe. This means that Tobias's choices are in fact very restricted.

Sarah too is an only child, and her only future is to find a husband from among her relatives. The situation is made worse by the fact that she is

TOBIAS EX CIVITATE ET TRIBV·

neptalim que est in superioribus galilee supra na
ason. que ducit ad occidentem in sinistro habes
ciuitatem sephet: cum captus esset in diebus sal
manasar regis assiriorum in captiuitate tamen t
positus uiam ueritatis non deseruit: ita ut omni
a que habere poterat cottidie concaptiuis fratri
bus suis qui erant ex genere suo impartiret. cum
q; esset iunior in tribu neptalim nihil tamen pu
erile gessit in opere. Deniq; cum irent omnes ad
uitulos aureos quos ieroboam fecerat rex israel
hic solus fugiebat consortia omnium: et perge
bat ad israelem ad templum domini: et ibi ado
rabat dommum deum israel omnia primitiua
sua: et decimas suas fideliter offerens. ita ut in
tertio anno proselitis et aduenis ministraret
omnem decimationem. hec et his similia secun
dum legem dei puerulus obseruabat. Cum uero
factus fuisset uir accepit uxorem annam de tri
bu sua genuitq; ex ea filium nomen suum impo
nens ei. Quem ab infantia timere deum docuit.
et abstinere ab omni peccato. Igitur cum per cap
tiuitatem deuenisset cum uxore sua et filio in ci
uitatem niniue: cum omni tribu sua: et omnes
ederent ex cibis gentium iste custodiuit ani
mam suam: et nunquam contaminatus est in es
cis eorum. Et quoniam memor fuit domini in
toto corde suo dedit ei dominus gratiam in co

spectu salmanasar regis. et dedit illi potestatem quo
cunq; uellet ire habens libertatem quecunq; facere
uoluisset. Pergebat enim per omnes qui erant in
captiuitate: et monita salutis dabat eis. Cumq;
ueniisset in rages ciuitatem medorum: et ex his
quibus honoratus fuerat a rege habuisset decem
talenta argenti: et cum multa turba generis sui
gabellum inderet egentem qui erat ex tribu
sua sub cirographo dedit illi memoratum pond'
argenti. Post multum uero temporis mortuo sal
manasar rege. cum regnaret senacherib filius eius
pro eo et exosos haberet filios israel in conspec
tu suo: tobias quotidie pergebat per omnem co
gnationem suam: et consolabatur eos. Diuide
debat unicuiq; prout poterat de facultatibus
suis Esurientes alebat: nudisq; uestimenta pre
bebat: et mortuis atq; occisis sepulturam exhibe
bat. Deniq; cum reuersus esset senacherib fugi
ens a iudea plagam quam circa eum fecerat de
us propter blasphemiam suam: et iratus multos
occideret ex filiis israel tobias sepeliebat corpo
ra mortuorum. At ubi nuntiatum est regi ius
sit eum occidi: et tulit omnem substantiam e
ius. Tobias uero cum filio et uxore fugiens nu
dus latuit: quia multi diligebant eum. Post
dies uero. xlv. occiderunt regem filii eius: et
reuersus est tobias ad domum suam: omnisq;

"Then Raguel summoned his daughter Sarah. When she came to him he took her by the hand and gave her to Tobias, saying, 'Take her to be your wife in accordance with the law and decree written in the book of Moses.' Then he called her mother and told her to bring writing materials; and he wrote out a copy of a marriage contract. Then they began to eat and drink."

TOBIT 7:12-14

threatened by an evil demon: each time she marries, he kills the husband on their wedding night but leaves Sarah untouched. This has now happened seven times, and her family have almost given up hope that their only child may still have a future. Since the only future for a person consists in the continuation of the family, and thereby of the Jewish people and of its religious tradition, the decisive question is whether it is still possible to free Sarah from this demon, who threatens her continued existence in every sense (cf. 3:7-15).

Tobias returns at the close of the story with a wife, but this was not originally planned; it is the result of events during his journey. The lives of the protagonists are skillfully interwoven: at the turning point of the story, Tobit and Sarah both send up a bitter lamentation to heaven, and both these prayers arrive simultaneously before the divine majesty, through the mediation of the angel Raphael. In heaven, the threads are woven together, to produce a happy ending: Tobit will be healed, and Sarah will be freed from the demon (3:16f.).

Tobias finds a companion for his journey, which leads not only to the restoration of the money but to a double healing: Tobias is able to free his father from his blindness, and his destined bride from the demon. While he is traveling, Tobias is threatened by a huge fish, but he draws it up out of the river Tigris and finds in it – with the help of his companion, who reveals at the close of the Book that he is the angel Raphael – both the medicine for the illness of his father and the means to drive away the demon.

He finds his bride in Ecbatana in Persia, in a manner reminiscent of a fairytale. Despite the immense distance involved, he is guided safely by the angel to the family of his relatives, to the house of Raguel, who gives him hospitality. It soon emerges that Tobias belongs to the same Jewish tribe, and that he is to marry Sarah. Nevertheless, they are afraid that the demon might kill this husband too on the marriage night.

The fears manifested here are found in many fairytales: a man must overcome many obstacles in order to obtain the woman he desires. Here, the obstacle is a demon, who bears the name Asmodeus and who kills only the husbands of Sarah, leaving her unharmed. In the Bible, seven is the number symbolizing completeness, but when we read here that Sarah has already lost seven husbands, this is certainly not meant in that sense. We are to assume that an eighth time is possible!

The popular fear of the woman who "murders her husband" is found in the Bible only here and in the story of Judah and Tamar (Gen 38); this fear of a woman who kills a man when he is at his most defenseless is probably generated by a profound masculine sexual fear. This is why such fears tend above all to be linked to the wedding night (as in the Book of Tobit). This also reflects a male fear of the woman's superiority in matters of love and sexuality, and perhaps also a secret male fear of procreation, for the man recedes into the background when his son is born. When the servants in Sarah's household accuse the young woman herself of murdering her husbands, the biblical text explicitly declares her innocence and blames a demon. In antiquity, inexplicable illnesses, terrible events, and other disasters which were hard to understand were often ascribed to the work of demons. The centerpiece of the story of Tobias and Sarah, their wedding night, shows how they get the better of this particular "demon."

THE MARRIAGE CONTRACT.
Jan Steen's painting (ca. 1667/1668) elaborates the biblical account (Tob 7:14) by drawing on contemporary customs. A notary puts the marriage contract down on paper. On the right, we see the preparations for the wedding feast.

"Wiping away the tears, Edna said to her daughter, 'Take courage, my daughter; the Lord of heaven grant you joy in place of your sorrow. Take courage, my daughter.'"

TOBIT 7:16

WEDDING NIGHT.
In contrast to the ethical code symbolized by the "Tobias nights," Rembrandt's painting (1647) emphasizes the importance of sensual fulfillment in the wedding night. His model was the painting Sarah Waits for Tobias *by his former teacher, Pieter Lastman; his own work has the title* Young Woman in Bed – *this needs to be expanded to include the words "waiting for her beloved."*

Before the marriage is consummated, the wedding is celebrated in the bride's house and a marriage contract is drawn up; this is the oldest scriptural evidence of a written marriage contract. Edna, Sarah's mother, brings in the writing materials and Raguel, Sarah's father, draws up the contract, which makes the marriage legally binding. Sarah is not consulted: as is customary in patriarchal societies, the marriage is arranged by the parents. Normally, it is the bridegroom's parents who do this, but in this case, since Tobias himself is already an adult and his parents live in the far distant city of Nineveh, Sarah's parents take the initiative (7:9-17).

Will Tobias escape with his life, so that the story can continue? This depends on what happens on the wedding night (8:1-9). By acting with prudence and piety, the young husband succeeds in driving off the demon by means of the heart and liver of the fish which he had earlier killed. Tobias burns those parts of the fish in which the vital forces were thought to reside, on a little incense-altar, and Asmodeus flees to Upper Egypt. This scene is reminiscent of magic, but it is accompanied by Tobias's prayers. He comes to his wife, not in blind lust, but with respect and the fear of God; and the demon has no power over those who fear God. It is only after the demon has been expelled and the appropriate prayers have been said that the marriage is consummated.

The wedding night of Tobias and Sarah had a considerable influence on Christian theology, especially moral theology, which reflected on it under the heading of "Tobias nights." The primary source here is not the Greek text of our book, but the exposition by Jerome and his Latin translation. The biblical narrative speaks of one single night, but Jerome extends this to three nights, and throughout the Middle Ages, Christian married couples were exhorted to live demurely and to begin their married life in chastity after the example of the young Tobias. Like Tobias, they were to invoke God's blessing before sleeping with one another. These exhortations are often generated by a profound hostility to the body, which is not found in the biblical story.

On the following morning, Sarah's parents find the two alive and asleep. They rejoice that nothing has happened to the young man, and Sarah's father fills in the grave that he has dug for the suitor (as a precautionary measure) during the night; and they rejoice that the two only children can now look forward to a happy married life in which they will continue the two families and their traditions (8:10-21).

This story is modeled on that of Isaac and Rebekah, who was asked if she wanted to marry Isaac. Sarah, however, is not consulted. Indeed, apart from her prayer at the beginning of the book, she says only one single word in the narrative, when she says the "Amen" at the end of Tobias's prayer on their wedding night. It is he alone who speaks, recalling the story of the creation of Adam and Eve, the exemplary couple, and asking that God may bless him and his wife even to great old age. Sarah merely joins him in saying "Amen." She is the most passive of all the women in the Book of Tobit, an object disposed of by men, first her father Raguel, and then Tobias. Nevertheless, this book also speaks of love, although it is completely one-sided: when the angel Raphael tells the young Tobias at the river Tigris about his relative Sarah, "he loved her very much, and his heart was drawn to her" (6:18). We learn at once about Tobias's love for Sarah, whom he has not yet met, but the narrative does not tell us whether Sarah returned this love. The author takes it for granted that she will show the respect and love of a good wife to this relative who has freed her from her distress and from the demon, and that she will accompany her husband to distant Nineveh. In other words, this story is told entirely from the perspective of men, and it is the men who are active – including the angel Raphael, who takes the outward form of a young man (and angels are always masculine in the Bible) and who secretly weaves the threads of the narrative together. Through the angel, the heavenly world guides the course of events on earth and blesses the young couple, who are finally able to continue the history of their families and thereby also to hand on the faith of Israel.

"When the parents had gone out and shut the door of the room, Tobias got out of bed and said to Sarah, 'Sister, get up, and let us pray and implore our Lord that he grant us mercy and safety'. . . And they both said, 'Amen, Amen.' Then they went to sleep for the night."

TOBIT 8:4.8-9

EDUCATION.
One of the leitmotifs of the Book of Tobit is education in piety as an aid to a good life. This is made clear by the medallion portraying Tobias between his father and his mother in the Urbino Bible *(1476-1478): note Tobit's finger pointing to heaven.*

SHECHEM AND DINAH

(Genesis 34)

"The sons of Jacob came in from the field. When they heard of it, the men were indignant and very angry, because he had committed an outrage in Israel by lying with Jacob's daughter, for such a thing ought not to be done."

GENESIS 34:7

Jacob, also known as Israel, had twelve sons, after whom the "tribes of Israel" are named. It is probable that he also had daughters, since statistically speaking, roughly as many girls as boys are born; but the genealogies of a patriarchal age do not register women. They record only men: "X begot Y." Women are mentioned only when they play a special role or when they are important in relation to one of the central masculine figures, e.g., as wife, as mother, or as daughter. For example, we are told about Jephthah's daughter, who is offered in sacrifice by her father as a consequence of his vow (Judg 11:29-40). Here, we know the father's name, but we are not told the name of the daughter he kills.

Things are different with Dinah, the daughter of Jacob: we know her name and her story. Since Jacob had four wives, the two sisters Leah and Rachel and their maids Zilpah and Bilhah, we need to know the name of her mother too. Dinah is the daughter of Leah, Jacob's first wife. Her story takes place in the nomadic period. Jacob does not yet have a settled place of residence, but lives on land belonging to others. He seeks and indeed needs contact with the local Canaanite population. Jacob and his family are living near Shechem, a town in the mountainous northern region of Canaan, between the mountains of Ebal and Garizim.

The story begins as follows: "Now Dinah the daughter of Leah, whom she had borne to Jacob, went out to visit the daughters of the region" (Gen 34:1). At first glance, these are extraordinary words, since we tend to assume that girls – and Dinah is presumably a young unmarried woman – are kept closely guarded in their father's house under the watchful eyes of numerous brothers. Clearly, this picture is wrong. Women in ancient times were relatively free to move around on their own; this is obvious from the stories about the ancestors, e.g., Sarah and Rebekah.

The story begins with freedom, with an innocent curiosity about the "daughters of the region"; today, we would say that she was looking for friends. But it soon takes a terrible turn, since she also meets the sons of the region. Dinah wanted to see; instead, she is seen, with appalling consequences for her. Shechem, the son of the prince of the city, sees Dinah and rapes her. This event is told in a brisk sequence of four steps, with no pause: he sees her, he seizes her, he lies with her, and he rapes her. In the story of Tamar, who is raped by her half-brother Amnon (2 Sam 13), we hear about her reactions, but Gen 34 tells us nothing about what Dinah felt. It seems that she has no time to try to stop Shechem from carrying out his purpose. She does not say one single word in the entire narrative: she is a pure victim of male violence, and later of the negotiations among men. In verse 3, however, the brutality of the narrative gives way to a very different tone. After raping her, Shechem comes to feel affection for the girl. Indeed, we are told that he loves her (unlike Amnon, whose lust changes into sheer hatred once it has been gratified: 2 Sam 13:15). After what has happened, Shechem asks his father to get him Dinah as his wife. It is only in verse 5 that Jacob makes an appearance, and from now on, all the negotiations are conducted between Jacob and his sons, and Shechem with his father Hamor, who offer a large sum of money as the bridal price. Once again, we are told that Shechem loves Dinah, but the narrative has nothing to say about her feelings. After the first sentence, in which she is portrayed as active and inquisitive, she is wholly passive.

Jacob's sons now hatch a plot to punish Shechem, the rapist of their sister. They say that they are unwilling to become the relatives by marriage of uncircumcised men. Before Dinah is given in marriage, therefore, Shechem and all the men in the city must be circumcised. This condition is accepted by the men of the city. But on the third day, before their traumatic fever has healed, Dinah's two brothers Simeon and Levi (both of them sons of Leah) attack the city and kill all the men, including Shechem and his father. They carry off the women and children, and plunder all the houses in the city. They take Dinah out of Shechem's house, where she is still living. This is the only verse where her name stands on its own. Otherwise, she is called "the daughter of Jacob" or "the daughter of Leah"; when the narrative speaks of the brothers, she is referred to as "their sister." Here, how-

BLOODY REVENGE.
This miniature in the Wenceslaus Bible *(ca. 1400) illustrates Gen 34:25f. by means of a simultaneous presentation: Simeon and Levi make their way into the city, kill the men (who are sick with traumatic fever after their circumcision), and bring their sister Dinah out of the city. The picture includes the robbery of all the animals as part of the ensuing plundering of the city.*

ever, Dinah is completely isolated: she has no relationships. She is not mentioned again in Genesis. She returns to her father's house, where she must spend the rest of her life as a disgraced woman, with no hope of marriage or a future. Unlike Shechem, she escapes with her life, but her future is gone.

Jacob's reaction at the end of the story shows that the violent reprisals taken by Dinah's brothers were not justified. The punishment of an entire city, not just of the one guilty man, was out of all proportion to the seriousness of Shechem's action; but the story of one family's honor has become inseparable from the story of a whole tribe. The blessing which Jacob pronounces in Gen 49 also denies the legitimacy of this deed of violence. Reuben has already lost his rights as the firstborn son, because he has had intercourse with Bilhah; now Simeon and Levi are told that they cannot be the bearers of God's promise. This means that it is Judah, Jacob's fourth son, who is now the bearer of the promise and the ancestor of all the Israelite kings. Jacob says (49:5-7):

> "Simeon and Levi are brothers;
> weapons of violence are their swords.
> May I never come into their council;
> may I not be joined to their company –
> for in their anger they killed men,
> and at their whim they hamstrung oxen.
> Cursed be their anger, for it is fierce,
> and their wrath, for it is cruel!
> I will divide them in Jacob,
> and scatter them in Israel."

Jacob's blessing condemns the violence of Dinah's brothers, but she herself is not mentioned. The legal tradition of the ancient east and of Israel had plenty of other means to deal with Shechem's crime, because there were clearly defined penalties for the rape of a virgin. Several such laws are transmitted in the Pentateuch. According to Ex 22:15f., the rapist must pay a bridal price and marry the woman. The father may refuse to give him his daughter, but in this case he still retains the bridal price. Shechem was willing to do all this, since he loved Dinah. According to the customs of the period, therefore, the brothers took a very exaggerated revenge; this is confirmed by the parallel story of Amnon and Tamar, where the rapist is dealt with rather mildly. It almost seems as if Shechem's action merely provided a pretext for the brothers' attack on his city. Deut 22:28f. likewise lays down regulations for what is to be done when a virgin is raped: the rapist must marry her and pay her father fifty silver shekels. Besides this, he is not permitted to divorce her – i.e., he cannot treat her arbitrarily a second time. Whether or not these laws were enforced in the period of the biblical ancestors, they show the rules in a patriarchal age where women and their sexuality were considered only under the aspect of property, and a fine had to be paid to the father (!) for the damage done to something he owned. In this wholly androcentric perspective, the damage done to the woman herself is not even mentioned. Gen 34 says nothing at all about Dinah's feelings.

Shechem and Dinah are a couple, but only for a brief period as the result of violence. This narrative does speak explicitly of love, but only in a very one-sided manner: we are only told that Shechem loved Dinah. The story might in fact have ended on a happy note, had it not been for another form of male violence, namely the destruction of an entire town. Why was this story told? One intention is doubtless to explain why the two brothers Simeon and Levi, although high on the list of Jacob's heirs, had lost their rights to be the bearers of the divine promise. But it is also possible that this story contains a warning to women: if you stay at home, nothing will happen to you! Outside, in public, danger is at hand. The delightful freshness of the first sentence – "Now Dinah … went out to visit the daughters of the region" – is in fact a trap for the young woman. Women who move around freely risk disaster. This may have been the point of the story of Dinah, from a male perspective; but women will see this as a very depressing tale.

The narrative has, however, an echo in the late Old Testament literature, where Dinah is mentioned again in the Book of Judith. The main character, Judith (whose name means "Jewess") represents the people of Israel as a whole, which is small and defenseless and must fight against the Assyrian foes with their heavy weaponry. Judith enters the camp of this enemy as a symbol of the defenselessness of Israel. Unlike Dinah, however, she is not raped, but cuts off the head of Holofernes, the Assyrian general. She invokes Yahweh as "God of my father Simeon" (9:2), tracing her ancestry directly back to the son of Leah who played the main role, with Levi, in the violence done to the city of Shechem. In Judith, the rape of Dinah symbolizes the disgrace inflicted on the city of Jerusalem/Zion (which the Bible often calls a "virgin"). Judith herself is a widow, and hence one of those who are defenseless and need protection. Unlike Gen 34, the Book of Judith does not condemn the action of the two brothers, but regards it as a just punishment for Shechem's crime. In the situation of political oppression in which the later book was written, this may be understandable. Judith continually calls on the God who is "the God of the lowly, helper of the oppressed, upholder of the weak, protector of the forsaken, savior of those without hope" (9:11). She does not seek to glorify violence or justify the revenge taken by her ancestors. Rather, she is giving one example of how God is on the side of weak Israel/Jerusalem. Thus, in a late period, Dinah becomes a positive symbol of those who are politically defenseless but – as Judith's story shows – need not simply abandon all hope.

AMNON AND TAMAR

(2 Samuel 13)

At first sight, the story of Amnon and Tamar looks like an incident in family life, but high political issues are in fact at stake, since the house of David plays a central role: his sons are competitors for the future succession to the throne. At the same time, it is the story of a relationship of a man and a woman, of lust and love, and finally of rape and hatred. Amnon and Tamar are half-siblings. Both are David's children, born to different mothers. We read about the relationship between brother and sister, and between father and son, but never between father and daughter.

"Then Amnon was seized with a very great loathing for her; indeed, his loathing was even greater than the lust he had felt for her."

2 SAMUEL 13:15

VICTIM AND RAPIST.
Instead of depicting the scene directly, Emil Wachter employs these water-colors of Amnon (1993) and his victim Tamar (1998) to show us the course of events.

Although Tamar is the only one of David's daughters whose name we know, she is never called "the daughter of David." David had six sons, born to various of his wives in Hebron; the Bible only mentions the name of the first-born of each wife, and we do not know how many other sons and daughters he had (cf. 2 Sam 3:2-5). In Jerusalem, the second city where he makes his royal residence, eleven other first-born sons are born to him, but the names of their mothers are not recorded (5:13-16). Daughters are not mentioned in either passage, because they could not succeed to the throne. David was a great king but a bad father. He does not intervene in the rivalry among his sons, nor in the conflict about

Tamar and Amnon, although that would have been his duty.

The narrative of the rape of Tamar served as a model for the story of the rape of Dinah, Jacob's daughter, which is found at an earlier place in the Bible (Gen 34). There too, it is not the father who directly intervenes to come to his daughter's aid; it is her brothers who act. In Gen 34, the violence of Shechem seems a spontaneous action; but Amnon plans his crime carefully over a long period, exploiting the sisterly love of Tamar, and he rapes her in his house, in the protected sphere of Amnon's private rooms, not in a foreign city as was the case with Dinah. The rapist is no stranger, but her own half-brother. Gen 34 and 2 Sam 13 do not mince words: these are disgraceful actions. "Such a thing is not done in Israel" (2 Sam 13:12).

The first verse of our story introduces all four royal protagonists, and each word is placed precisely: "*David's son Absalom* had a beautiful *sister whose name was Tamar*; and *David's son Amnon* fell in love with her." Absalom and Amnon, half-brothers, are both called "the son of David," but Tamar, who is the king's daughter, is introduced as the "sister of Absalom." Like Absalom, she is a daughter of Maacah, and was born to David in Hebron. We are told something else about her, something that will be important in the continuation of the narrative: she is "beautiful." And this seals her fate, for the fact that Amnon falls in love with her presages conflicts to come.

The drama begins in the very next verse: Amnon falls sick with desire, and wishes to "do something" to his sister, but this is impossible, since she is still a virgin. The vocabulary employed here is typical of sexual actions: Amnon wants to sleep with Tamar, but he is at a loss to see how he can gratify this wish until a friend notes his depression, and the two men hatch an effective plot. This friend, Jonadab, is also related to the house of David: he is the king's nephew, the son of David's brother Shimeah and thus the cousin of Amnon – and of Tamar! He is presented as "very crafty" and he advises Amnon to pretend to be ill and to take to his bed. When his father David visits him, he is to ask permission for his sister Tamar to come to him. This presupposes that David will be concerned about his sick son and that Tamar will follow without question the command of her father. In this male conspiracy, the virgin princess is a helpless victim. Everything turns out as Jonadab has said: David does not visit Tamar (indeed, in the whole story he never once speaks with her); he simply "sends home to Tamar, saying, 'Go to your brother Amnon's house, and prepare food for him'" (13:7).

We are told in detail how Tamar carries out this order, kneading the dough and making heart-shaped cakes for her sick brother. He watch-

es her the whole time, and this gazing at her almost amounts to touching her – it is an erotic action. The story does not say whether Tamar realizes what is going to happen to her. Amnon cleverly exploits the fact that women were responsible for preparing food everywhere in the ancient east (just like the first woman, who plucked the fruit from the tree), and that Tamar, as his sister, is obliged to care for him. This means that she will not suspect anything.

When the meal is ready, Amnon refuses to eat: first, he sends out all the servants, and then he asks Tamar to bring the food to him in his bedroom, where he seizes her and demands that she sleep with him. Now she speaks for the first time in the story. She does not yield, but reproaches him, appealing to him as her "brother" and reminding him of the customs that prevail in their land: "No, my brother, do not force me; for such a thing is not done in Israel; do not do anything so vile!" (13:12). The vocabulary and the customs of the time make it clear that this "vileness" does not refer to incest, since the king had the right to give Tamar in marriage to her half-brother; she herself goes on to suggest this, speaking prudently and wisely to her brother. Amnon's "vileness" is the violence he uses against her. He refuses to listen to Tamar, and rapes her.

Immediately after this act, Amnon's attitude to Tamar changes completely, and he suddenly feels a great revulsion: "indeed, his loathing was even greater than the lust he had felt for her." This change leads to a final action which displays the same brutality and insensitivity as the rape itself: Amnon demands that she leave. Once again, Tamar replies. She does not yet give up the struggle, but addresses him once again as "brother" and tells him: "This wrong in sending me away is greater than the other that you did to me" – for if the crime becomes public knowledge, it will irreversibly alter her situation. The possibility of marriage, which she has suggested, still exists; this would not cancel the fact of rape, but it could reduce the consequences. Even for the son of a king, the penalty for rape was death, especially when the victim was the virgin daughter of the sovereign. And polygamy, especially in royal families, was possible at that time, as the examples of David and Solomon show. This makes it hard to understand why Amnon rejects this solution to the situation. "He would not listen to her" (13:16), although he had listened to the advice given by Jonadab. Instead, he calls his servants and has them throw out Tamar and bolt the door of the house after her. Once he has raped her, he no longer speaks of her as his "sister," but only as "this woman."

Tamar has made three objections, prudently and calmly, both before the rape and afterwards, since she wishes to defuse the drama of

---

"But she said to him, 'No, my brother; for this wrong in sending me away is greater than the other that you did to me.' But he would not listen to her. He called the young man who served him and said, 'Put this woman out of my presence, and bolt the door after her.'"

2 SAMUEL 13:16-17

the situation for herself and for Amnon. But when she is thrown out of his house like dirt – and not even by Amnon himself, but by his servants – she gives up the fight. She had been wearing the garments of an unmarried princess, but now she has lost her right to do so. She strews ashes on her head as a sign of grief, and tears her garment, a symbolic action pointing to the loss of her virginity. She goes home weeping (clearly, she has her own house, from which David had summoned her).

WARNING AGAINST SEDUCERS.
Jan Steen's painting (ca. 1668/1670) uses the theme of Amnon and Tamar to warn against having anything to do with frivolous playboys who have the money to indulge in all the luxury they desire. This warning is vividly underlined by the malicious gloating on the face of the servant.

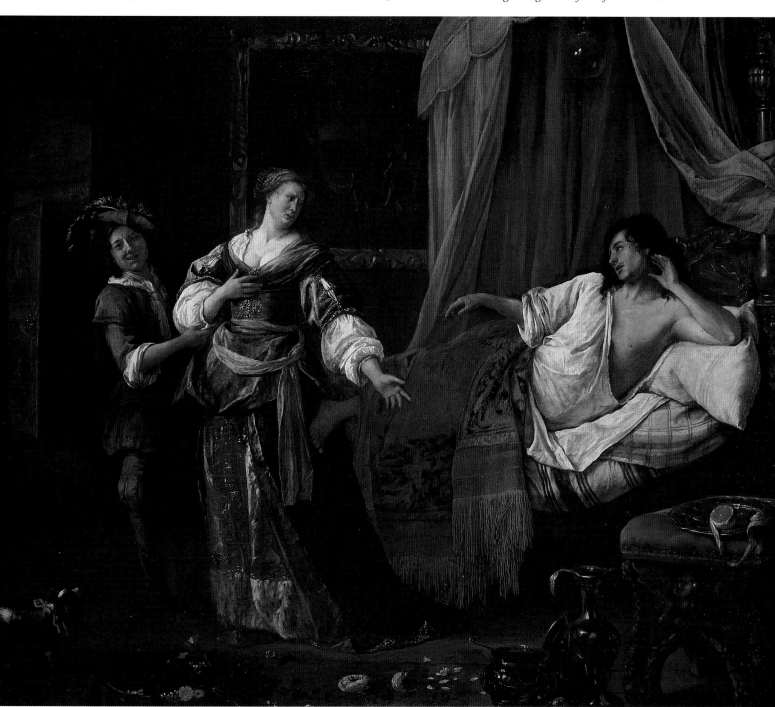

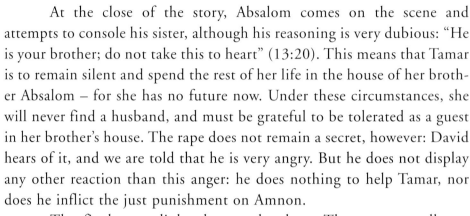

"But Tamar put ashes on her head, and tore the long robe that she was wearing; she put her hand on her head, and went away, crying aloud as she went."

2 SAMUEL 13:19

DESPAIR.
*The upper half of this miniature
in the* Wenceslaus Bible *(ca. 1400)
depicts Amnon's command to his
servant to throw "this woman" out
and bolt the door behind her.
This takes place in the lower half, where
Tamar becomes the main figure.
In despair, she strews ashes on her
head (2 Sam 13:19).*

At the close of the story, Absalom comes on the scene and attempts to console his sister, although his reasoning is very dubious: "He is your brother; do not take this to heart" (13:20). This means that Tamar is to remain silent and spend the rest of her life in the house of her brother Absalom – for she has no future now. Under these circumstances, she will never find a husband, and must be grateful to be tolerated as a guest in her brother's house. The rape does not remain a secret, however: David hears of it, and we are told that he is very angry. But he does not display any other reaction than this anger: he does nothing to help Tamar, nor does he inflict the just punishment on Amnon.

The final verse links the two brothers. The narrator tells us: "Absalom *hated* Amnon" because of the disgrace inflicted on his sister Tamar – just as Amnon *hated* Tamar after he had raped her. This concludes the story of an unhappy relationship. The most unfortunate of all is Tamar, who has lost her honor and prestige and has been cheated of any future with a husband and children.

The reference to Absalom's hatred indicates that Amnon will not escape his punishment. Two years later, Absalom has his half-brother murdered during a banquet, and it is Jonadab – the same nephew of David who had advised Amnon how to get Tamar into his bed – who tells the king that Absalom had in fact made up his mind to kill Amnon as soon as he heard of the rape (13:32). Nevertheless, this is not merely a punitive reaction to Amnon's disgraceful deed, for the two brothers are rivals for the succession to the throne, and Amnon is David's firstborn! In other words, Absalom both takes revenge for the rape and eliminates his most dangerous rival; the family story and the political interests are inseparably linked. However, a later verse does show that Absalom had a special relationship to his sister: we are told that he had three sons "and one daughter whose name was Tamar; she was a beautiful woman" (14:27). Normally, the Old Testament genealogies mention only the names of the sons, but here they remain nameless. It is clear that the daughter named Tamar was a kind of "substitute" for Absalom's sister, and the author underlines her beauty. This means that the unhappy story of Tamar is given at least a hint of promise of a future through this niece who bears her name – though David's daughter herself remains shut out from any future as a woman.

JUDITH AND HOLOFERNES

(Judith 8-16)

The late Book of Judith presupposes many Old Testament stories. Its events are set in a period in which Israel was no longer free, but had to live under various foreign rulers. In this time, people liked to remember the old traditions – the stories of Shechem and Dinah, of David and Goliath, and many others. This book relates a fictitious story with a woman as the central character. The name Judith means "the Jewess," and she not only represents her people: she also saves them.

Her opponent is a soldier, the general Holofernes, who brims over with an exaggerated view of his own prowess and weaponry. The king who is named in the Book of Judith, Nebuchadnezzar, is known to history as the conqueror of Jerusalem in 587 B.C.E. At 1:1, he is called an Assyrian. This is an anachronism: the whole history of Israel's oppression from the time of the Assyrians onwards is "compressed" here, so to speak, since the Assyrian empire had already perished in 612 B.C.E., and its capital Nineveh had been a ruin for four hundred years by the time this book was written. These historicizing data are intended to give examples of the tremendous superiority of the Gentile powers, and of the threat they posed to the defenseless Israel. A woman, Judith, is chosen to represent the weak and defenseless. She also symbolizes the endangered city of Zion/Jerusalem, which is always described by means of female symbols. Like Judith, Jerusalem too is sometimes called a widow, though sometimes also a virgin. As in the story of Shechem and Dinah in Gen 34, the story of Holofernes and Judith is a story of male lust. But unlike the earlier narrative, here it is not the woman who is the loser, but the man.

The events of this book may seem terribly cruel, but we ought not to read them from a moral perspective. Rather, they are the expression of an extreme threat, a matter of life and death for Israel. Even in the ancient east, the Assyrians were regarded as exceptionally cruel, and women and children suffered most under the savagery of their conquests. The irony of history now sees a woman taking in hand the rescue of her people. The narrative is set in an Israelite city named Bethulia, probably a cipher for the holy city, Jerusalem. As was customary in sieges in the east, the water supplies have been cut off, so that the population are on the verge of dying of thirst. They are ready to surrender to the enemy, but at this moment Judith comes on the scene. We are told that she is a rich widow, and very beautiful. Her plan to save the city means that she must leave it and enter the camp of the enemy. Before she sets out, she prays to the God of Israel, invoking him as "God of my ancestor Simeon" (9:2), thus putting the bloody deed of

DEADLY EROS.
In his version of Judith *(1926), Franz von Stuck portrays the danger that lies slumbering in the sensuality of women. The style of his picture evokes the demonic element which generates those seductive charms to which men like Holofernes blindly succumb.*

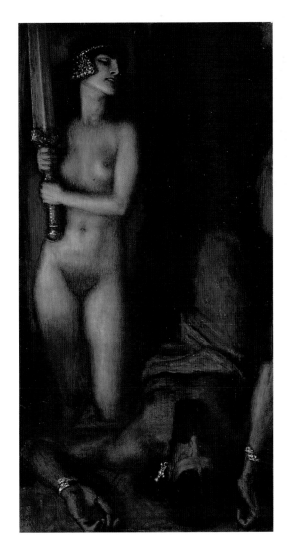

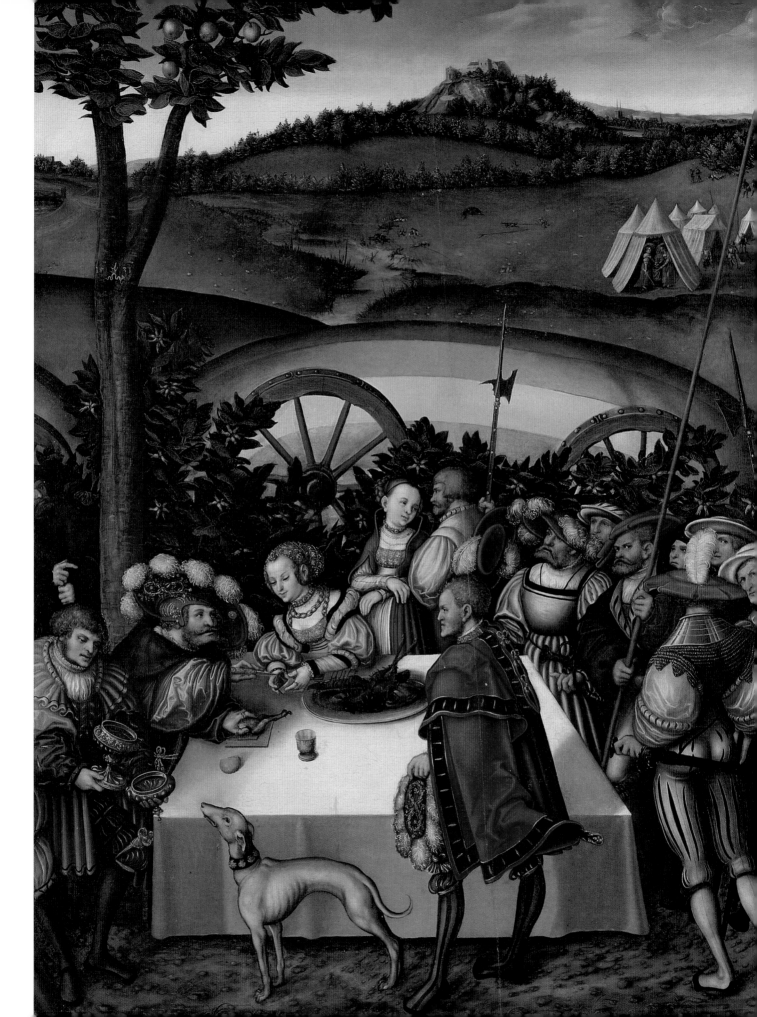

her ancestor in a positive light, as vengeance on the enemies of the Jewish faith. After her prayer, she anoints herself and puts on her jewels and her festal garments, then leaves the city with her maid. The reason for this finery is stated clearly: "to entice the eyes of all the men who might see her" (10:4). She succeeds in this. Blinded by her beauty, the soldiers bring her to the tent of Holofernes, who is lying on his bed under a precious canopy. With numerous flatteries of his greatness, she dupes the general, and all marvel not only at her exceptional beauty, but also at her wisdom. Holofernes and his servants say: "No other woman from one end of the earth to the other looks so beautiful or speaks so wisely!" (11:21).

Three days later, Holofernes holds a great banquet, for ever since he set eyes on Judith, he has burned with lust for her, and he seeks an occasion to lie with her. Judith once again wears her festal garments and all her jewels, since her outward appearance is vital to her plan. She eats and drinks with Holofernes, but only from the supplies she has brought with her – Judith is pious and does not wish to make herself impure by eating Gentile food. Holofernes drinks more wine than ever before in his whole life (12:20). After this, all the servants leave his tent, supposing that the general wishes to spend an undisturbed night making love with Judith. This, however, does not happen, since he is completely drunk and lies motionless on his bed. The seducer has reduced himself to impotence. Whereas Judith reflects, plans prudently, and then acts, Holofernes digs his own grave with his unbridled lust. Judith draws near, but before she acts, she once again prays and asks God to help her destroy the enemy. Then "she went up to the bedpost near Holofernes's head, and took down his sword that hung there. She came close to his bed, took hold of the hair of his head, and said, 'Give me strength today, O Lord God of Israel!' Then she struck his neck twice with all her might, and cut off his head" (13:6-8). The sword (symbolizing Holofernes's masculinity) hangs there with no one to guard it, and Judith can take hold of it easily. She wraps his head in the canopy under which she first saw him lying, then goes out, giving the head to her maid. Both arrive safely in the city of Bethulia. The Assyrian soldiers suspect nothing, since Judith had wisely made the petition beforehand that she might be allowed to go out each night with her maid to pray in a nearby valley (Judith repeatedly emphasizes her fidelity to the God of Israel). Thus the two women are able to escape undetected from the camp after the killing of Holofernes.

When the soldiers discover the headless corpse of their general next morning, they all flee in confusion, and this disarray allows the Israelites to defeat their enemies. The special characteristic of Judith's behavior is that she goes completely defenseless, without any weapons, into the camp of the enemy. Like David when he beheaded Goliath, she too slays Holofernes with his own sword. The weak and defenseless woman triumphs over a strong man armed to the teeth. What an encouragement and consolation for Israel, a small and

LIFE IN THE CAMP.
Lucas Cranach the Elder transposes Judith and Holofernes into his own period, when generals attached great importance to a luxurious life in their military camps. An anecdotal detail in his painting (ca. 1520) shows that the attractive "deserter" has won the favor of Holofernes: Judith enjoys the privilege of handing him the choicest morsels of his food (opposite page).

SONG OF PRAISE.
This miniature from a fourteenth-century Biblia pauperum *employs the figure of the harpist to emphasize the religious aura attaching to Judith's deed when she beheads Holofernes. She holds his head in her hand.*

THE VICTIM'S ROLE.
This painting by Cristoforo Allori (1613) is a chapter of the painter's autobiography, so to speak: his mistress was the model for Judith, the servant maid has the face of his mistress's mother, and the head of Holofernes is a self-portrait (opposite page).

THE END.
There are many paintings of the beheading, but this picture by Tintoretto (ca. 1530) resembles the closing of a curtain at the end of a tragedy (below).

oppressed people, in the second century before Christ! Women were regarded as inferior and weak, but here a woman conquers a Gentile general despite all his weapons. He loses his life because of his unrestrained lust. This is the obvious first meaning of the story, and this alone would make it worth telling. When foreign armies conquer, their first victims are the women whom they rape and the weak persons whom they humiliate. The story of this "couple" – which existed as such only in the wishes of Holofernes – would give them courage.

But the story has a deeper dimension too, since Judith symbolizes the oppressed and tormented Jewish people, while Holofernes/Nebuchadnezzar represents the Gentile superpower, all those who rely on weapons and military equipment, horses and brute force. Israel is to rely on its God alone, as Judith does. We see this in the many prayers which are interspersed in the narrative at every critical juncture. The Gentile opponents are portrayed as lascivious, lustful, and incapable of thought or understanding, but Judith is portrayed as one

POLITICAL SYMBOLISM.
Donatello's statue of Judith was commissioned by the Medici ca. 1456-1460. After their expulsion from Florence in 1495, it became public property and was taken as a symbol of the liberation of the republic from tyranny.

who acts prudently, temperately, and from a position of superiority. In her prayers, she mocks the armament and the clinking weapons of the enemies. It is only on the surface that the story seems to take a delight in war or cruelty: if we look more closely, we see that God is continually invoked as the one "who crushes wars" (16:2, etc.). These words begin Judith's song of exultation, which is modeled on the song of Miriam in the Book of Exodus and concludes the story. In the older text, Miriam sings of the destruction of Pharaoh with his army when they tried to cross the Red Sea; now, Judith rounds off the narrative by singing of the destruction of Israel's foes at the hand of a woman.

When we read of Judith's bloody deed, it is good to remember both the intention of the narrative and its Old Testament models. Once before in the history of Israel, about a thousand years earlier, a woman had done a similar deed. There too, a defenseless woman encountered an enemy general, who had fled into her tent. The narrative of Jael and the Canaanite general Sisera, who threatened the existence of Israel in the period before the formation of a state, is one of the great stories on which the Book of Judith draws. The narrative is embedded in Deborah's song in Judg 5, where once again a woman – the judge and prophetess Deborah – plays the central role. Jael, a defenseless woman, spontaneously takes up a tent-peg and drives it through the enemy general's head as he lies sleeping. After she has nailed him to the ground in this way, Israel is saved: the death of their leader throws the Canaanite foes into confusion, just as the death of Holofernes scatters the soldiers in the Book of Judith. Judith acts with premeditation, Jael acts spontaneously. But Jael had been raped: there could be no doubt about the general's intention when he enters her tent, and we are told that afterwards, when he lies exhausted "between her legs" (cf. Judg 5:24-27), Jael seizes the opportunity to kill him.

Violence – especially when practiced by women, whom a widespread cliché expects to be meek and peaceful – often appears problematical, and this means that we pay close attention to the difference between women like Judith and Jael. Violent measures are justified in self-defense. Judith is not in such a situation, since she is not required to defend herself personally against Holofernes, whose drunken stupor makes it impossible for him to attack her. But her action is the response to a deeper situation of distress: she is not saving her own person but her whole people, who face certain annihilation at the hands of a dangerous enemy. She deliberately employs her erotic attractiveness as a means to gain her end: it is precisely as a woman that she can exploit Holofernes's passion for her and thus do what she has in mind. She is conspicuous for her breadth of vision and prudence, Holofernes for his insensitivity and blindness. Only a woman could save her people, because her supposed weakness and defenselessness entailed an element of surprise which would not have been available to a man in her situation.

SAMSON AND DELILAH

(Judges 16)

The tale of Samson and Delilah is one of the best-known love stories in world literature and has often inspired artists and musicians (e.g., Camille Saint-Saëns' opera *Samson and Delilah*, composed in 1877). The story is set in the period of the judges, when Israel was a loose confederation of tribes, before the first kings, Saul and David, united the land. Many sagas are told about the heroic figures of the various tribes in those years, and one such hero is Samson, a figure of mythical strength whose deeds are comparable to Hercules of Greek mythology.

His birth is remarkable: for a long time, his mother is infertile, but an angel of Yahweh announces Samson's birth, making it clear that this is no ordinary child. The Spirit of God will rest upon him (Judg 13). The narrative of the annunciation of Samson's birth has the same structure as the later annunciation of the birth of Jesus (Lk 1:26-38). We are told the name of Samson's father, Manoah, while his mother remains nameless; nevertheless, the angel comes to his mother, and the father has a more passive role. During her pregnancy, the woman must not drink wine or beer, nor eat anything that is ritually impure – another sign of the exceptional character of the child she will bear, who is to be a Nazirite, a man consecrated to God.

After he has grown up, the first story about Samson relates how he falls in love with a Philistine woman from Timnah (Judg 14:1). He lived in a period of intense struggles against the Philistines, who were Israel's most dangerous enemies until David defeated them once and for all. The Philistines lived in the regions along the Mediterranean coast and were culturally superior to the Israelites. The Philistines were uncircumcised, whereas the Israelites (like all Semites) had a high esteem for circumcision; the Book of Judges often speaks contemptuously of the Philistines as "the uncircumcised."

Samson asks his father and his mother to get him the Philistine woman as his wife; when we bear in mind the patriarchal structures of the Old Testament, it is very striking that his mother too should be involved here. While on his way to Timnah, Samson displays his exceptional strength by tearing a lion apart with his bare hands. He later finds a honeycomb in the corpse of the lion, and this provides him with a riddle that the Philistines cannot solve during the wedding feast: "Out of the eater came something to eat. Out of the strong came something sweet" (14:14).

His wife weeps for seven days on end, until Samson discloses the solu-

A WOMAN AS INSTRUMENT.
Delilah is the main character in this miniature in the Wenceslaus Bible *(ca. 1400); we see Samson sleeping in her lap. But the second scene makes it clear that her marriage with Samson is merely a means to an end: she disappears altogether, and we see only Samson's mortal enemies.*

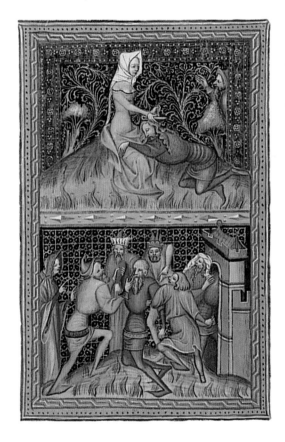

"By then he was very thirsty,
and he called on the Lord, saying,
'You have granted this
great victory by the hand of your
servant. Am I now to die of thirst,
and fall into the hands of
the uncircumcised?'
So God split open the hollow place
that is at Lehi, and water came from
it. When he drank, his spirit
returned, and he revived."

JUDGES 15:18-19

THE END OF A HERO'S LIFE.
This illuminated page in the Crusader
Bible *(ca. 1250) depicts the end of chapter
15 and chapter 16 in the Book of
Judges. After Samson has won victory with
the jaw-bone of an ass, a miraculous spring
of water opens up for him. The final
high point is his adventure in Gaza,
before Delilah delivers him up to his
enemies (opposite page).*

tion to his riddle; she then hands this on to her fellow countrymen, who want to take Samson captive. In his fury at his wife's betrayal, Samson goes to Ashkelon, where he kills thirty Philistines (14:19). His wife is given to another man, who had been Samson's best man at the wedding. In the clash of interests, she had not sided with her husband, but with the members of her own people.

Nevertheless, Samson wants to visit her again, and brings a goat kid as a present (15:1). When however her father refuses to admit him to the house, Samson takes revenge by setting fire to the fields of the Philistines: he "caught three hundred foxes, and took some torches; and he tied the foxes tail to tail, and put a torch between each pair of tails. When he had set fire to the torches, he let the foxes go into the standing grain of the Philistines" (15:4f.). The Philistines in turn take revenge by burning his wife and her father alive. Samson's first marriage was more than just a sexual relationship; it was a special kind of marriage that was still possible at the end of the second millennium B.C.E., whereby the wife remained living in the house of her parents and her husband came occasionally to visit her. For the wife, this marriage ends in her death, a punitive action which the Philistines take against Samson, who had taken revenge for the loss of his wife. The hero himself escapes unscathed.

After various heroic deeds have been related, the story of chapter 14 is repeated; probably this is a doublet of Samson's first marriage, with the difference that here the woman has a name, Delilah. Once again, Samson falls in love with a Philistine woman (16:4), but this time the conspiracy begins even before she marries him, because she is bribed by the Philistines to get the better of her husband: his mighty deeds have become too dangerous for them. Delilah is promised a huge amount of money if she can outwit Samson and hand him over to his enemies, and she immediately begins the attempt to find out the secret of his strength. Samson sees through her attempts, and it is he who outwits her three times. First, he tells her that she should bind him with seven fresh bowstrings, but when the Philistines appear, he snaps these as if they were mere string; then he tells her to bind him with new ropes, but he snaps these as if they were threads. Then he tells her to bind the seven locks of his head to the peg of her loom; but this time too, he easily frees himself. The Philistines lie in wait each time, but they never succeed in seizing Samson. After this threefold failure, in which the number seven plays an important role, Samson ought really to have been convinced of the faithlessness of his wife, but she tries one more time: "How can you say, 'I love you,' when your heart is not with me? You have mocked me three times now and have not told me what makes your strength so great.' Finally, after she had nagged him with her words day after day, and pestered him, he was tired to death. So he told her his whole secret, and said to her, 'A razor has never come

upon my head; for I have been a Nazirite to God from my mother's womb. If my head were shaved, then my strength would leave me; I would become weak, and be like anyone else'" (16:15-17).

Samson's strength lies in his hair – a symbol both of his mighty deeds and of sexual potency. Samson is so blinded by his love that he tells Delilah the whole truth this time. "She let him fall asleep on her lap" (a poetic circumlocution for intercourse, after which the man is exhausted). She then cuts off his seven locks. His strength leaves him, and the Philistines blind him and carry him off in bronze fetters to the coastal city of Gaza, where they put him in prison.

But this is not the end of the story. The text at 16:22 signals that more is to come: "But the hair of his head began to grow again after it had been cut off." We hear nothing more of the woman who had betrayed Samson. The Philistines hold a great feast in Gaza, and all the nobles assemble in a house. All the princes of the Philistines are present, and as many as three thousand men and women are on the flat roof alone (16:27); this may well be an exaggeration typical of sagas, but we are certainly to understand that a great many persons were present. The Philistines fetch Samson, so that they can mock him publicly. They make him stand between the pillars, and he gropes helplessly to find them since he is blind. Samson senses that his strength has returned and that this is his chance to strike a truly serious blow against the Philistines. First he prays to Yahweh his God, then he takes hold

TREACHERY.
Peter Paul Rubens' painting (ca. 1620) makes a contrast between Samson, sleeping trustfully without a thought of danger, and the busy activities of his enemies who hope that now, with Delilah's help, they have at last achieved their goal (opposite page).

CONFLICTING EMOTIONS.
Rubens' pupil Anthonis van Dyck presents an unusual interpretation of the relationship between the traitor and her victim in his painting of the capture of Samson (ca. 1628/1630): Samson is forcibly parted from Delilah, but he is as it were chained to her through the gaze with which she answers his uncomprehending terror. Delilah is tortured by profoundly conflicting emotions (below).

of the central pillars which support the entire house and strains with all his might, so that the house collapses and all are buried under its ruins – both the princes of the Philistines and Samson himself. "So those he killed at his death were more than those he had killed during his life" (16:30).

Samson pays for his love with his death; the narrative says nothing about what happened to the treacherous Delilah. The hair in which Samson's strength lay is a symbol of his potency; in the Bible, seven is always a sacred number signifying completeness or perfection, and this is why the story specifies that he has seven locks. The love story itself was only a means to an end; its conclusion reveals the strength and superiority of the hero. Samson's love for Delilah is one-sided; he falls in love and throws all caution to the winds, but nothing like this is said about Delilah. From the outset, she is a spy who plans to ensnare Samson and hand him over to the Philistines.

This narrative is more than just the tale of a man who falls in love and is outwitted by a crafty woman. Ultimately, he does not lose his power, as his parents had feared when they asked why their son did not seek a wife among the women of his own people. The narrator comments: "His father and mother did not know that this was from the Lord; for he was seeking a pretext to act against the Philistines" (14:4). It is indeed true that Samson's love for the woman who betrays him brings him to his death; but at the same time, Israel has taken one more step along the road to liberation from its worst enemies.

The love story between Samson and Delilah is constructed along similar lines to the other well-known story in which a man falls in love and is blinded by passion, so that he loses his life: Holofernes and Judith. But the roles are reversed in the late story of Judith, where the heroic figure is a woman; in the Book of Judges, the hero is a man. The account of his annunciation and birth shows that Samson will be a deliverer of Israel, just as Judith will deliver Israel later on. In both cases, the man falls in love and is swept away by passion, while the calculating woman employs her charm to ensnare him. Neither woman seeks love or a life in common with the man involved; each wishes to help her own people by using her attractiveness to outwit a man who is in love with her, and this succeeds in both cases. The good and evil roles are reversed: in Judges, the good and heroic figure is Samson, but in the Book of Judith, the woman is the deliverer, while Holofernes is the incarnation of evil, personifying the enemies of Israel. The perspective in each of the two narratives is decisive. Both women behave in a very similar manner, seeking to save their own people by making use of the possibilities open to them precisely as women; but Delilah must play the negative role in her story, because she is on the side of Israel's enemies. All the reader's sympathies belong to the courageous Samson; Delilah is stuck with all the clichés about seductive women who betray men.

THE GREATEST VICTORY. *This stained glass window (ca. 1300) employs symbols to concentrate on the essential point in the last mighty deed of the prisoner Samson (Judg 16:23-30). By shattering the middle pillars of the palace with newly acquired strength, Samson causes the entire house to collapse. Great numbers of the Philistines are gathered on the flat roof and in the hall of the house: "So those he killed at his death were more than those he had killed during his life" (16:30).*

JOSEPH AND THE WIFE OF POTIPHAR

(Genesis 39)

The stories about Joseph form a narrative cycle (Gen 37-50) which follows the stories about the ancestors of Israel. Joseph, the second youngest son of Jacob, is sold by his brothers into slavery in Egypt and is now in the house of Potiphar, a high Egyptian official. As a slave, he has risen to the responsible post of domestic administrator, and his master entrusts to him all his possessions: "with him there, he had no concern for anything but the food he ate" (39:6). Chapter 39 has a theme and a dynamic of its own. It assumes that the reader is familiar with the Egyptian tale of the "two brothers," a story of the seduction of the wife of one of the brothers.

The introduction tells us about the circumstances of Joseph's work (39:1-6) and emphasizes above all that "Yahweh was with Joseph." He is under the special protection of God, like David later on in the biblical story (1 Sam 16:18); this is a leitmotif of the narrative. And as with David, God's special favor includes outstanding beauty: "Joseph was handsome and good-looking" (Gen 39:6). The young man's beauty causes the wife of Potiphar to fall in love with him. Once again, we meet an unnamed woman who is defined only by means of her husband. This woman and Joseph are the protagonists in chapter 39, a tale of lust and passion – here, not on the part of the man (as with Holofernes and Samson), but of the woman. It is she who takes the initiative each time, while Joseph remains passive. His only reaction is to flee.

The course of events might be called the reverse of the story of Amnon and Tamar: the woman throws herself on Joseph and wants to sleep with him; but he resists, using some of the arguments that Tamar uses with her brother. Joseph does not wish to commit so great a crime (cf. 2 Sam 13:6). In this case, the crime would be adultery, incurring the death sentence for Joseph, since Potiphar has not withheld anything in his house from the slave. Everything is in his hands – except his master's wife. But more would be involved than disloyalty to Potiphar, since adultery is a sin against God: "How then could I do this great wickedness, and sin against God?" (Gen 39:9).

Joseph's faith in God obliges him to resist. The text does not say whether the woman's passion was contagious but compresses the dramatic situation into one single sentence: "And although she spoke to Joseph day after day, he would not consent to lie beside her or to be with her" (39:10; Thomas Mann gives a lengthy epic description of this scene in his novel

CALUMNY.
This two-part miniature in the Wenceslaus Bible *(ca. 1400) illustrates* Gen 39:12-18 *with considerable artistic freedom – Potiphar and his lying wife are given crowns, elevating them to royal rank. In the lower picture,*

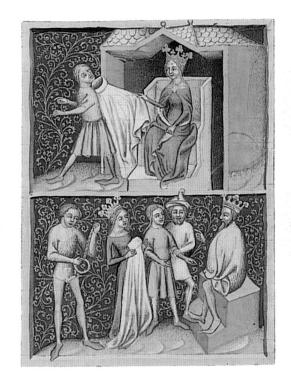

a servant on the left is holding a collar of iron which will be put on Joseph's neck as soon as he is pronounced guilty.

Joseph and His Brothers). This goes on for some time, but Joseph resists the temptation. For this reason, he is often referred to as "the chaste Joseph." Then things come to a crisis. The woman seizes her chance on a day when none of the servants is present, in order to bend Joseph to her will. She doubtless finds it incredible that this foreign slave is not willing to sleep with his master's wife. Like Amnon, she chooses a time when there are no witnesses. She seizes Joseph's garment and cries: "Lie with me!" But Joseph leaves his garment in her hand and flees. He thus avoids being compelled to have intercourse (unlike Tamar), but the woman retains his garment in pledge, as it were, so that she can use it to construct a false accusation. She calls the servants together and exclaims: "See, my husband has brought among us a Hebrew to insult us! He came in to me to lie with me, and I cried out with a loud voice; and when he heard me raise my voice and cry out, he left his garment beside me, and fled outside" (39:14f.).

Thus she takes revenge for her humiliation. Her accusation sounds very credible, for there are no witnesses to speak in Joseph's favor. Clearly, her passion has turned into hatred, as we are told explicitly of Amnon after the rape of his sister (2 Sam 13:15). Her indignation is a pretense, born of her disappointment that her lust remained unsatisfied. In her accusation, she does not even mention Joseph's name but calls him "a Hebrew," expressing her contempt for this foreigner. The other servants are certainly receptive to her story, for her words kindle or deepen their envy of this young man who has risen to such a high position. Later, she tells her husband the same story,

SENSUALITY.
Tintoretto employed the narrow horizontal format of his painting (ca. 1550) to depict a female nude figure in the tradition of depictions of Venus, goddess of love. Joseph, who refuses to yield to her sensual longings, seems like a second Adonis; this figure from classical mythology also corresponds to the description of Joseph as an attractive and desirable young man.

"This one is the woman
who made false
accusations against Joseph;
the other is Sinon, the
Greek mad with love: so great
is the torment of their
hot fever that they give off smoke."
DANTE, DIVINE COMEDY

EPISODE.
*In six circular paintings, the so-called
Master of the Legend of Joseph relates
the story of the last of the patriarchs
(ca. 1490/1500). This panel depicts
the wife of Potiphar. To the right, she
makes her false accusation; in the
background, we see Joseph's arrest.*

ACCUSATION.
This medallion in a thirteenth-century Bible
moralisée *depicts the accusation of Joseph. This*

somewhat more briefly, and here too she alludes to Joseph's background and
his subordinate status. Once again, she uses the plural ("us"), forming a common front with her servants against the despised foreigner: "The Hebrew servant, whom you have brought among us, came in to me to insult me; but as
soon as I raised my voice and cried out, he left his garment beside me, and
fled outside" (Gen 39:17f.).

This is the end of the "love story." What are its consequences for
Joseph and for the wife of Potiphar? We hear nothing more about her; she
simply disappears from the narrative, and we do not know whether she went
on with her life as before. For Joseph, however, the consequences are grim. In
his anger, Potiphar has him thrown into prison among the king's prisoners
(39:20). It is not entirely clear whether Potiphar believes his wife; he could in
fact have killed Joseph for this deed. This remains an open question, but the
subtext of the narrative suggests that Potiphar does not simply believe everything his wife has told him; nevertheless, he must preserve his honor, above
all vis-à-vis the rest of his domestic slaves, and this is why he is obliged to have

*begins a series of narrative pictures which
compares this miscarriage of justice with the
accusations made against Jesus before Pilate.*

Joseph imprisoned. The episode in the prison is, however, only one further stage in Joseph's ascent to still higher honors. For Joseph – and from the perspective of the narrator – the attempt of Potiphar's wife to seduce him is only one step on his upward path, where he must prove his worth. Joseph himself later marries an Egyptian woman, so the point here is not that it is a foreign woman who tries to seduce him. The challenge for him is to avoid committing adultery and breaking faith with his master. Joseph must prove his worth until the time comes when he can exercise power fully; it is only then that he himself can have a family of his own.

This is how the narrator sees things. But how different the story is when the one who seduces – and the one who has power – is a woman! The "partners" Amnon and Tamar are equal in rank, but the rape means for Tamar the end of her life, at any rate in the sense of an honorable existence with a future. The consequences for Potiphar's wife prove similar, even when, externally speaking, her life is unchanged: she too has no longer any historical visibility. The women are always the losers, even when they have the more powerful position. Besides this, later generations have often laughed at the nameless wife of

BODY LANGUAGE.
Rembrandt's etching (1634) employs the expressive power of excited bodies to portray the antithesis between seduction and resistance as a drama in which the two persons are completely caught up.

"She caught hold of his garment, saying, 'Lie with me!'
But he left his garment in her hand, and fled and ran outside."

GENESIS 39:12

Potiphar as one who tried to seduce a man, but failed; she has sometimes even been used as proof that women easily accuse men of sexual assault when none has taken place. This can of course happen, but the cases in which men do in fact sexually assault women are very much more numerous. This means that the story of the attempted seduction of Joseph has had negative consequences for many women even today, since it supports the image of women as dangerous seducers, from the first woman in the Bible, Eve, onwards. Such ideas have a very long tradition, but they have no place in serious argumentation.

The wife of Potiphar has a bad reputation, although she cannot be charged with anything more serious than we find in the stories of many male heroes. Between his marriages to his first Philistine wife and to Delilah, Samson visited a prostitute (Judg 16:1), but this does not affect in any way his reputation as the hero who rescued Israel. Nor is David – a brilliant and heroic figure like Joseph – evaluated on the basis of his excesses and adulteries. A woman, however, is judged according to sexual aspects alone, as if these made up the totality of her existence. This is not only because a man in Old Testament times could have several wives, whereas a woman could have only one husband. Even today, in a period which accepts the obligation to monogamy, two different sets of criteria are applied to stories of seduction. This is why later times have painted the wife of Potiphar in exclusively negative colors, although her attempt to seduce Joseph did not even succeed.

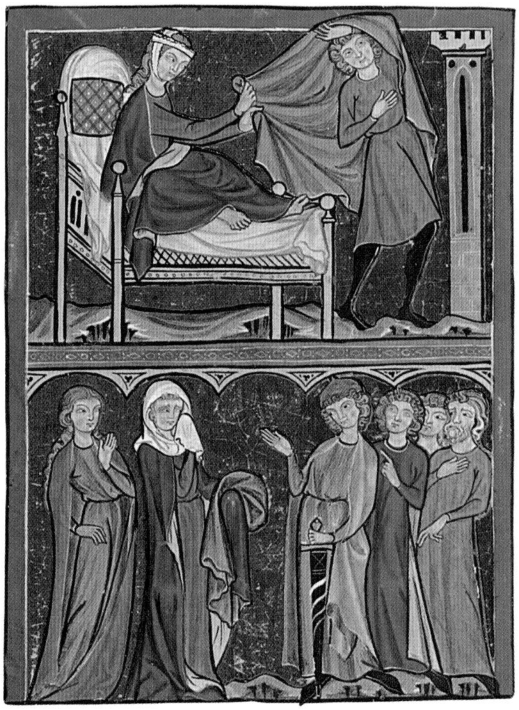

The late apocryphal *Testament of the Twelve Patriarchs* takes up the attempted seduction of Joseph anew and devotes considerable space to this narrative. In these so-called Testaments, the twelve sons of Jacob lie dying as old men, and look back on their earlier lives, giving moral exhortations to their descendants. Joseph speaks here in great detail of his former mistress's intention to seduce him. The author employs a style which was modern in the late Greek Hellenistic period, and elaborates numerous erotic details: "For even when I was in her house, she uncovered her arms and breasts and legs, so that I might lie down upon her. For she was very beautiful, and she decked herself out in all her glory in order to seduce me. But the Lord preserved me from her plotting" (Test. XII, 9:5). The woman's attempts at seduction occupy many chapters of this work. She even goes as far as to suggest poisoning her husband, but Joseph remains steadfast.

In this late text, Joseph is always the self-controlled, wise man, while the wife of Potiphar is the one who loses control. She is the antithesis of Joseph as the seductive woman who embodies folly. These two types – Lady Wisdom and Lady Folly – were very common in the literature of that period, and they are exemplified here in the figures of Joseph and the wife of Potiphar.

HISTORY.
The story of Joseph and the wife of Potiphar is one of the biblical themes in the World Chronicle *of Rudolf of Ems. The magnificent manuscript of this book (written after 1300) contains this depiction of the two decisive scenes, with Joseph's cloak as the alleged proof of his attempt to have intercourse with the wife of his master.*

ABRAHAM AND HAGAR

(Genesis 16 and 21)

Abraham, the first of the three great patriarchs in the Book of Genesis (Abraham – Isaac – Jacob), has a wife who emigrates with him from Ur in Chaldea. At the command of his God, Abraham leaves his country and his relatives, to go to the country Yahweh will show him. He takes his wife, his servants, his livestock, and his other possessions with him.

Sarah (whose name means "princess"), Abraham's primary wife, is infertile (Gen 11:30). Abraham has been promised not only the country but also many descendants, but they are both getting older. In her desperation, Sarah resorts to a method which was customary at that period, by giving her husband a secondary wife. There was nothing exceptional about this in a time when men were allowed to have numerous wives. However, the secondary wife Hagar is not free, but is a slave of Sarah. This means that she is the personal property of her mistress. We meet a similar instance later in the Book of Genesis, in the story of the patriarch Jacob, where slave women are "lent out" (so to speak) by their mistress to her husband. His two wives, the sisters Leah and Rachel, give him their personal maids as secondary wives, so that Jacob can have even more sons by means of these two women; and he ends up with twelve sons, born to four different mothers. In legal terms, the children born to the slave women are counted as legitimate children of the mistress. In Abraham's case, this means that any child of Hagar is a legitimate child of Sarah. Thus, the infertile Sarah can use her slave Hagar to have a son in whom the promise to Abraham will be accomplished.

In this transaction, Abraham is completely passive: it is Sarah alone who acts. Nor is Hagar consulted. As a slave, she must obey the commands of her mistress, and this includes obedience in the sexual sphere. Nevertheless, slave women who become concubines or secondary wives of their masters are not completely without rights. They enjoy legal protection, and their owner cannot simply sell them to another master. A series of laws in the so-called book of the covenant (Ex 21ff.), with parallels in other legal texts from the ancient east, regulate this situation. Besides this, Israel is admonished in many passages of scripture to treat male and female slaves humanely, since the people of Israel itself was "a slave" in the land of Egypt. This means that they ought to know what it means to be a slave!

The situation changes when Hagar realizes that she is pregnant. Now she looks down on her mistress, feeling superior to her, for she is expecting a son, but Sarah remains infertile. Sarah is rich and powerful; Hagar is a slave,

ABRAHAM.
A water-color by Emil Wachter (1982) depicting the first of the three great patriarchs, or to put it more precisely: the ancestral fathers and partners of the ancestral mothers Sarah and Hagar, Rebekah, Leah, Rachel, Bilhah, and Zilpah.

but she is young and fertile. The rivalry which grows up between the women may seem natural and understandable in human terms, but Sarah is deeply hurt by it. In her despair, she turns to Abraham and complains about the situation. He dismisses her with the remark that Hagar is under her authority and that she can do with her as she pleases. Abraham does not get involved in the conflict, but refers to a legal situation which leaves him in a very comfortable position. Earlier on, he had presented his wife Sarah as his sister, thus in a sense abandoning her in order to save his own life (Gen 12). Here, he is abandoning his unborn son without intervening to help him. Abraham appears not merely passive but cowardly.

Sarah exploits her position of power to treat Hagar harshly, and the slave woman flees. The verb used here for Sarah's "oppression" is the same word used later for the "oppression" of the Israelites in Egypt; since Hagar is an Egyptian, this choice of vocabulary is certainly intentional. Sarah oppresses her Egyptian slave just as the Egyptians will later make slaves of the people of "Israel," who then flee to the wilderness. In this context, "Egypt" is an emotive word. The ancestral couple, Abraham and Sarah, do not appear in a good light in this story.

Hagar flees to the southern wilderness near the Egyptian border. The text mentions Shur, where Israel will later wander without finding water (Ex 15:22). Hagar, however, at once finds a spring of water, and a messenger from Yahweh (whom later tradition makes an angel) comes to meet her. Unlike Sarah and Abraham, who never address a word directly to Hagar, he treats her as a person and addresses her by her name and her social status as Sarah's slave. He commands her to return to her mistress and endure her harsh treatment. Hagar is promised descendants – a promise that otherwise in the Book of Genesis is made only to men: "Now you have conceived and shall bear a son; you shall call him Ishmael, for the Lord has given heed to your affliction" (Gen 16:11).

The Bible contains numerous annunciations of forthcoming births; the last of these is made to Mary (Lk 1:26-38). Usually, they include the name of the child that is to be born, and this is explained at once: "Ishmael" means "God has heard." It is unusual for a woman to receive a divine revelation of this kind. Hagar reacts at once by giving the God who has "seen" her a name, El-roi ("the God who sees me"). The slave woman acts with great self-awareness in this scene. She obeys the angel's command, returns to Abraham, and gives birth to her son, but it is Abraham who gives him the name Ishmael and thereby acknowledges him as his own child. Ishmael is Abraham's first legitimate child, for in the patriarchal ordering of society it is only the father (not the mother) who plays the decisive role here.

Although Hagar is expecting his child, Abraham shows no concern for

BROTHERLY LOVE.
In his painting of the expulsion of Hagar (ca. 1700), Adriaen van der Werft emphasizes the separation between the two brothers – Ishmael, the firstborn son of Abraham, and Isaac, his second son. Abraham blesses Ishmael, while Sarah looks on unmoved (opposite page).

DOUBT.
Rembrandt's etching (1637) depicts Abraham as the patriarch who expels Hagar but whose outstretched arms reveal that he himself has doubts about this decision. On the left, Sarah looks out of the window with a satisfied face.

her but gives Sarah a free hand to do as she pleases. The relationship between Abraham and Hagar has a purely legal character; love is never mentioned. Hagar has intercourse with Abraham only in order that he may have a son. Even when this purpose is put at risk by her flight, Abraham simply accepts the situation. Hagar is merely a means to an end, so that the promise made to Abraham may be fulfilled. Nor is there any communication between Sarah and Hagar, only command and obedience; the Bible does not mention any direct contact between the two women. If we want to speak of a "relationship," we might say that chapter 16 is the story of a relationship between two women which breaks down.

This is not the final word, however. Things take a dramatic turn in Gen 21, which is not simply a doublet of chapter 16, since the situation has changed fundamentally in the meantime. Despite her advanced age, Sarah herself has now borne a son, Isaac, who is to be the bearer of the promise of Abraham. Hagar's son is by now several years old. The conflict which erupts now is not between a fertile and an infertile woman, but between the claims of the two boys to inheritance. Legally speaking, Ishmael is and remains the firstborn, and Sarah therefore fears that her son Isaac may not be Abraham's heir. This occurs to her one day as she watches the two children at play (21:9), and this leads to the second expulsion of Hagar. Sarah demands that Abraham drive out the slave and her son, so that he may not be a joint heir with Isaac (21:10). She speaks with lofty contempt not of the mother of Ishmael, but of Hagar as "this slave" – a person with whom she has no longer any relationship.

This time, we are told of a reaction on Abraham's part. Although he is "distressed" by Sarah's demand, since it is a question of his own son, he accepts it after God has told him that Isaac is to be the bearer of the divine promise. He loads Hagar with provisions for one day and sets the child on her shoulder, then sends her off to the wilderness. Hagar wanders around in despair, half dying of thirst. She casts her son under a bush because she cannot bear to look on his death. She weeps loudly, but then an angel of God appears to her, shows her a well, and saves both her life and that of the child. He promises her that the boy will become a great people. After this, she lives with him in the wilderness, and the last we hear of her is that she gets Ishmael an Egyptian woman as his wife. Hagar is the first woman in the Bible who is directly addressed from the heavenly sphere, when this promise is made about her son. On the level of her relationship to God, she is treated as a person, and she is promised descendants.

We should not read this narrative, in which Abraham does not hesitate to abandon his firstborn son, without looking briefly at the following chapter, Gen 22, where he is charged by God to offer his son Isaac in sacrifice. After Ishmael has vanished from the scene, Isaac is Abraham's last

CHANGE OF MOOD.
Before Hagar is expelled for good, she flees a first time from the harsh treatment which Sarah metes out to her pregnant slave woman, but then returns. This painting by Pietro Berrettini da Cortona (ca. 1630) shows the angel who encourages Hagar to return (opposite page).

HEAVENLY CONSOLATION.
These two scenes in the magnificent manuscript of the World Chronicle *of Rudolf of Ems (written after 1300) contrast the harshness with which Sarah treats her maid and rival Hagar, and the consolation which Hagar receives from the angel when she flees into the wilderness (above).*

guarantee of a future. In both cases, with Ishmael and with Isaac, an angel of God intervenes at the last moment to deliver each boy from a certain death. In both cases, therefore, the child is saved not by the courageous or well-considered action of the patriarch but only by the intervention of God.

Hagar and Abraham are a very unequal couple: Abraham is powerful, rich, and the ancestor of innumerable persons, while Hagar is poor, enslaved, and a foreigner. In the first narrative, she flees alone into the wilderness; in the second narrative, she flees with her son, who will never see his father again. But Hagar does not simply acquiesce in Sarah's endeavor to use her as an instrument and then get rid of her. Besides this, God himself takes the side of Hagar and her son. Although she is the weakest and most disadvantaged person in these stories, she proves to have the strongest character, whereas the ancestral couple cut a poor figure.

Hagar has been remembered in later history as a desperate mother who flees for safety. Oppressed, humiliated, and foreign women can identify with her. The Arab peoples regard Ishmael as their ancestor, and this means that Hagar could function as a bridgehead for dialogue among the three monotheistic religions, precisely as a woman with a threefold disadvantage: as a woman, as a slave, and as a foreigner.

"It is written that Abraham had two sons, one by a slave woman and the other by a free woman."

PAUL,
LETTER TO THE GALATIANS 4:22

MOSES AND ZIPPORAH

(Exodus 2, 4 and 18)

RETURN.
This column in the Wenceslaus Bible *(ca. 1400) relates in text and image how Moses and his family travel from Midian to Egypt (Ex 4:18-31). Zipporah holds her firstborn in her arms; three other children are in the saddle bag (opposite page).*

ENCOUNTER.
This miniature in the Wenceslaus Bible *at Ex 2:17 emphasizes two figures: Moses and his future wife Zipporah. Her six sisters and the inconsiderate shepherds are much smaller figures (above).*

Moses is the great legislator who, according to the biblical tradition, received the ten commandments from God on Mount Sinai. Later tradition traced the entire legal corpus of commandments and laws back to him.

Moses is born in Egypt, the son of an Israelite couple, but he is given an Egyptian name (names such as Tuth-Mosis are recorded in ancient Egypt) three months after his birth, when he is exposed in a papyrus basket on the Nile and the daughter of Pharaoh rescues him. When he has reached adulthood, he sees how the Israelites are oppressed (Ex 2:11). He kills an Egyptian and is forced to flee into the wilderness, to the land of Midian, where he settles. At a well where the animals are watered, he sees the shepherds driving off some young women who want to water their sheep. Moses helps them; he has already intervened to help his oppressed fellow countrymen, and this is the second time that he helps the weak.

We recall the similar situations when Eliezer, Abraham's servant, meets Rebekah (Gen 24) and Jacob meets Rachel (Gen 29). The well, with the daily fetching of water and giving drink to the animals, was the most important meeting place, where one heard the latest news and people could get to know each other. The stories of the biblical ancestors tell us that many marriages came about as a result of meetings at wells, and this is what happens here too.

The young women are the daughters of a Midianite, and they invite the helpful stranger to their father's tent. Moses is welcomed warmly, in keeping with the traditions of hospitality, and he is very soon given one of the daughters in marriage. Like Abraham and Joseph before him, Moses too now has a foreign wife – and not only a woman of Midian but the daughter of the high priest of that land. The Midianites were a desert tribe at the Gulf of Aqaba and in the Sinai peninsula, merchant Bedouins who rode on camels; it was Midianites who drew Joseph out of the cistern and took him to Egypt (Gen 37:28). In Ex 2, the priest is called Reuel; other passages call him Jethro. We are also told the name of the woman Moses marries: Zipporah ("bird"). She is one of Jethro's seven daughters, and we may take it as certain that he had no sons. A capable son-in-law like Moses was very welcome.

Immediately after mentioning the wedding, the text tells us of the birth of a son, whom Moses names Gershom ("guest" or "foreigner"): "I have been an alien residing in a foreign land" (2:22). The name of his firstborn points to the situation of Moses, who is regarded as "an Egyptian" (2:19). It has a double meaning, designating both one who resides in a foreign land and one who enjoys the status of a guest. The peoples of the ancient east esteemed hospitality very highly, and it is clear that Moses was a guest who was treated extremely well: Zipporah's family has not only welcomed him hospitably but has made him their relative by marriage.

We next hear about Moses and Zipporah in chapter 4. Between this narrative and the marriage of Moses lies the scene in which God reveals his name YHWH in the burning bush, while Moses is looking after the flock of his father-in-law Jethro (3:1). The name Yahweh is connected in some way with the desert tribe of the Midianites; scholars today agree that this name comes from the wilderness of Sinai, where the mountain of God, on which the ten commandments will later be given, is also located.

After the revelation of the name of Yahweh, Moses wishes to return to Egypt and see how his kindred are getting on. He does not travel alone but takes his wife and his sons with him (4:20). This means that some time has passed, since Moses apparently now has not only his firstborn, but other sons too, whom he puts on a donkey. So much time has passed that the Egyptians have forgotten the incident that forced Moses to flee from Egypt. We are not told the names of his other sons; only the firstborn is important to the narrator, because the ensuing negotiations in Egypt concern Israel, the "firstborn" of Yahweh: if Pharaoh does not allow the Israelites to leave, his own firstborn will die. The concept of "firstborn" is central here, and the author plays variations on it. Moses goes down to Egypt with his family. The illustration in the margin recalls the flight of the Holy Family to Egypt (cf. Mt 2:13-15), and the two journeys were doubtless similar.

In the course of their journey, an incident takes place in which only Moses' firstborn son and Zipporah play a role. While they are resting one night, Yahweh meets Moses and wishes to kill him (Ex 4:24); we are not told the reason for this, but this attack is strongly reminiscent of the patriarch Jacob's fight with God by night at the river Jabbok (Gen 32:23-33). This is a very ancient story with some strange aspects – indeed, so strange that later generations simplified things by substituting a demon for God (although he appears under his own name, Yahweh). It is God himself who attacks the man he has chosen, perhaps in order to put him to the test, just as other great men are tested or tempted before they can carry out the task God has given them (cf. the temptations of Jesus in the desert). In the Bible, God is neither as harmless nor as straightforward as we might like to think; both good and evil are said to come from him. In the last analysis, we do not know the reason for this attack on Moses.

It is, however, clear that the story has a happy ending, thanks to Zipporah's action. Only her name and that of her firstborn son Gershom are

mentioned here. She takes the initiative to ward off the peril that threatens her husband. She takes a sharp stone and circumcises her son. This very ancient rite was originally carried out with a knife of stone. Part of the foreskin was cut off, probably as a rite of initiation in the period of puberty or shortly before a man married (in ancient times, these two more or less coincided). Later, infants were circumcised on the eighth day; Jesus was circumcised in Jerusalem on the eighth day after his birth (Lk 2:21). Circumcision was interpreted as a sign of the covenant between Yahweh and his people, and this is why all men in Israel had to be circumcised; the Bible has nothing to say of circumcision for girls or women, such as is customary even today among many other peoples.

In the entire Old Testament, there is no other passage in which a woman performs circumcision. This is always done by men, and in later times it was specialized professional work. The Midianites, to whom Zipporah belonged, and all the surrounding Semitic peoples practiced circumcision. How does Zipporah in our story know what needs to be done? By doing what is right, she saves Moses – the savior of his people. She takes a sharp stone, cuts off part of the foreskin of her firstborn son, and touches Moses' genitals with this (the "feet" in the Hebrew Bible are often a circumlocution for the sexual organs). Through this "blood rite," she confirms the covenant with God. To understand this fully, we probably need to remember the rite which the Israelites perform when they leave Egypt (cf. Ex 12): the blood of the Passover lamb, which is smeared on the doorposts, prevents the slaughter of the firstborn of the Israelites. In the nocturnal scene in the wilderness, Zipporah prevents the death of Moses by performing an ancient blood rite. (Obviously, her son Gershom had not yet been circumcised.)

In this narrative, Zipporah is the protagonist. Through her quickness of mind, she saves her husband Moses shortly before he enters the land of Egypt, where he and Aaron must negotiate with Pharaoh. Thanks to the prudent wisdom of a woman, Moses was placed as a little child in his basket on the Nile, so that Pharaoh's desire to kill him was thwarted. Here too, a woman – his wife Zipporah – saves him from God himself, when God attacks her husband. Clearly, the daughter of the high priest of Midian has learned much about how to deal with the Holy One and the perils which the encounter with God involves. After this, she returns with her children to her father's house, as Ex 18:2 tells us. There she meets Moses later on.

The protagonist in the last narrative about Moses and Zipporah (Ex 18:1-27) is his father-in-law, Jethro, who shows himself to be a wise man when he visits Moses in the wilderness with Zipporah and their sons. Jethro eats with Moses and gives him advice about how to reduce his excessive workload. The priestly family in Midian stuck together; Moses had not separated

from his wife but remained united to her, although his nomadic life meant that he could not always take her with him. Zipporah lives with her children for a lengthy period in her father's house. In Israel, especially in the early generations, a great variety of forms of marriage were possible. For nomads, the structures were not so stable as in later times when people had fixed dwellings and a woman normally came to live in the house and family of her husband and spent all her life there.

In ancient times, no one took offense at the fact that Moses, the great lawgiver, married a Midianite woman who was the daughter of a high priest. We must suppose that Zipporah was his first wife, since Moses was obliged to flee from Egypt as a fiery young man, after he killed an Egyptian. As was customary at that time, the marriage was agreed upon with no great preliminar-

"Moses looked this way and that, and seeing no one he killed the Egyptian and hid him in the sand."

EXODUS 2:12

A MAN OF ACTION.
Emil Wachter's portrait study of Moses emphasizes his character as a man of action, who is sometimes carried away by his emotions (above). This underlines all the more strongly the mildness in Zipporah's face (above right).

ies. It was a pragmatic matter, which did not involve love. As the first story makes clear, the intention was to have sons who would continue the man's name and family. Mutual help was prized very highly. Moses receives Zipporah as his wife, because he had intervened to help those who were weak; and Zipporah in turn helps her husband when God attacks him by night and his life is at risk. Married couples in a barren and hostile land take it for granted that each will help the other. No matter what happens, one can rely on this help.

Only at a later period, after the fourth century B.C.E., were marriages between Israelite men and foreign women sharply criticized, as we see most clearly in the Books of Ezra and Nehemiah, which demand that all the Israelite men send away their foreign wives and children (cf. Ezra 9f.; Neh 13:23-31). There is as yet no trace of such rigorism in the ancient narratives of the patriarchs, of Joseph, or of Moses.

JOSEPH AND ASENATH

(Genesis 41)

JOSEPH IN DISTRESS.
*The two parts of an illuminated page in
the* Crusader Bible *(ca. 1250) depict
the two lowest points in Joseph's life.
He is sold by his brothers to Midianite*

After Joseph is released from the prison in which he has spent two years upon being falsely accused by the wife of Potiphar, he rises to high office in Egypt and finally marries a high-ranking woman. The Book of Genesis relates the marriage of Joseph and an Egyptian woman in one single sentence: "Pharaoh gave Joseph the name Zaphenath-paneah; and he gave him Asenath daughter of Potiphera, priest of On, as his wife" (41:45). The new name bestowed on Joseph is found only here in the Old Testament. It means: "God speaks and he lives." It was customary in Egypt to bestow a new name on one who was given such a high office.

This marriage is astonishing for a number of reasons. Joseph has risen to great heights in Egypt, where he is now the second man after Pharaoh. This is almost a literal echo of the story in chapter 39, where Joseph (then still a slave) was the second man after his master Potiphar. That story too involved a wife, Potiphar's wife, from whom Joseph was obliged to keep his distance, since he could not countenance the idea of committing adultery. And Potiphar had the same name as Joseph's father-in-law. In keeping with the leitmotif of chapter 39, "God was with Joseph," we now see how God accompanies Joseph in his ascent. This narrative reads like the second act, the sequel to the first act which was set in the house of Potiphar.

After Joseph interprets for Pharaoh his dreams of the seven fat and seven lean cows, he is rehabilitated, and chapter 41 relates the measures Joseph undertakes during the seven fat years. He gathers stores of food in order to keep the whole population of Egypt – and thereby his own family too, his father Jacob and his brothers – from dying of hunger. It is during these fat years that he marries his Egyptian wife. Gen 41:46 tells us that he was thirty years old, and hence no longer a youth but a mature man. In the world of the Bible, it is very unusual to put off marrying until one is so old. Normally, sons are married off by their parents at the early age of fifteen or sixteen, and daughters roughly two years before that. The wait is probably due to Joseph's unparalleled career, his brilliant ascent to office: in this long period, he must prove his worth. Usually, his father would arrange the marriage; the fact that Pharaoh performs this function here emphasizes how important Joseph's position was.

Asenath is an Egyptian. Later generations called this non-Israelite woman a pagan; even worse, she was the daughter of the priest of On, the sun god in Heliopolis – a foreign god for Joseph. Such marriages with foreign women were viewed in various ways in Israel. At certain periods, they were a

*traders, who bring him as a slave to
Egypt (Gen 37:28), where he is the
victim of calumny by the wife of
Potiphar and is thrown into
prison (39:17-29).*

JOSEPH'S FAMILY.
Rembrandt's painting Jacob Blesses the Sons of Joseph *(1656) differs from other contemporary depictions of this scene (Gen 48:1-22) by including Asenath, wife of Joseph and mother of the children.*

matter of course. David's great-grandmother Ruth was a Moabitess who came to Bethlehem with her mother-in-law (cf. Ruth 1:6ff.), and Solomon's mother Bathsheba was likewise a foreigner, a Hittite married to Uriah the Hittite and a member of the high aristocracy in the Jebusite city of Jerusalem. Nor was Moses' marriage to the Midianite woman Zipporah judged negatively.

At a later period, however, there was much polemic against foreign women, because it was thought that they would seduce their husbands to apostasy from Yahweh. Once the idea had taken root that a Jew was one who had a Jewish mother, it was held that foreign wives would not be able to bring up their children in the Jewish faith. We do not know when this idea hardened into a matter of principle, but when we consider the tremendous insistence in the Book of Tobit (second century B.C.E.) that the young Tobias should seek and find a wife from his own people and tribe, it is striking that marriage with foreign wives should have been seen as a perfectly natural occurrence in earlier days. The traditions about the marriages of heroes from the past with foreign wives had obviously not been forgotten, and no one took offense at the marriage of Joseph, a central savior figure in the Old Testament, to an Egyptian woman. Otherwise, later tradition would have passed over this marriage in silence. What then do we know about Asenath, and about Joseph and Asenath as a couple?

Apart from the brief mention of their marriage, Genesis tells us that two sons were born to the couple: "Before the years of famine came, Joseph had two sons, whom Asenath daughter of Potiphera, priest of On, bore to him. Joseph named the firstborn Manasseh ['Making to forget'], 'For,' he said, 'God has made me forget all my hardship and all my father's house.' The second he named Ephraim ['Making fruitful'], 'For God has made me fruitful in the land of my misfortunes'" (41:50-52).

Otherwise, the Hebrew Bible has nothing more to say about Asenath, the mother of Ephraim and Manasseh, who later give their names to two of the tribes of Israel. The sequence of their births does not determine their inheritance, for Jacob crosses his hands when he blesses them, passing over the firstborn so that the story of Jacob himself and his brother Esau is repeated: the younger son is preferred (Gen 48:14; cf. Gen 27). Rembrandt depicts this scene in his famous painting of Jacob's blessing, where Asenath too stands, somewhat apart, by the deathbed of Jacob and is present when the patriarch blesses the children. In the other narratives of the patriarchs, it is usually the mother who gives children their names, but here this is done by Joseph alone. In the Book of Genesis, therefore, Asenath has a subordinate function.

It is only in the late period that she becomes an important figure. An apocryphal book, which was not included in the Bible but had a long-lasting influence both on literature and on art until the nineteenth century, tells her story. *Joseph and Asenath* is a Greek hellenistic novel written between 100 B.C.E. and 100 C.E. and belongs to the intertestamental texts. The Septuagint, the Greek translation of the Hebrew Bible, had been completed by this date, and the author of the novel was able to draw on all the traditions and personages of the Old Testament in the language which was spoken throughout the educated world at that time, i.e., Greek. The novel was probably written in Egypt, where large colonies of Greek-speaking Jews had existed for a long time. Alexandria, the important center of learning on the Mediterranean Sea, had a large Jewish quarter and philosophical circles (including groups of women). What could be more natural than to write a novel about an important savior figure from the biblical tradition, who had married an Egyptian wife? The main point of the story is Asenath's conversion to Judaism, in order that she may marry Joseph. This shows that a later period found it offensive that Joseph should have married the daughter of a pagan priest and that she remained a Gentile even after her wedding.

"Jacob said to Joseph, 'God Almighty appeared to me at Luz in the land of Canaan, and he blessed me, and said to me, "I am going to make you fruitful and increase your numbers; I will make of you a company of peoples, and will give this land to your offspring after you for a perpetual holding." Therefore your two sons, who were born to you in the land of Egypt before I came to you in Egypt, are now mine; Ephraim and Manasseh shall be mine, just as Reuben and Simeon are.'"

GENESIS 48:3-5

"So the girl Asenath was sent with twenty-four hand-picked female slaves up to Memphis, to Joseph's house, for her virginal wedding. Her high-priestly parents, deeply stricken that they should be bereft of their daughter in so incomprehensible a manner, came up from On, and Pharaoh himself came down from Nowet-Amun to take part in the mysteries of this wedding. He himself handed over the choice bride to his favorite and, as an experienced husband, ensured Joseph once again of all the pleasures that accompanied the married state." Thomas Mann,

JOSEPH AND HIS BROTHERS, PART IV: JOSEPH THE PROVIDER

BRIDAL COUPLE.
Emil Wachter's water-color Isaac and Rebekah *draws from Rembrandt's painting* The Jewish Bride *(illustration: p. 49), which probably also depicts Isaac and Rebekah (opposite page).*

The protagonist of this Greek novel from the period between the two Testaments is Asenath; Joseph has only a minor role. The genre of such works demands a happy ending, and this is what we get: not because of the great love of this couple but because of Asenath's conversion. The name Asenath is derived from the Egyptian goddess Neith. When therefore this young woman converts to the God of Israel, this means that the Egyptian goddess submits to Yahweh, the God of the Jews.

At the beginning of the novel, Asenath, the daughter of the priest of Heliopolis, is described as follows: "And he had a daughter, a virgin eighteen years of age, tall and shapely and more beautiful in appearance than all the other virgins on earth. Nor was she comparable to the virgins of the Egyptians, but resembled in everything the daughters of the Hebrews. She was tall like Sarah and shapely like Rebekah and beautiful like Rachel. And the name of this virgin was Asenath" (1:4f.). Her beauty is compared to that of all the ancestral mothers (with the exception of Leah), but she is also described as proud and exceedingly arrogant. She hates all men and initially despises Joseph because he is a foreigner, a Canaanite who has turned up in Egypt. Joseph is afraid of the women of Egypt, not only because he recalls the attempts of the wife of Potiphar to seduce him, but because there is no end in this novel to the temptations he must face – *all* the women of Egypt fall in love with Joseph when they see his outstanding beauty, and Joseph is afraid of their plots. All the women love Joseph, but he despises them. His suffering is described in great detail in chapter 7 of *Joseph and Asenath.*

Joseph loses his fear when he hears that Asenath is a virgin, and she in turn abandons her hatred when she sees Joseph and learns that the story told by Potiphar's wife is untrue and that Joseph too is still a virgin. Joseph pronounces a blessing on Asenath, and their relationship develops initially as that of brother and sister. Asenath returns to the tower in which she lives, does penance, and abjures her idols. She must pass through a series of tests (recalling Mozart's *Magic Flute* at many points), until this "prince and princess" finally come together and Pharaoh himself presides over their wedding.

The emphasis on Asenath as the main character suggests that women were involved in the composition of this late novel. Asenath is not a passive figure here but takes an active share in events. She does not simply let herself be married off; she makes her own essential contribution to the decision that she should wed Joseph. The two divergent versions of the novel show that a great disagreement existed in the educated circles of Greek-speaking Jews over the correct role for women. In Christian circles too there were ascetic tendencies which rejected marriage altogether – this was probably true especially of educated women. Thus, this late novel presents a quite different picture of a traditional couple. The ancient biblical tradition is interpreted anew.

JOB AND HIS WIFE

(Job 1 and 2)

NEW HAPPINESS.
After he is declared innocent, Job is depicted between his seven sons and three daughters (Job 42:13). The scrolls declare: "And the Lord gave Job twice as much as he had before" (42:10). Illuminated page of a Hebrew manuscript, the Rothschild Miscellany, *written in northern Italy ca. 1450/1475 (opposite page).*

COUNSELORS.
This miniature by Jean Bourdichon in a Book of Hours *from Tours (ca. 1480/1485) depicts Job at the feet of his self-righteous friends, who advise him – and accuse him (above).*

Everyone knows Job, but his wife remains anonymous, although she plays an important role in his life. Job lives in Uz in Arabia. He is a rich and pious man who meets disaster. Devastating reports reach him, one after the other: he loses all his children, his animals, and all that he possesses. Only the messengers escape the catastrophes and come to tell Job about them. His world collapses, and he can no longer understand God.

Naturally, Job does not know that he is the object of a "wager" between Yahweh and Satan, who wishes to prove that Job believes in God only for as long as things go well with him. The narrative framework of the book is furnished by the wager, the catastrophes, and the subsequent rehabilitation of Job. Ultimately, the book asks: What is a human being? How does he behave when suffering comes his way? Does he despair or can he find some meaning in his suffering? A second author integrated his own poetry into the ancient folk-tale, and it is here that we find the disputations between Job and his three friends, highly theological discussions of the question: Who is God? Are the human notions of God confirmed when suffering comes, or must they be corrected? Can we reckon on a "redemption"? Many theologians and philosophers have sought answers to this question of theodicy, for Job's suffering is intolerable; it is not his own fault, and remains inexplicable. There is no answer. The experiences of our own times call God into question.

Modern scholars increasingly tend to see a close connection between the two parts of the Book of Job, and we can see in the figure of Job's wife how they belong together. She stands at the interface of the story, both in terms of form and in terms of substance. At the end of the prologue, which emphasizes the discontinuity in Job's piety and the beginning of a contrary movement in which his humility vis-à-vis God is replaced by accusation, Job is abandoned by God and the world at the lowest pitch of disaster, where the reader cannot imagine that anything worse could befall him. He is sitting, reduced to nothing, on the dunghill outside his village, close to death, when his wife comes out to him and asks: "Do you still persist in your integrity? Curse God, and die!" (2:9). This is all we are told about her, but these words are very informative, not only about her relationship to Job but also about the significance of this relationship for Job's piety.

What impels her to come out of the village to Job? Is it love, the desire to see him rescued from his sufferings? Is it a compassion that has intensified to the point where she can no longer bear to look on? Perhaps we will understand this woman better if we recall what has happened to her. She was rich, the mistress of a large household, but now she has been reduced to poverty. She had seven sons, but

now the name of her family has been extinguished. Without her husband and sons, she has lost her position in society. There is no one to look after her and she stares doom in the face. She too has lost everything. And she too is innocent.

One might perhaps have thought that the catastrophes would bring the couple together, and that their love would prove its worth now. Instead, she attacks him verbally, posing a shocking question which clearly implies that her husband is a fool. She shows no understanding of his situation, and can give him neither consolation nor help.

What is this piety of Job that drives the couple apart? In the Old Testament, "piety" means first of all the fear of God, i.e., an attitude of submission to the Lord. The concept has also a social component: one who grasps one's relationship to God, belongs to the people of God and therefore has obligations to society. This means that one must lead a just and ethically responsible life. God in turn is responsible for the life of the one he protects. This relationship is similar to that of master and servant, and Job feels secure and safe in his God. It is this personal relationship between Job and his God that his wife now calls into question, employing the same words with which Yahweh justifies Job when he tells Satan: "He still persists in his integrity" (2:3).

In antiquity, curses were not merely a way of letting off emotional steam. The curse had a terrible magical power: once uttered, it took effect, like a power which automatically generated destruction. Satan has prophesied that Job would curse God to his face (1:11), and now his wife urges him to do precisely this. She clothes Satan's thoughts in words, taking thereby an attitude diametrically opposed to that of her husband. She drives Job to bitterness and despair – and that is exactly where Satan wants him to be.

Cursing God was a crime deserving death: "One who blasphemes the name of the Lord shall be put to death" (Lev 24:16). But even more important for Job is the realization that, if he were to curse God, the confidence and obedience which unite him to the Lord would be broken asunder and the very foundations of his existence would perish. Perhaps his wife only wants to suggest that he should part company with his God, since this particular deity is useless; it is possible that she belongs to the native population and that she retains her Babylonian faith in the stars even after she marries Job. The great speech in which he justifies himself shows indirectly that her religion had once been a snare for Job (31:26-28):

> "If I have looked at the sun when it shone,
> or the moon moving in splendor,
> and my heart has been secretly enticed,
> and my mouth has kissed my hand;
> this also would be an iniquity to be punished by the judges,
> for I should have been false to God above."

"Satan answered the Lord, 'Skin for skin! All that people have they will give to save their lives. But stretch out your hand now and touch his bone and his flesh, and he will curse you to your face.' The Lord said to Satan, 'Very well, he is in your power; only spare his life.'"
JOB 2:4-6

A WAGER.
This illuminated page of the Romanesque Gumbertus Bible *(ca. 1200) introduces the Book of Job. God is enthroned in a mandorla, and Satan offers him a wager (Job 1). The four medallions depict the catastrophes which afflict Job, culminating in the death of his sons and daughters when the house collapses (1:19). His wife is included in the two lower scenes, where Job is covered in sores (opposite page).*

MOCKERY AND CONTEMPT.
A fragment of the Jabach altarpiece by
Albrecht Dürer (ca. 1503/1506).
His wife pours water over Job: this can be
considered an expression of her contempt.

"Then his wife said to him:
'Do you still persist in your integrity?
Curse God, and die.'"

JOB 2:9

But perhaps Job's wife has lost all religious faith. Job calls her a "foolish woman," and "folly" in the vocabulary of the Old Testament is not only a sign of stupidity but also an ethical deficiency.

Job is alone. His wife is against him. God leaves him to his own devices, and his friends accuse him, insisting that if Job is suffering, he must be guilty – for there is a causal link between our own actions and what happens to us. Job remains unshaken: since I am suffering, then either God is wicked (cf. 9:24), or else something is wrong with your theological system. He cannot abandon God, and so he must therefore question his previous notions of God. At the end, God himself pronounces the verdict. Job's friends are wrong, since they heartlessly insist on theological principles. Job is correct to see a contradiction between his notion of God and reality, but he is wrong to absolutize his own small stock of experiences and make these the criterion for God's behavior. God's final word is the affirmation that human beings cannot bring him under their control nor understand him fully. No answer is given to the problem of innocent suffering in this world. All we can do is endure it in the hope that a God nevertheless exists.

Job's wife plays a key role in this exciting process because she makes the specifically theological question more acute. She emerges from the darkness and disappears in darkness. She is herself dark in her existence and her thinking, and she seems to exist only in order that she may pose this question. Like Eve, her function is to impel the narrative forward, prompting a further development and raising consciousness to a new level. Ultimately, Job is rewarded for his insight, but she remains a radically questioning figure. One might even say that she is an anticipation of the atheist worldview. Job's wife thinks the problem through to its logical conclusion. She becomes the spokeswoman of Satan, and thus separates herself from Job.

WHERE THERE IS LOVE, THERE IS GOD

When I think of the concept of "love," I immediately think of a mediaeval verse which today, thanks to the Taizé movement, is widely known and is sung very often. *Ubi caritas et amor, Deus ibi est*, "Where there is love, there is God." These words are based on a verse from the Bible. The heart of religion is not the worship of God in humility and submission, not the adoration of a higher and incomprehensible being, but love in the twofold sense of this word: we are beloved and we are lovers. Believing in love means that we experience ourselves as beings who are affirmed, desired, and accepted, and as beings who ourselves become love. The goal of our life is that we should become capable of love. Tradition uses an expression that many find hard to understand today, "eternal bliss": what this means is that love and justice display their power in everyone and for everyone.

The remarkable conjunction of *amor* and *caritas* in the mediaeval verse (the corresponding Greek terms are *erôs* and *agapê*) is at the very center of the

THE FORMS OF LOVE.
The Gumbertus Bible *(ca. 1200) contains this allegorical distinction among various forms of human love. On the right of the throne of Wisdom* (sapientia) *we see* amor coniugum *(married love),* amor proximorum *(love of one's*

Christian religion. In classical antiquity, the word *erôs* – yearning or longing – was the name of a "demon" that could impel the human person to transcend himself or herself and find complete fulfillment. Eros is born of the sense of incompleteness, of something lacking, of a yearning for something that does not exist now –

neighbors), and amor fratrum *(love between siblings). The figures to the left of Wisdom embody the opposite: an arrogant poor man, a lying rich man, and a foolish old man.*

AGAPE MEAL.
The Last Supper of Jesus with his disciples was the model for the meals in which Christians expressed their *agapê*. At the same time, the sacramental understanding of the Last Supper developed, and this dominates the pictorial tradition. This painting (1652) is in the stave church of Gol in Norway (above).

A RELATIONSHIP OF LOVE.
The encounter between the risen Jesus and Mary of Magdala (Jn 20:11-18) is depicted in the painting Noli me tangere *by Titian (ca. 1510). The Latin words mean literally: "Do not touch me," but can also be translated: "Do not hold me fast, do not embrace me" (opposite page).*

something that not only "ought" to be, but that actually "wants" to be. This erotic power lives in all human beings, since they are made (or, to put it more correctly and more piously, created) for relationship.

When the earliest Christians needed a vocabulary for their fundamental concept and praxis of love, they did not employ the word *erôs* but a much more inconspicuous term, *agapê*, a concept with its roots in the tradition of eating together as brothers and sisters, i.e., in the celebration of the Lord's Supper. Agapê meant that both slaves and masters, both women who worked as dyers (and could not get rid of the stink of the animals' skins) and rich businessmen, both Jews and Greeks, both local residents and foreigners shared what they had with one another in the celebration of their faith. The act of eating was the sensuous expression of their fellowship, and the meal of love united them. The body was not a troublesome matter of no importance, something that hindered their ascent to higher things: on the contrary, it belonged to the very heart of the new, liberated life.

In later theological reflection, church fathers and bishops attempted to make a clean-cut distinction between a love from above and a love from below. The

"The Samaritan woman said to him, 'How is that you, a Jew, ask a drink of me, a woman of Samaria?' (Jews do not share things in common with Samaritans.) Jesus answered her, 'If you knew the gift of God, and who it is that is saying to you, "Give me a drink," you would have asked him, and he would have given you living water.'"

JOHN 4:9-10

AT THE WELL.
The conversation between Jesus and the Samaritan woman at Jacob's well (Jn 4:1-26) is one in a long line of encounters between men and women at the well which gives the water that keeps us alive and possesses a symbolic significance as "water of life." This depiction of Jesus and the "foreigner" is a recently rediscovered sketch by Michelangelo (1530).

former love proceeded from God, while the latter love among human beings ought at best to mirror God while excluding as far as possible all sexual connotations. From the very beginning, the Jesus movement undermined this separation of "divine" from "earthly" love, as we see above all in the "love stories" (to use Luise Schottroff's term) which the Gospel of John relates about Jesus and his relationships to people like Mary, Martha, and Lazarus, and John his beloved disciple. The Gospel is not afraid to include erotic traits in these stories. They are wonderful examples of the creative power which blazes up where what we call eros and agape become one.

"Whoever does not love does not know God, for God is love" (1 Jn 4:8).

BRIDE AND BRIDEGROOM.
The depiction of the risen Christ taking leave of Mary in a Bohemian Passionale *(ca. 1320) employs the symbolism of bride and bridegroom in the Song of Songs: "O that his left hand were under my head, and that his right hand embraced me!" (8:3; left).*

MERCY.
The canon of the seven works of mercy is based on the words of Jesus in Mt 25. These include taking care of prisoners ("I was in prison, and you came to me," 25:36), exemplified here in the charity of Tobit in a medallion in the Urbino Bible *(cf. p. 115; above).*

This little clause – "God is love" – is the only "definition" in the New Testament of the indefinable God, and it includes the two qualities of love, giving and receiving, becoming new and making new. The patriarchal understanding of sexuality, which splits off genital sexuality from the great web of relationships between our bodies and souls and other people and the world, is wholly absent here.

Agape is the ability of the ego to make a gift of itself. Martin Buber, the Jewish philosopher of religion, expresses this fundamental datum of human existence by saying: "In the beginning was the relationship." We are not simply *homo oeconomicus*, the "economic person" for whom it is enough to follow one's own self-interest. We need more for our life than that. Society may seek to make us the *homo oeconomicus*, this individual with a capacity for business and for pleasure; but "in the beginning" was something else, that is, the self-transcendence of love.

"If I speak in the tongues of
mortals and of angels,
but do not have love,
I am a noisy gong or a clanging
cymbal.
And if have prophetic powers,
and understand all mysteries
and all knowledge,
and if I have all faith, so as to
remove mountains,
but do not have love,
I am nothing."

PAUL,
FIRST LETTER TO THE CORINTHIANS 13:1-2

REFUGE.
In his painting Jesus and the Adulteress *(1917), Max Beckmann depicts the narrative of Jn 8:1-11 as a dramatic instance of persecution. The woman, who has broken the societal norms for love, finds refuge in Jesus, the "law breaker."*

The experience of being loved awakens our own ability to love. But do we need religion in order to understand this? Is not a rational analysis enough? Does not psychology offer the tools needed to clear up the problems caused by the parent-child relationship? Why should anything more be needed? Is not *religio*, the "link back," especially in its institutionalized forms, a decrepit structure that obscures the glowing core and distracts rather than edifies? I myself believe that our capacity for relationship needs a language which is more than merely the language of arguments. The mystery of life, to which people in the various religions have given names such as the Eternal, the Triune, Allah, Energy, the Power of Goodness, the Unutterable, needs to be communicated. In Meister Eckhart's words, "God is supremely communicative" – a sentence that has often infuriated me, since it so often appears utterly impossible to hand on to others even the tiniest part of this

TENDERNESS.
The first meeting between Jacob and Rachel is illustrated by Palma Vecchio (ca. 1520/1525). The spontaneous emotion is mentioned in the Old Testament text: "Then Jacob kissed Rachel, and wept aloud" (Gen 29:11; left).

CERTAINTY.
This reclining female nude embodies the security experienced in the joy of love: a woodcut by Ernst Ludwig Kirchner (1909) for an edition of the poems of Francis Petrarch.

mystery. Religion is born of the necessity to find a language encompassing the totality, a language which demands and invokes more than what human beings can quantify and achieve.

It is in love's interest to point to the necessity of a language which binds us to others and to a tradition which transcends pure subjectivity. We are all "incurably religious," as Nikolai Berdyaev said. To bid farewell to this "illness" would mean abandoning the divine eroticism, without which no life exists. As the economy spreads its tentacles into every corner of our lives, I find myself harboring increasing doubts about those who think they have been "healed" of this illness, those who are indifferent to religion. For can we truly live without "the love of God, which transcends all reason"? To say of a human being that he or she is "unerotic" seems to me a kind of death sentence. In tandem with the discarding of religion goes the tendency to destroy our other wishes and dreams for the lives of all persons on this planet of ours. Many speak of an "enlightened understanding," but does not this really amount to saying: "The illness (i.e., religion) has been successfully treated, but unfortunately the patient died"?

Sometimes, I wonder why the Christian confessions have so little to say about the love of God. Mostly, all we hear is a pale account of a Lord God who loves us and protects us but expects nothing of us miserable little beings. One of the reasons for the weakness of institutionalized religion in our world seems to me to be a religious wish to remain a child for as long as possible, indeed forever. This childlikeness to which people cling so desperately is itself childish and has nothing to do with the open eyes of children, so full of amazement, of which Jesus spoke. Growing up, both against and with the religious institutions, means above all taking love seriously in all its mutuality. The mystic Angelus Silesius said: "I know that without me / God could not live for one moment." This expression of mutuality transcends every orthodoxy that thinks hierarchically in a pattern of "above" and "below."

The "kingdom of heaven" of which we hear in the Gospel means something quite different. We are to have a share in this kingdom, in which the last become the first. We are to love the Eternal by receiving a share in its own being. This is put most clearly in the New Testament in the writings of John, who is regarded as the "apostle of love" and traditionally represents the mystical element in the Christian religion. "The portion of God in us" of which the Quakers (mystics of the modern age) speak is in fact nothing other than the radical acceptance of the fundamental Jewish commandment, which concerns the love of God: "Love then Him your God, with all your heart, with all your soul, with all your might" (Deut 6:5, following Martin Buber's translation).

What kind of love is this? Let me mention two points that I find important. First, this text speaks of a totality: you are to love God "with all your heart, with all your soul, with all your might." When do we ever do anything complete-

A VICTIM.
This detail from Rembrandt's painting Bathsheba with David's Letter *(1654, cf. p. 85) displays the awareness of a connection between love and guilt (opposite page).*

THE JUDGE.
Michelangelo depicted the head of Christ in his fresco The Last Judgment *(1536-1541), behind the altar in the Sistine Chapel, with the beauty and inaccessible remoteness of an Apollo.*

"And if I give away all my
possessions,
and if I hand over my body
so that I may boast,
but do not have love,
I gain nothing.
Love is patient;
love is kind;
love is not envious or
boastful
or arrogant or rude."

PAUL,
FIRST LETTER TO THE CORINTHIANS 13:3-4

THE HUMAN PERSON.
*The artistic tradition of depicting the creation
narrative interprets the first words which God
addresses to "the human person" (Gen 2:16f.)
as addressed to the first human couple. This
detail from the ceiling painting in the stave
church of Ål in Hallingdal in Norway stands
in this tradition (opposite page).*

ly, without reservations, without attaching conditions, without expecting a reward or fearing a punishment, without coercions and without the deadly question about what will happen in the future, the question that destroys the experience of the present moment? When do we ever live something that is purely "now," where we are totally what we do? "I am what I do" is a classic mystical formulation of this existential totality. In love, being and action coalesce. When do we ever achieve this recollection, this undistracted attention, which is an essential characteristic of love? The Buddhist monk Thich Nhat Hanh expresses the same fundamental way of being as: "washing the dishes in order to wash the dishes." It is an act of the undistracted gift of self which presupposes the individual's capacity to bind oneself to the totality. The ego is not the final horizon of the self. We can emerge from our own selves. We can become the cloud that we see passing overhead; we can become the song that we are singing. We are not only the limited and calculable product to which we often reduce ourselves. In the beginning was the relationship which constitutes us. We exist, as Emmanuel Levinas has said, "in the accusative": in other words, we are addressed, we are breathed upon, we are seen, we are needed. Holistic existence means the joy expressed in the biblical word: "behold!"

The second point that seems to me important in our reflection on love is mutuality. It is an essential characteristic of love to undermine the division between giving and receiving, actor and object, giver and vessel, active and passive. Love expresses the unity of acting and receiving. The gift of self whereby we bind ourselves to something larger than our own ego cannot be described exclusively with the help of concepts that have their roots in the sexual experience of only one half of humankind.

Love not only thinks interpersonally; it lives in the structural observation of reality. One of the great strengths of the Jewish and Christian traditions is their refusal to separate love from justice, which is the political name of love. More and more people are suffering as a result of our economy and our ecology. A market economy which does not intervene to protect the weakest or to guarantee a human right to work cannot function in favor of humankind as a whole; at most, it can function in favor of a few rich people. At present, more than 75 percent of all the states in the world are organized according to our neoliberal system. In 90 percent of these states, people go hungry – and starve to death. Is the market completely unconnected to this fact? The market recognizes no needs, only demands for goods, and acts on this principle. If you have nothing to offer for which a demand exists, you are dead. For need itself does not make you a player in the market.

For God, however, the human person's need is the most important of all, taking priority over productivity and achievements. Even today, God hears the cry of the people, as once in Egypt: "I have heard the cry of my people." God is the one who knows our needs, and God lives where we hear with God's ears. "God has no other hands than ours," said Teresa of Avila. To love God does not mean throw-

THE COMMON HOME.
*The left wing of the triptych with the middle
panel depicting* The Garden of Delights
*(ca. 1480/1490; illustration on p. 12)
by Hieronymus Bosch does not follow
the sequence from the creation of human
beings, via the fall, to the expulsion from
paradise (cf. p. 33). Instead, the Garden of
Eden is depicted as the earthly paradise
where all creatures live in fellowship.*

SEPARATION.
*A detail from the reliefs decorating the early
Christian sarcophagus of Junius Bassus
(died 359), depicting Adam and Eve
after the fall, which separates the man
from the woman: they lose sight of
each other, so to speak. The specific
reason why they turn away their
eyes from each other is their shame.*

ing off responsibility, but rather joining God in bearing responsibility. The best translation of what the early Christians meant by *agapê* remains "solidarity" – and this is at risk in our world because the love of neighbor is considered a private hobby, and people refuse in this context to think in terms of structures. The love of justice remains harmless, because our stories of justice are becoming thin: in a world which is free of religion and of tradition, we forget the story of our liberation from Egypt, that rich slave-owning land. All that seems conceivable is a little "fairness" (the new substitute concept for "justice" in the economy).

An interpersonal and structural love in accordance with the religious tradition requires more than transient feelings: it also needs choreography. It needs stories, for it must be narrated, played, danced, sung, and whistled. It withers and dies in the wordlessness of a world in which everything can be obtained, bought, and produced – while it becomes ever more obvious that people are not truly at home in this world, which is more than an object that can be used. Love needs nourishment by traditions and stories. If these are lacking, or damaged, we must notice this and draw attention to it. Love must be invoked again and again. God is not "private property."

The Jewish people taught that we should imitate God. When Adam and Eve had to leave paradise, God made clothes for them: we too should clothe the naked. God buried Moses: we too should honor the dead and bury them. God gave bread to the hungry widow through Elijah: we too should imitate God's power and give food to the hungry. God forgives people their guilt: why cannot we forgive our debtors (e.g., the starving people in Nicaragua)? The idea that we should fall down and worship the market as the ultimate force which organizes everything runs contrary to this understanding of human life, which shows that it resembles God by imitating him. A false theology, in thrall to dogmatic concepts, pictures God as an unmoved, unweeping Lord who needs no one in order to be alive. The knowledge that God needs me is the most attractive aspect of Christianity for me.

I believe that the gravest danger threatening us today is a spiritual matter: that we declare ourselves unable to act, and remain trapped in this sensation of our own powerlessness. Perhaps nothing separates us so effectively from love as this anthropological pessimism which has no confidence in love, since it is unaware that love articulates in us our sharing in God. Nothing is so godless as the sentence: "You can't change that – that is just how things are." This way of thinking denies our union with God, this enduring power that rises up again and again to demand that everyone has a right to life. This power that carries us forward is not some supernatural intervention. God does not "intervene" in that way. Rather, God reveals God's will to us: life is for everyone.

One of the central tasks flowing from a religious unity with the entire human family and with the life of all our brothers and sisters is the formulation of

"Love never ends.
But as for prophecies, they will
come to an end;
as for tongues, they
will cease; as for knowledge,
it will come to an end.
For we know only in part,
and we prophesy only in part;
but when the complete comes, the
partial will end."
PAUL,
FIRST LETTER TO THE CORINTHIANS 13:8-10

our existential intentions, our wishes. Religion helps us to renew our wishes and to prevent them from an excessive restriction to present possibilities, to goals we can attain now. Religion unites things that are isolated. Its most important language is prayer, a wishful thinking that is not content to accept things as they now are. Love needs this language in order to transcend the realm of the realistic and the probable. Love of our neighbor and of the world in which we live is caught up in love for God. In such wishes, God is not an idol who decrees human fate and ordains that things shall be as they in fact are. Prayer unites us to a God who is not the omnipotent victor but stands on the side of the poor and the disadvantaged, a God who is as yet hidden in the world, but wants to become visible.

The Letter to the Romans proclaims that nothing can separate us from the love of God (8:35). We do not experience this deepest certainty if we attempt to wrap ourselves in God's cloak like little children and then believe, once we have grown up, that we no longer need it. It is too cold in the world for us to think we could live without God's cloak. Grace gives us warmth, but at the same time it prompts us to join in sewing God's cloak for others.

In the ninth century, a Muslim believer used an image to express the strange experience of making the transition from belief in a fate decreed on high to a life shared with God here below. The mystic Bayazid al-Bistami had gone on pilgrimage to Mecca and visited the house of God with the sacred stone, the Ka'ba. He writes: "For a while, I walked around the house of the Ka'ba. When I came to God, I realized that the house was walking around me." His seeking had become an experience of being found; the acceptance of dogmas and theological propositions had given place to a mystical life with God. We can feel helpless when faced with the alternatives of total submission to God or abandoning God as a pre-modern illusion; but this helplessness can give place to a different kind of strength when we become one with God's love. We think that we are walking around the house, but in reality the house is walking around us, and we have already been in that house for a long time.

FAITH, HOPE, LOVE.
Among the seven virtues of the Christian tradition, the four cardinal virtues – prudence, justice, courage, and temperance – have their origin in Greek antiquity, and found their way into the Old Testament, e.g., in the Book of Wisdom: "And if anyone loves righteousness, her labors are virtues; for she teaches self-control and prudence, justice and courage; nothing in life is more profitable for mortals than these" (8:7). The three divine virtues (known as "theological" virtues since the thirteenth century), i.e., faith, hope, and love (1 Cor 13:13), must be considered Christian in their origin, especially when love is defined as caritas*. They can however be applied to biblical affirmations about the figures – beginning with the ancestors – in whom our human conduct is mirrored. They too lived in faith, hope, and love. The subject of this watercolor by Emil Wachter (1978) is Abraham and Sarah.*

"For now we see in a mirror, dimly;
but then we will see face to face.
Now I know only in part;
then I will know fully, even as I have been fully known.
And now faith, hope, and love abide, these three;
and the greatest of these is love."

PAUL,
FIRST LETTER TO THE CORINTHIANS 13:12-13

NOTES ON ILLUSTRATIONS

The captions that accompany the illustrations to the text of this book are expanded here either by information about the place and time of their creation, about materials, techniques, format, and present location; or else by help to a better understanding of the works reproduced here.

Abbreviations:
BAV: Biblioteca Apostolica Vaticana (Apostolic Vatican Library).
ÖNB: Österreichische Nationalbibliothek (Austrian National Library).
SMPK: Staatliche Museen Preussischer Kulturbesitz (State Museums of the Prussian Cultural Possessions).
Manuscripts: fol. = folio; r = recto (obverse); v = verso (reverse).

Manuscripts frequently used in this book:
Biblia pauperum of the British Library (Kings MS 5) is an unusual fifteenth-century manuscript of the "Bible of the poor." Its horizontal format (17.9 x 38.4 cm) and its use of gold and silver are unusual. – The *Biblia pauperum* was one of the typological books of devotion in the Middle Ages, which aimed to explain the salvation-historical relationship between the Old Testament and the New: Old Testament personages and scenes are "types" which point to corresponding "antitypes" in the New Testament. For example, the Old Testament "type" Eve corresponds to the New Testament "antitype" Mary.
    Facsimile edition: Faksimile Verlag, Lucerne.
    Illustrations: pp. 8, 131.

Gumbertus Bible, named after Gumbertus Abbey in Ansbach, which can be shown to have possessed this book ca. 1200. It was written in Bavaria at the end of the twelfth century. The codex, consisting of 394 parchment leaves in the format 67 x 43 cm, contains the Latin Bible (Vulgate). With 39 groups of scenes, sometimes taking up a whole page, and 65 decorated initial letters, it has one of the most extensive pictorial cycles on the Bible in the Romanesque period.
    Erlangen, University Library, Ms. 1.
    Illustrations: pp. 75, 164, 167.

Psalter of Ingeborg, named after its owner, Ingeborg of Denmark: a manuscript of the 150 Psalms, introduced by 27 illustrated pages with themes from the Old and New Testaments.
    Chantilly, Musée Condé Ms. 9.
    Illustrations: pp. 24l., 41.

Crusader Bible, so named because it was commissioned by Louis IX, a king who was deeply committed to the Crusade movement. It was produced in Paris ca. 1250. Louis IX (born 1214), became king in 1226. He died on his last Crusade in 1270, and was canonized in 1297. Another reason for the name is the depiction of battle scenes

from the Old Testament, which could help legitimate the contemporary military campaigns as just and pleasing to God, by linking these to the victorious battles of God's people Israel.
    The codex is a purely pictorial manuscript which goes from the creation to the story of David. It consists of 46 parchment leaves in the format 39 x 29.5 cm, with 283 individual pictures. It has survived in three fragments which are located today in New York (Pierpont Morgan Library, M 638), Los Angeles (J. Paul Getty Museum, 83 MA 55), and Paris (Bibliothèque nationale de France, Ms. nouv. acq. lat. 2294).
    Facsimile edition: Faksimile Verlag, Lucerne.
    Illustrations: pp. 9, 26, 27, 64, 72, 81, 86r., 137, 157.

Book of Hours from Tours, produced ca. 1480/1485. It consists of 116 parchment leaves in the format 15.8 x 9.5 cm. The principal Master who provided the miniatures was Jean Bourdichon (1457-1521).
    Rome, BAV, Vat. lat. 3781.
    Facsimile edition: Belser Verlag, Stuttgart.
    Illustrations: pp. 86l., 162.

Farnese Book of Hours, commissioned by Cardinal Alessandro Farnese (1520-1589), a member of one of the most influential Italian families, many of whom commissioned works of art and were cultural patrons. They assembled a valuable collection of art (Palazzo and Galleria Farnese, Rome).
    The manuscript was produced in Rome in 1546. The principal Master of the miniatures in the late Renaissance style is the Croatian miniaturist Giulio Clovic, also known as Clovio (1498-1578).
    The codex consists of 114 folios (128 pages) in the format 11 x 17.3 cm. 26 of these are miniatures (with principal and subordinate scenes) covering an entire page. 37 pages have an elaborate border decoration and a rich but not excessive use of gold.
    New York, Pierpont Morgan Library, M 69.
    Facsimile edition: Akademische Druck- u. Verlagsanstalt, Graz 2001, Codices Selecti, Vol. 106. Limited editions have also been produced for sale.
    Illustrations: pp. 2, 25, 97.

Urbino Bible (the Bible of Federigo da Montefeltro), so called because it was kept in the Ducal Library in Urbino, or else because it was commissioned by Federigo da Montefeltro (1422-1482; from 1444 Count of Urbino, from 1474 Duke of Urbino). This codex, consisting of 552 parchment leaves in the format 60 x 44.33 cm, is an edition in two volumes of the entire Latin Bible (Vulgate), produced in Florence in 1476-1478. Each book of the Bible is introduced by splendid border decorations and by a picture in a horizontal format which is usually set in a framework.
    Since 1657, it has been in Rome:
    BAV, Urb. lat. 1+2.
    Illustrations: pp. 21, 56, 66, 115, 119, 171.

Wenceslaus Bible, named after Wenceslaus (1361-1419) who commissioned it. He became king of Bohemia as Wenceslaus IV in 1363, and was Roman-German king from 1376/1378 to 1400. It was produced ca. 1400 in the Wenceslaus atelier in Prague. The codex, with 1214 parchment leaves in the format 55.5 x 37 cm, contains the Old Testament (from Genesis to Sirach) in the fifteenth-century translation into Prague German. The text is written in two columns with miniatures occupying one column and a rich border decoration. Today, the codex is divided into six volumes.
    Vienna, ÖNB, Cod. 2759-2764.
    Facsimile edition: ADEVA (Akademische Druck- und Verlagsanstalt, Graz).
    Illustrations: pp. 40, 47, 50 (2), 51, 54, 59, 63, 67, 86, 88, 89, 105, 121, 125, 128, 135, 141, 152, 153.

World Chronicle of Rudolf of Ems. Rudolf (ca. 1200 - ca. 1254) composed a world history in Middle High German for the Staufer King Conrad IV (1228-1254, Roman king from 1237, as Conrad III Duke of Swabia). His text, which sticks close to the Old Testament, runs from the creation to the death of King Solomon. This rhymed chronicle is transmitted together with the *Vita* of Charlemagne by the so-called "Knitter" in a splendid manuscript from ca. 1300. The codex consists of 294 parchment leaves in the format 29.5 x 20 cm.
    St Galen, Kantonsbibliothek Vadiana, Ms 302 Vad.
    Facsimile edition: Faksimile Verlag, Lucerne.
    Illustrations: pp. 146, 150.

2
Giulio Clovic, "Solomon and the Queen of Sheba," in the Farnese *Book of Hours*, fol. 39r.

3
Albrecht Dürer (1471-1528), woodcut 1511, detail from the illustration on p. 34.

4
"Fall and expulsion from Paradise" in the "Very Rich Book of Hours of the Duke of Berry" (*Très Riches Heures du Duc de Berry*), named after Jean de France, Duc de Berry (1340-1416), who commissioned this work. It was begun ca. 1412 and completed ca. 1485; Chantilly, Musée Condé, Ms 65, fol. 25v.
    This miniature is one of the works created for this book by the brothers Jan, Pol, and Herman of Limburg (who died, like the Duke, in 1416). This leaf was inserted in the Office of the Virgin before the picture of the annunciation to Mary, in keeping with the connection between the fall and the renewal of the history of human beings through the incarnation of God in Jesus: Mary is the "new Eve" and Jesus the "new Adam."

5
Gustav Klimt (1862-1918), *Judith II*, Vienna 1909; oil on canvas, 48 x 17 cm; Venice, Galleria

d'Arte Moderna.

In this second version, Klimt reacted to the criticism of the eroticism of his first depiction of the heroine who brought freedom to her people. Nevertheless, his Judith in her precious garments remained a *femme fatale* in keeping with the *Zeitgeist* at the turn of the nineteenth and twentieth centuries. It is only at a second glance that one notices the head of Holofernes.

6
Marc Chagall (1887-1985), *Song of Songs I*, Vence 1956; oil on paper, mounted on canvas, 148 x 172 cm; Nice, Musée Nationale Message Biblique Marc Chagall.

This painting begins a cycle in five parts on the Song of Songs, which Chagall, who married his second wife, Valentina (Vava) Brodsky in 1952, interpreted autobiographically. He gave the cycle the following dedication in 1980: "To Vava, my wife, my joy and my cheerfulness."

8
"The creation of Eve" in the *Biblia pauperum* of the British Library, fol. 18r.

The corresponding New Testament scene depicts the crucifixion: as Eve comes out of the opened side of Adam, so the blood of redemption flows from the wound in Jesus' side.

9
"Creation and fall" in the *Crusader Bible*, fol. 1v.

10
Michelangelo (1475-1564), "The creation of Adam," ceiling fresco in the Sistine Chapel, 1508-1512.

The pictorial program which Julius II commissioned Michelangelo to carry out in the barrel vaulting of the papal chapel has nine sections, running from the creation to the story of Noah. The fourth section shows the creation of Adam; one of the figures covered by the Creator's cloak is a woman, who has been interpreted as Eve or as an allegory of Wisdom. The sixth section has a double scene: the fall (illustration, p. 36) and the expulsion from paradise (illustration, p. 37).

11
Michelangelo, "Eve," detail from the illustration on p. 10.

12
Hieronymus Bosch (ca. 1450-1516), "The Garden of Delights," 's-Hertogenbosch, ca. 1480/1490; oil on wood, 220 x 195 cm; Madrid, Museo del Prado.

This is the middle panel of a triptych; the wings depict "The Garden of Eden" (illustration, p. 178) and "hell."

13
Three details from the illustration on p. 12. The middle detail with the loving couple may be related to a passage in the Song of Songs where the bride replies to the "daughters of Jerusalem," the

aristocratic ladies with pale skins who do no work in the fields and therefore need not expose themselves to the sun: "I am black but beautiful" (1:5; in the Latin version of the Vulgate, *nigra sum sed formosa*). The slogan of the Black movement in the USA in the 1960's, "Black is beautiful," is based on this verse. It protests against the dominance of the white ideal of beauty.

14
Heinrich Friedrich Füger (1751-1818), "Bathsheba in the bath," Vienna ca. 1790.

A maid opens a casket of jewels which David has sent.

15 left:
Giotto (1267-1337), "The meeting of Anne and Joachim at the Golden Gate" (detail), ca. 1305/1306, fresco, ca. 150 x 140 cm; Padua, Arena chapel.

15 right:
A "loving couple" in the tendrils of a border in the fifteenth-century *Ottheinrich Bible* (Munich, Bayerische Staatsbibliothek, Cgm 801 O/1,2), named after Elector Ottheinrich of the Palatinate (1502-1559), who possessed it for a period. He acquired it for the Bibliotheca Palatina in Heidelberg.

16
Giovanni Baglione (1566-1643), "The victory of the heavenly love over the world, the flesh, and the devil," Rome ca. 1602; oil on canvas, 183.4 x 121.4 cm; Berlin, SMPK, Gemäldegalerie.

17
Titian (ca. 1490-1576), "Heavenly and earthly love," Venice 1515/1516, oil on canvas, 118 x 279 cm; Rome, Galleria Borghese.

The customary title given to this allegorical painting most probably gets its original function wrong. It was probably intended to encourage a timid lady to embrace the delights of sensual love. In this context, the "heavenly" love is not antithetical to the "earthly" love, but is its highest intensification.

18
"Wedding" in a Hebrew manuscript of the legal collection *Arba'a Turim* ("Four ordinances" or "ranks") by Isaac ben Asher (1296-ca. 1343), Mantua 1435; Rome, BAV, Ross. 555, fol. 220v.

19
Michael Pacher (ca. 1435-1498), "Jesus and the adulteress," panel of the altar of St. Wolfgang, completed 1481; tempera on wood, 175 x 130 cm; St. Wolfgang (Salzkammergut), St. Wolfgang's church.

20
Raphael (1483-1520), "The Marriage of Mary and Joseph," Perugia 1504; oil on wood, 170 x 117 cm; Milan, Pinacoteca di Brera.

21
"The marriage of Mary and Joseph" in the *Urbino Bible*, Urb. lat. 2, fol. 201r.

22
Tintoretto (1518-1594), "Jesus in the home of Mary and Martha," Venice ca. 1580; oil on canvas, 200 x 132 cm; Munich, Alte Pinakothek.

23
Raphael (1483-1520), "Mary Magdalene," detail from the painting "St. Cecilia," Rome 1514; Bologna, Pinacoteca Nazionale.

24 left:
"The Risen Jesus and Mary Magdalene (*Noli me tangere*)," in the Ingeborg Psalter, fol. 29r.

24 right:
Peter Paul Rubens (1577-1640), "Jesus and Mary Magdalene (Christ and the repentant sinner)," Antwerp ca. 1618; oil on wood, 147.4 x 130.2 cm; Munich, Alte Pinakothek.

25
Giulio Clovic, "The baptism of Jesus" in the Farnese *Book of Hours*, fol. 35f.

26
"Jacob and Rachel/Jacob's encounter with Esau" in the *Crusader Bible*, fol. 4v. (upper half).

27
"Jacob wrestles with the angel/Jacob meets Esau" in the *Crusader Bible*, fol. 4v. (lower half).

28
"The fall" in a Hebrew biblical manuscript, northern France ca. 1280/1290; London, British Library Add. Ms. 116639, fol. 520v.

29
"From the creation to the dream of Pharaoh" in the Hamilton Bible, Naples ca. 1350; Berlin, SMPK, Kupferstichkabinett, Ham. 94, fol. 4r.

30
"The creation," ca. 1220; mosaic in the dome of the vestibule of San Marco, Venice.

31
Hieronymus Bosch (ca. 1450-1516), "Creation of human beings, fall, and expulsion from paradise": left wing of the "Heuwagen triptych," 's-Hertogenbosch, ca. 1490; oil on wood, 135 x 45 cm; Madrid, Museo del Prado.

32
Albrecht Dürer (1471-1528), "Adam and Eve," Nuremberg 1507; oil on wood, each panel 209 x 80 cm; Madrid, Museo del Prado.

33
Peter Paul Rubens (1577-1640) and Jan Brueghel the Elder (1568-1625), "Adam and Eve in paradise (the fall)," ca. 1620; oil on wood, 74 x 114

cm; The Hague, Mauritshuis.

The painting is a joint work of Rubens and Jan Brueghel the Elder (known as "Flowers Brueghel"), who was a specialist in painting flora and fauna.

34 left:
Albrecht Dürer (1471-1528), "The fall" in the cycle "The life of Mary," published 1511; woodcut, 12.9 x 9.9 cm.

This woodcut reminded those with a humanistic education of the classical myth of the originally "undivided" human person. This is why Dürer's human person is depicted as a being with four legs; only with the upper part of the body does this separate into two beings. An essential characteristic of the separation is their mutual perception through their eyes, which both bridges the distance and makes them aware of it.

34 right:
Hugo van der Goes (ca. 1440-1482), "The fall," Ghent ca. 1470/1475; oil on wood, 32.2 x 21.9 cm; Vienna, Kunsthistorisches Museum. This is the left panel of a diptych; the right panel depicts the women weeping over the dead Christ. The theological connection is supplied by the doctrine of Jesus' sacrificial death on the cross.

35
Francesco Zuccho (according to a drawing by Vittorio Bigeri), "The expulsion from paradise," 1740; copperplate engraving, 19 x 11.5 cm.

This illustrates the twelfth canto of John Milton's epic *Paradise Lost* (1667) in a splendid edition in Italian published in Paris in 1740.

36
Michelangelo, "The fall": cf. p. 10.

37
Michelangelo, "The expulsion from paradise": cf. p. 10.

38
"Abraham's bosom," southern Russia ca. 1830/1840; an icon of the patriarchs Abraham, Isaac, and Jacob; formerly in the Peter und Paul Ikonengalerie, Vaduz, now in a private collection.

39
Vladimir-Susdal school, "Holy Trinity," fourteenth century. This icon depicts the "three men" who visit Abraham and Sarah in the grove of Mamre; Pittsburg, G.R. Hann Collection.

40
"Abraham and Sarah in Egypt," in the *Wenceslaus Bible*, Cod. 2759, fol. 11v.

41
"God as Abraham's guest," Psalter of Ingeborg, fol. 10v.

42
"God as Abraham's guest/The sacrifice of Isaac," ca. 550; mosaic, Ravenna, San Vitale.

43
"Abimelech gives back to Abraham his alleged sister Sarah," seventeenth century; tapestry; Freiburg i.Br., Münster church.

44
"A son is promised to Abraham and Sarah" in the *Octateuch* (manuscript of the first eight books of the Bible) of Smyrna, twelfth century; fol. 170v (burnt).

45
Rembrandt (1606-1669), "Abraham and Isaac," Amsterdam 1645; etching, 16 x 13.1 cm; Hamburg, Kunsthalle.

46
Andrea Vaccaro (1598-1670), "The first meeting between Isaac and Rebekah" (detail), Naples, ca. 1650; Madrid, Museo del Prado.

47
"Eliezer and Rebekah at the well" in the *Wenceslaus Bible*.

48
Bartolomé Estéban Murillo, "Eliezer and Rebekah at the well," Seville ca. 1650; Madrid, Museo del Prado.

49
Rembrandt (1606-1669), "The Jewish bride," Amsterdam ca. 1665; oil on canvas, 121 x 166.5 cm; Amsterdam, Rijksmuseum.

This title was given in the nineteenth century. One of the numerous hypotheses about this picture says that it depicts the Persian King Cyrus and the shepherdess Aspasia, the protagonists in a play (1656) by Jacob Cats which was successful in the theater in Amsterdam. However, a pen-and-ink drawing by Rembrandt, "Abimelech eavesdrops on Isaac and Rebekah" (ca. 1656, in a private collection) makes it probable that the painting depicts Isaac and Rebekah. At the same time, this could be a portrait of a bridal or married couple playing the roles of Isaac and Rebekah, for such *portraits historiés* were very popular at that period.

50 above:
"Rebekah with Esau and Jacob in childbed/Jacob and Rebekah with the growing twins" in the *Wenceslaus Bible*.

50 below:
"Isaac blesses Jacob" in the *Wenceslaus Bible*.

51
"Leah and Rachel with the mandrakes that Reuben brought to his mother Leah/Jacob sleeps with Leah" in the *Wenceslaus Bible*.

52
Hugo van der Goes (ca. 1440-1482), "The first meeting between Jacob and Rachel" (detail), Ghent ca. 1470; pen-and-ink drawing on paper,

34 x 57 cm; Oxford, Christ Church Library Collections.

53
"The first meeting between Jacob and Laban," Brussels, sixteenth century; tapestry.

54
"Jacob, Leah, and Rachel leave their home/Laban in Jacob's camp" in the *Wenceslaus Bible*.

55
Bartolomé Estéban Murillo (1618-1682), "Laban in Jacob's camp," Seville ca. 1650. This scene, the subject of many pictures, contains one precious detail: Rachel (who has robbed her father) assures him that she cannot get up, because of her menstruation. Laban is tricked, and does not notice the stolen goods under Rachel's saddle.

56
"Jacob and his family on the way to Egypt" in the *Urbino Bible*, Urb. lat. 1, fol. 27r.

57
Giovanni Benedetto Castiglione (1609-1663/1665), "Jacob's journey," Mantua ca. 1650; Madrid, Museo del Prado.

Castiglione is one of the best known painters of animals in the Baroque period; his specialties included the entry of the animals into Noah's ark. Jacob's journey looks like that of a cattle drover.

58
"Judah and Tamar" in the *Viennese Codex 2554*, ca. 1210.

59
"Judah and Tamar" in the *Wenceslaus Bible*, ca. 1400.

61
Horace Vernet (1789-1863), "Judah and Tamar," ca. 1840.

62
"Ruth in the field" in the Bible of the Duc de Berry, Paris ca. 1390; Rome, BAV, Vat. lat. 50, fol. 145r.

This splendid manuscript of the Bible, commissioned by Jean de France, Duc de Berry, restricts the illuminations to initials which are decorated with figures or with scenes.

63
"Ruth and Boaz on the threshing floor" in the *Wenceslaus Bible*.

We see the high artistic quality of the painters in the Prague atelier in the mimic power in the facial expression of Boaz: he is surprised, curious, and considerate. A detailed realism in the depiction of objects corresponds to this psychological realism. The ornamentation is employed to enhance the meaning of the picture.

64
"Ruth and Naomi/Ruth and Boaz on the threshing floor" in the *Crusader Bible*, fol. 18r.

65
"Ruth and Boaz in the field" in the *Octateuch* of the monastery of Vatopédi on Mount Athos.

66
"Naomi with her family on the way from Bethlehem to Moab" in the *Urbino Bible*, Urb. lat. 1, fol. 110v.

67
"Ruth and Boaz in the field/Ruth shares in the meal of Boaz and his servants" in the *Wenceslaus Bible*.

68
Nicolas Poussin, "The triumph of David," Rome ca. 1630.

69
"Abishag is brought to David/Abishag caresses David" in a *Bible moralisée*, ca. 1410; Rome, BAV, Vat. reg. 25, fol. 81v.
    Abishag "scratches" David on the chin, a standard gesture in mediaeval art, depicting a caress.

70 left:
"David playing the harp" in a Hebrew manuscript Miscellany (containing various texts including Psalms), northern France ca. 1380/1390; opaque water colors on parchment, 15.7 x 12.1 cm; London, British Museum, Ms. Add. 11639.

70 right:
Marc Chagall, "King David," Vence 1962/1963; oil on canvas, 180 x 98 cm; in a private collection.

71
"The wedding of David and Michal," Constantinople ca. 610/620; silver vessel, diameter 27 cm; Nicosia, Museum of Antiquities.

72
"David brings Saul the bridal price/Wedding of David and Michal" in the *Crusader Bible*, fol. 30r (upper half).

73
"Michal helps David flee" in a *Biblia pauperum*, ca. 1430/1440; Rome, BAV, Pal. lat. 871, fol. 5v (detail).

74
"David dances before the ark of the covenant" in a German-language Historical Bible, Lower Rhineland, ca. 1450; SMPK, Ms. germ. fol. 516, fol. 129r.

75 left:
Star of David on the city wall of Jerusalem.

75 right:
"Michal laughs at David" in the *Gumbertus Bible*, fol. 161v (detail).

76
"The first meeting between David and Abigail" in a "Mirror of Salvation," ca. 1430/1440; Chantilly, Musée Condé.

77
"The first meeting between David and Abigail" in the *Book of Hours of Anne de Montmorency*, 1549; Chantilly, Musée Condé, Ms. 1943, fol. 27v.

78-79
Lucas Floquet, "The story of David and Abigail" (after a lost work by Hugo van der Goes), 1517; oil on canvas, 130 x 325 cm; Waarschoot, Saint-Ghislain.

80
Lucas Cranach the Elder, "David and Abigail," Wittenberg 1509; woodcut.

81
"Abigail and Nabal/The death of Nabal" in the *Crusader Bible*, fol. 33v (lower half).

82
Hans Memling, "David gives his servant a ring for Bathsheba" (excerpt from "Bathsheba in the bath").

83
Hans Memling, "Bathsheba in the bath" (detail), Bruges ca. 1485/1490; oil on wood, 191.5 x 84.6 cm; Stuttgart, Staatsgalerie.
    The narrow vertical format of the panel and Bathsheba's turning to the left (from the viewer's perspective) indicate that this was originally the right panel of a triptych which probably depicted the last judgment on the central panel and was employed as an "image of justice." In this context, the story of David and Bathsheba was an example of unjust conduct, which incurred a divine penalty (the death of their firstborn child).

84
"Bathsheba in the bath" in the Barberini *Book of Hours*, Paris ca. 1510; opaque water colors on parchment, 21.4 x 14 cm; Rome, BAV, Barb. lat. 487, fol. 67v.

85
Rembrandt (1606-1669), "Bathsheba with David's letter," Amsterdam 1654; oil on canvas, 141 x 142 cm; Paris, Musée du Louvre.
    The model was Hendrickje Stoffels, the housekeeper and lover of Rembrandt, whose wife died in 1642. Until the end of her life, Hendrickje Stoffels suffered under the contempt shown her as a "harlot." On the expression of the face of Bathsheba/Hendrickje, cf. the illustration on p. 175. Here too, the painter Rembrandt shows that

he is an incomparable interpreter of human situations.

86 left:
Jean Bourdichon (1457-1521), "David at prayer" in the *Book of Hours* from Tours, fol. 74r.

86 right:
"The story of David and Bathsheba" in the *Crusader Bible*, fol. 41v.

87
Bernardo Strozzi (1581-1644), "David with Abishag and Bathsheba," ca. 1530.

88
"Josaphat and Ahab in Samaria/Zedekiah makes horns of iron" in the *Wenceslaus Bible*, Prague ca. 1400.

89
"Jezebel tells calumnies about Naboth/Naboth is stoned outside the city gate" in the *Wenceslaus Bible*.

90-91
"The death of Joram, Ahaziah, and Jezebel" in a *Bible moralisée*, ca. 1410; Vatican City, Biblioteca Apostolica Vaticana.

92
Thédore Chassériau (1819-1856), "Esther at her toilet," 1842; oil on canvas; Paris, Musée national du Louvre.

93
Johann Creszenz Meyer, "Esther and Ahasuerus," 1778; *verre églomisé*; Beromünster, Haus zum Dolder, Dr. Edmund Müller's Foundation.

94
Hans Burgkmair (1473-1531), "The story of Esther," 1528; oil on wood, 103 x 156.3 cm; Munich, Alte Pinakothek.
    This is one of a cycle of historical paintings which were made for William IV of Bavaria and his consort, Jacobea of Baden, ca. 1530, depicting events of world history in connection with heroes or heroines of antiquity. Esther belongs to the group of outstanding women in world history.

96
Filippino Lippi (1457-1504), "Esther on her way to Ahasuerus," Florence ca. 1489.

97
"Esther before Ahasuerus" in the Farnese *Book of Hours*.

98
Friedrich Wilhelm Kleukens, cover of a limited edition of the Song of Songs, 1909.
    This picture was one of the preliminary works for a mosaic in the dining room of the Palais Stoclet in Brussels.

99
Gustav Klimt (1862-1918), "The Kiss (Fulfillment)," 1907/1908; oil, with layers of silver and gold, on wood, 180 x 180 cm; Vienna, Österreichische Galerie in the Belvedere.

100 left:
"King Solomon and his chosen bride" in the *Winchester Bible*, ca. 1150.

100 right:
Master of the Upper Rhine, "The little garden of paradise," ca. 1410; oil on wood, 26 x 33 cm; Frankfurt am Main, Städelsches Kunstinstitut.

102
Emil Wachter (born 1921), "Bathsheba," 1989; water-color.
   The artist studied theology and philosophy before beginning his studies at the Academy of Art in Karlsruhe in 1949.

103
Robert Wyss (born 1925), Illustration of the Song of Songs, 1983; woodcut.

104
Åke Gustavsson, Illustration in an edition of the Song of Songs, 1971.

105
"The arrival of the Queen of Sheba in Jerusalem" in the *Wenceslaus Bible*.

106-107
Apollonio de Giovanni, "The journey of the Queen of Sheba to Jerusalem," fifteenth century; Florence, Galleria Luigi Bellini.

108 left:
Model of the temple built by King Solomon.

108-109:
Edward Poynter, "The Queen of Sheba visits King Solomon," 1890; oil on canvas, 234.5 x 350.5 cm; Sydney, Art Gallery of New South Wales.

109
Steles from the palace of Marib.

110
"Solomon and the Queen of Sheba," Ethiopia, fifteenth century.

111
"Solomon and the Queen of Sheba (Charles V, the Wise, of France, and his sister, Marie de Hongrie)," Brussels, sixteenth century; Brussels, Collections de la Banque Nationale de Belgique.

112
"The adoration of the kings/Solomon and the Queen of Sheba" from the famous Turin-Milan *Book of Hours* (Turin, Museo Civico d'Arte Antica, Inv. nr. 47), a part of the comprehensive project involving prayers and missals which was initiated by Jean, Duc de Berry, but was completed only in the mid-fifteenth century, after his death.

113
"The story of the Queen of Sheba," Ethiopia.

115
"The story of Tobit, Tobias, and Sarah" in the *Urbino Bible*, Urb. lat. 1 fol. 213v.

117
Jan Steen (1626-1679), "The wedding of Tobias and Sarah," Haarlem ca. 1667/1668; oil on canvas, 131 x 172 cm; Brunswick, Herzog-Anton-Ulrich-Museum.

118
Rembrandt (1606-1669), "Sarah awaits Tobias (Young woman in bed)," Amsterdam 1647; oil on canvas, 81.3 x 68 cm; Edinburgh, National Gallery of Scotland.
   The model was probably Geertje Dircx. After Saska's death, she took care of Rembrandt's son Titus as foster mother, and hoped to marry the painter. After Rembrandt set up house with Hendrickje Stoffels, Geertje Dircx brought charges of breach of promise against him in 1649.

119
"Tobias with his father and mother" in the *Urbino Bible* (detail from the illustration on p. 115).

121
"The vengeance of Simeon and Levi" in the *Wenceslaus Bible*.

124
Emil Wachter (born 1921), "Tamar" and "Amnon," 1988; water-colors.

125
"David sends a request to Tamar that she visit Amnon/Amnon rapes Tamar" in the *Wenceslaus Bible*.

127
Jan Steen (1626-1679), "Amnon and Tamar," Haarlem 1668/1670; oil on wood, 67 x 83 cm; Cologne, Wallraf-Richartz-Museum.

128
"Amnon has Tamar thrown out of his house/Tamar's despair" in the *Wenceslaus Bible*.

129
Franz von Stuck (1863-1928), "Judith and Holofernes," Munich 1926; oil on canvas, 157 x 83 cm; Schwerin, Gemäldegalerie.

130
Lucas Cranach the Elder (1472-1553), "Judith in the camp of Holofernes," ca. 1520.

131
"Judith with the head of Holofernes," *Biblia pauperum* of the British Library, fifteenth century, fol. 9r.

132
Tintoretto (1518-1594), "Judith covers the corpse of Holofernes," Venice ca. 1530.

133
Cristofano Allori (1577-1621), "Judith with the head of Holofernes," Florence 1613; oil on canvas, 139 x 126 cm; Florence, Palazzo Pitti.

135
"Samson's hair is cut by Delilah while he sleeps/Samson is taken captive and blinded" in the *Wenceslaus Bible*.

137
"The miracle of the spring/Samson in Gaza/Samson's hair is cut by Delilah while he sleeps/Samson is taken captive and blinded" in the *Crusader Bible*, fol. 15r.

139
Peter Paul Rubens (1599-1641), "Samson is taken captive," ca. 1638/1630; oil on canvas, 146 x 254 cm; Vienna, Kunsthistorisches Museum.

140
"Samson and the pillars in the house of the Philistines," ca. 1300; stained glass window; Bad Wimpfen.

141
"Joseph and the wife of Potiphar/The calumny before Potiphar" in the *Wenceslaus Bible*.

142
Tintoretto (1518-1594), "Joseph and the wife of Potiphar," ca. 1550.

143 left:
The Master of the Legend of Joseph, "Joseph and the wife of Potiphar," *floruit* ca. 1490/1500, probably in Brussels; oil on wood, a circular painting, diameter 57 cm; Munich, Alte Pinakothek.
   This is one of six surviving circular paintings with scenes from the life of the patriarch Joseph (Berlin, Gemäldegalerie; Munich, Alte Pinakothek; New York, Metropolitan Museum of Art). We know neither the original extent of this cycle nor the function it was intended to have. As a cycle, the circular paintings are in the tradition of pictorial narratives about Joseph as a forerunner of Jesus. Besides this, Joseph came increasingly to be seen as the model of an ideal ruler.

143 right:
"Joseph is accused" in a *Bible moralisée*, ca. 1300.

144 left:
Johann Peter Abesch, "Joseph and the wife of Potiphar," 1725; *verre églomisé*; Beromünster, Haus zum Dolder, Dr. Edmund Müller Foundation.

Johann Peter Abesch was a clergyman. His picture was meant to serve as a warning against adultery.

144 right:
Rembrandt (1606-1669), "Joseph and the wife of Potiphar," Amsterdam 1634; etching; Haarlem, Teyler's Museum.

145
Carlo Count Cignani (1628-1719), "Joseph and the wife of Potiphar," ca. 1700.

146
"Joseph and the wife of Potiphar/The calumny before Potiphar" in a splendid manuscript of the *World Chronicle* of Rudolf of Ems.

147
Emil Wachter (born 1921), "Abraham," 1982; water-color.

148
Rembrandt (1606-1669), "The expulsion of Hagar," Amsterdam 1637; etching, 12-6 x 9.6 cm; Berlin, SMPK, Kupferstichkabinett.

149
Andriaen van der Werft (1659-1722), "The expulsion of Hagar," ca. 1700.

150
"Sarah drives away Hagar/An angel shows Hagar the way to a spring" in a splendid manuscript of the *World Chronicle* of Rudolf of Ems.

151
Pietro Berrettini da Cortona (1596-1669), "The return of Hagar," ca. 1630.

152
"Moses defends Zipporah and her sisters against the shepherds at the well" in the *Wenceslaus Bible*, Prague ca. 1400.

153
"Moses and his family on their way to Egypt" in the *Wenceslaus Bible*, nr. 145.

154
"Moses and Zipporah are reunited" in a *Biblia figurata*, fifteenth century.

155
"Vocation of Moses at the burning bush/Moses and his family meet Aaron/Moses and Aaron before the elders/Moses and Aaron before Pharaoh" in the *Golden Haggadah*, Catalonia ca. 1320/1330; London, British Library, Add. Ms. 27210, fol. 10v.

156
Emil Wachter (born 1921), "Moses" and "Zipporah" in *Paare der Bibel. Gesichter und Geschichten, gesehen und erzählt von Emil Wachter*, Stuttgart 1978.

157
"Joseph is sold by his brothers to the Midianite traders/Joseph is falsely accused by the wife of Potiphar and thrown into prison" in the *Crusader Bible*, fol. 5r.

158
Rembrandt (1606-1669), "Jacob blesses the sons of Joseph," Amsterdam 1656; oil on canvas, 175.5 x 210.5 cm; Kassel, Gemäldegalerie.
   This is probably a family portrait with *portraits historiés* of the family members in the roles of Jacob, Joseph, and Asenath.

161
Emil Wachter (born 1921), "Isaac and Rebekah"; water-color.

162
Jean Bourdichon (1457-1521), "Job and his friends" in the *Book of Hours* from Tours, fol. 88v.

163
"Job after his justification" in the *Rothschild Miscellany* (a Hebrew collection of various texts), northern Italy ca. 1450/1475; opaque water colors on parchment, 21 x 16 cm; Jerusalem, Israel Museum, Ms. 180/51.

164
"The story of Job" in the *Gumbertus Bible*, fol. 247v.
   The damage done to the figure of Satan is no accident. This was a deliberate "attack" in order to ward off the threat of evil which was thought to be present even in a picture.

166
Albrecht Dürer (1471-1528), "Job's wife pours water over him" (fragment of the Jabach altar, formerly the outside of the left panel), Nuremberg ca. 1503/1505; oil on linden wood, 96 x 51 cm; Frankfurt, Städelsches Kunstinstitut.
   On what was formerly the outside of the right panel of the altar (Cologne, Wallraf-Richartz-Musem), two musicians playing pipes and drums observe this event in a detached manner. A comparison with contemporary medical depictions might suggest that Job's wife is pouring water over her sick man in order to give him some relief from his sufferings; but this "therapeutic" interpretation fails to do justice to the expression of contempt on her face and to the vigor with which she swings the bucket.

167
"Allegory of wisdom" in the *Gumbertus Bible*, fol. 146v.

168
"The Last Supper," 1652; painting on wood; stave church in Gol, Norway.

169
Titian (ca. 1490-1576), "The Risen Jesus with Mary Magdalene (*Noli me tangere*)," Venice ca.

1510; oil on wood; 109 x 97 cm; London, National Gallery.

170
Michelangelo (1475-1564), "Jesus and the Samaritan woman at Jacob's well," 1530.

171 left:
"The Risen Jesus takes his leave of Mary" in a *Passionale*, Bohemia, ca. 1320; Prague, University Library, Cod. XIV A 17, fol. 16r.
   This codex was commissioned by Cunigundis, daughter of Ottocar II, who was abbess of the Benedictine convent of St. George in Prague from 1314 until her death in 1321.

171 right:
"Tobit comforts prisoners" in the *Urbino Bible* (detail from the illustration on p. 115).

172
Max Beckmann (1884-1950), "Jesus and the adulteress," Frankfurt 1917; oil on canvas, 150 x 128 cm; St Louis, Art Museum.

173 left:
Palma Vecchio (ca. 1480-1528), "Jacob and Rachel" (detail), Venice ca. 1520/1525; oil on canvas, 146.5 x 250.5 cm; Dresden, Gemäldegalerie Alte Meister.

173 right:
Ernst Ludwig Kirchner (1880-1938), "Love's triumph," Dresden 1909; woodcut.

174
Michelangelo (1475-1564), "The Judge of the world," detail from the "Last Judgment," 1536-1541; fresco; Rome, Sistine Chapel.

175
Rembrandt (1606-1669), "Bathsheba," detail from "Bathsheba with David's letter" (illustration, p. 85).

177
"Adam and Eve before God," detail of the ceiling painting in the stave church of Ål in Hallingdal; Oslo, Historical Collection of the University (copy in Ål).

178 left:
"Adam and Eve after the fall" on the sarcophagus of Junius Bassus (died 359); marble; Rome, grottoes of St. Peter's basilica.

178 right:
Hieronymus Bosch (ca. 1450-1516), "The Garden of Eden," left panel of the triptych with the central panel "The Garden of Delights" (illustration, p. 12); oil on wood, 220 x 97 cm; Madrid, Museo del Prado.

181
Emil Wachter (born 1921), "Abraham and Sarah," 1978; water-color.

AUTHORS

HERBERT HAAG was born in Zurich in 1915. He studied philosophy, theology, and oriental languages in Rome (Licentiate in philosophy), Paris (Licentiate in theology), Fribourg in Switzerland (Doctorate in theology), Jerusalem, Leiden, and Boston. From 1948 to 1960, he was professor of Old Testament at the Academy in Lucerne, and from 1960 to 1980 at the Faculty of Catholic Theology in the University of Tübingen. His home was in Lucerne, where he died on August 23, 2001. His many publications on the world and environment of the Bible and on the present and future of the Catholic church, some of which were written together with Katharina Elliger, include most recently: *Wenn er mich doch küsste – Das Hohelied der Liebe* (with Katharina Elliger), 1994 and 1995; *Am Morgen der Zeit*, 1995; *Worauf es ankommt*, 1997; *Zur Liebe befreit*, 1998; *Nur wer sich ändert, bleibt sich treu*, 2000.

KATHARINA ELLIGER was born in Upper Silesia in 1929. She studied German, Latin, and theology and taught in high schools first in Münster, and from 1962 in Tübingen, where she lives today. She works in adult education and has written theological works, frequently in collaboration with Herbert Haag. In addition to numerous articles, essays, and contributions to books, her publications include: *Wenn er mich doch küsste – Das Hohelied der Liebe* (with Herbert Haag, and twenty woodcuts by Robert Wyss), 1994; Katharina Elliger, *Paare in der Bibel – was damals alles möglich war*, 1996.

MARIANNE GROHMANN was born in Vienna in 1969 and studied Protestant theology and German in Vienna and Berlin. After study periods at the Hebrew University in Jerusalem (1992/1993 and 1995/1996), she became Assistant at the Institute for Systematic Theology in Vienna and took her doctorate in 1999; she lives in Vienna. Her publications include the essays: "Sara und Hagar. Anfragen an die Exegese von Gal 4,21-31 von der Wirkungsgeschichte her," in Protokolle zur Bibel 7 (1998) 53-74; "Die Erzmütter: Sara und Hagar, Rebekka, Rahel," in Markus Öhler, ed. *Alttestamentliche Gestalten im Neuen Testament. Beiträge zur Biblischen Theologie*, 1999, 97-116; her book *Aneignung der Schrift. Wege einer christlichen Rezeption jüdischer Hermeneutik* appeared in 2000.

HELEN SCHÜNGEL-STRAUMANN was born in St. Gallen in 1940. After attending evening classes in Zurich, she studied theology in Tübingen, Paris, and Bonn, and took her doctorate in Old Testament in 1969 at the Faculty of Catholic Theology in the University of Bonn. After teaching at various schools, including the Teacher Training College in the Rhineland (for Cologne and Bonn), she became Professor of Biblical Theology at the University Academy of Kassel in 1987. Helen Schüngel-Straumann lives in Kassel and Graubünden. She has published extensively in the fields of Old Testament, biblical ethics, and feminist theology, most recently the book *Die Frau am Anfang – Eva und die Folgen*, 1999.

DOROTHEE SOELLE was born in Cologne in 1929 and studied classical philology and philosophy, then theology and German. In 1969, she became widely known thanks to the working party "Political Night Prayer" which she and F. Steffensky founded. After her Habilitation in 1972, it was impossible for her to obtain a professorship in Germany. She succeeded Paul Tillich as Professor at Union Theological Seminary in New York, where she taught from 1975 to 1987. Her books, her poetry, and her involvement in the peace movement brought her international recognition. She lived for many years as a freelance author in Hamburg. She died on April 27, 2003. Her more recent publications include: *Es muss doch mehr als alles geben. Nachdenken über Gott*, 1992; *Mutanfälle. Texte zum Nachdenken*, 1993; *Große Frauen der Bibel*, 1993; *Gegenwind. Erinnerungen*, 1995; *Maria – Kunst, Brauchtum und Religion in Bild und Text*, 1997; *Den Rhythmus des Lebens spüren. Inspirierter Alltag*, 2001.

CHRISTOPH WETZEL was born in Bautzen in 1944 and studied art and art history, German, and history at the academies or universities of Stuttgart, Munich, Vienna, and Constance. After teaching at high school in Rottweil, he began work as a publishing consultant in 1976. He has written on the history of literature, of religion, and of art. His wide knowledge of religious art made him the ideal consultant for the illustrations to several editions of the Bible, including: *Die Bibel. Die Stuttgarter Bibel der Buchmalerei*, 1996; *Die große Bibel der Moderne*, 1999; and *Die Lutherbibel. Mit Meisterwerken aus dem Zeitalter der Reformation*, 2000. His most recent works are: *Jesus – 2000 Jahre Glaubens- und Kulturgeschichte* (with other authors), 1999; *Das Reclam Buch der Kunst*, 2001.

INDEX OF PERSONS

SOURCES OF ILLUSTRATIONS

The publishers wish to thank all the archives, libraries, photographers, museums, and collectors who supported the program of illustrations for this book by kindly making material available.

In particular, we thank the Prefect of the Biblioteca Apostolica Vaticana, Don Raffaele Farina, and the Vatican Archive of the Belser Verlag in Stuttgart for permission to include reproductions, especially from the facsimile editions of the Rouen *Books of Hours*, of Jean Bourdichon, and of the *Biblia pauperum* in the Palatine;

Dr. Manfred Kramer and the Faksimile Verlag in Lucerne for permission to include reproductions from the facsimile editions of the *Crusader Bible* (1998), the *Biblia pauperum* (1993), the *Très Riches Heures* (1984), the *Ottheinrich Bible* (in preparation), *Les Heures de Turin-Milan* (1994), and the *World Chronicle* of Rudolf of Ems (1982);

Mr. Alexander Wilhelm and the Akademische Druck- und Verlagsanstalt in Graz for permission to include reproductions from the facsimile editions of the Farnese *Book of Hours* (2000) and the *Wenceslaus Bible* (1981-1991).

Despite intensive researches, it proved impossible to clarify who has the copyright to a number of reproductions; we ask pardon for this.

THE SONG OF SONGS.
Woodcut by Robert Wyss.

Akademische Druck- und Verlagsanstalt, Graz: 2, 25, 40, 47, 50 (2), 51, 54, 59, 67, 88, 89, 97, 105, 121, 125, 128, 135, 141, 152, 153

Archiv EMB, Lucerne: 10, 11, 12, 14, 32, 36, 37, 39, 46, 53, 55, 57, 58, 63, 80, 87, 92, 96, 106/107, 130, 132, 133, 134, 140, 149, 151, 173 (l), 174

Archiv für Kunst und Geschichte, Berlin: 17, 61, 155, 167

Archiv Christoph Wetzel: 3, 34 (l), 35, 71, 98

Art Gallery of New South Wales, Sydney (photograph: Ray Woodbury): 108/109

Artothek, Peissenberg: 17, 24, 33, 95, 100 (r), 127, 143, 166

Atlantis Verlag, Zurich: 44, 65

Bentschev Ivan, Bonn: 38

Biblioteca Apostolica Vaticana, Vatican City (photographs: Belser Studio in the Vatican, Federico Sardella): 21, 29, 41, 56, 62, 66,69, 73, 84, 86 (l), 90/91, 115, 119, 162, 171 (r)

Bildarchiv Preussischer Kulturbesitz, Berlin (photographs: Hans-Jörg Anders): 16, 74

Faksimile Verlag, Lucerne: 4, 8, 9, 15 (r), 26, 27, 64, 72, 81, 86 (r), 112, 131, 137, 146, 150, 157

Freiburger Münsterbauverein, Freiburg (photograph: Vieser): 43

Gemäldegalerie, Kassel (photograph: Brunzel): 158

Giraudon Bridgeman, Paris: 70 (r), 76, 77

Gustavsson Åke, Göteborg: 104

Herzog-Anton-Ulrich-Museum, Brunswick (photograph: Keiser): 117

Kunsthistorisches Museum, Vienna: 139

Maertens Hugo, Bruges: 12 (m + r), 78/79

Mauritshuis, The Hague: 34 (r)

Mercatorfonds, Antwerp: 52, 138, 148, 154

Motovun Book, Lucerne: 18, 19, 20, 22, 23, 24 (l), 28, 70 (l), 75 (r), 100 (l), 108 (l), 109 (r), 110, 113, 144 (r), 163, 171 (l), 172, 173 (r)

Musée de la Banque Nationale de Belgique: 111

Musei Civici Veneziani: 5

Musei Civici, Padua: 15 (l)

Museo del Prado: 12 (l), 13, 31, 48, 68, 142, 178 (r)

National Galleries of Scotland, Edinburgh: 118

National Gallery, London: 169

Österreichische Galerie Belvedere, Vienna: 99

Private collection (photograph: courtesy of Sotheby's, London): 170

Rijksmuseum-Stichting, Amsterdam: 49

RMN, Paris (photograph: Gérard Blot): 6, 85, 175

Sächsische Landesbibliothek, Dresden: 145

Sakuma Yasuo, Tokio: 168, 177

Schlensog Stephan, Tübingen: 75 (l)

Staatliches Museum, Schwerin (photograph: Walford): 129

Staatsgalerie, Stuttgart: 82, 83

Stiftung Dr Edmund Müller, Beromünster: 93, 94, 144 (l)

University Library, Erlangen: 164, 167

Wachter Emil, Karlsruhe: 102, 124 (2), 147, 156 (2), 161, 181

Wyss, Robert, Adlingenswil/Lucerne: 103, 191

Zentralbibliothek, Lucerne: 45, 143